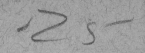

JAMES FORD RHODES

JAMES FORD RHODES

From a crayon portrait by John S. Sargent, 1920

JAMES FORD RHODES

American Historian

by

M. A. DeWolfe Howe

D. APPLETON AND COMPANY

New York   ::   London

1929

PRINTED IN THE UNITED STATES OF AMERICA

PREFACE

SINCE a preface is an author's *apologia*, it must be forgiven for dealing far more freely in the first personal singular than any pages that follow it. Here, then, I would say first that during the life-time of James Ford Rhodes it never occurred to me that I might one day become his biographer. It was soon after his death in January, 1927, that his son, speaking for his mother and himself, proposed this undertaking, and told me that twenty years ago, and more than once in the time since then, Mr. Rhodes had expressed a wish of which this would be the fulfilment. It hardly needs to be said that such a mark of confidence on the part of a greatly valued older friend was at once a touching circumstance and a compelling incentive to engage upon the proposed undertaking.

To these considerations a word must be added. It came to my mind, before arriving at a decision, that in 1908, just twenty years before this book could be completed, my first considerable venture in the field of biography, "The Life and Letters of George Bancroft," was published, and that, among its first readers, Mr. Rhodes was one of the most sympathetic. In matching this memory with the newly acquired knowledge that in about 1908 he had thought of me as his possible biographer, I could hardly escape the suspicion that my Life of Bancroft may have prompted the thought. Nor could I ignore the appeal of attempt-

[v]

ing, long after my study of the one, a corresponding study of the other, perhaps most nearly his modern counterpart as the foremost American historian of his time. Had I needed any suggestion of the sharp and provocative contrast between these two writers, with the younger of whom I am now concerned, it would have been found in the discerning words of Mr. G. P. Gooch about Rhodes's history: "The work marks the immense distance which American scholarship has travelled since Bancroft. The crude elation and national arrogance are dead and buried, and a younger generation has learned to respect the motives of men whose actions the world has agreed to condemn."

Especially in view of Mr. Rhodes's evident contemplation of the possibility that this book might be written, and of his early training as a man of business, it is extraordinary that he himself took not the slightest pains to assemble any material relating to his life. Apparently his ancestry had no interest for him, and if others had not preserved certain personal records which he was called upon to set down for special passing needs, and also a number of letters of which he himself kept scarcely a single copy, there would have been the scantiest provision of autobiographical material for this book. The letters, nearly all in his own handwriting, are remarkably free, as the reader will discover, from any of those tokens of an eye to ultimate publication which are not unknown in the correspondence of writers. Fortunately it has been possible to assemble a number of these letters, quite innocent of any "literary" self-consciousness, together with other memorials of a long, active life, and to supplement this material with the personal remembrances of friends. For the help I have received from many of these—too many to enumerate—and from Mr. Rhodes's immediate family, I wish to record something more than a conventional gratitude.

M. A. DeW. H.

Boston, October, 1928.

CONTENTS

ILLUSTRATIONS

I

INTRODUCTORY

I

INTRODUCTORY

On May 1, 1918, the seventieth birthday of James Ford Rhodes was celebrated in Boston by a dinner in his honor. Twenty-nine of his friends sat down with him at a great oval table in the Somerset Club. Others, unable to be present, expressed through memorable letters their admiration for the central figure of the evening. Among these were Woodrow Wilson, President of the United States, Theodore Roosevelt, his predecessor, and two English friends, Lord Bryce and Sir George Otto Trevelyan. Out of the letters that have been preserved, one must be quoted in this place. It came from Charles W. Eliot, President Emeritus of Harvard University, and read as follows:

To William Roscoe Thayer

Cambridge, Mass., May 1, 1918.

Dear Mr. Thayer:

I very much regret that a heavy cold makes it impossible for me to attend the dinner tonight in honor of Mr. Rhodes's seventieth birthday. I much desired to be one of the friends who should meet him on his birthday with hearty congratulations on his past career and good wishes for his future.

Mr. Rhodes's career as a student and writer of

[3]

history has always been of great interest to me as an educational administrator and an advocate of individualism in school and college training and in the conduct of life. I know no other case in this country in which a successful business man of irregular education came to the conclusion while still young that he had acquired as much property as his family would need, and thereupon gave up business, changed his residence, put himself among scholars and libraries, and set deliberately and persistently to work to make himself an historical scholar and a good writer.

In this remarkable undertaking he has had prompt and wonderful success. He selected as his period for study the very difficult period of the thirty years after the Compromise of 1850, exhibited great diligence and sound discrimination in the pursuit and choice of his material, an impartial judgment in ranking men and events according to their relative importance, and a keen appreciation of the motives, often mixed, which governed the actions of individuals and masses. His historical writings will always be valued for the justice as well as the sagacity which they exhibit.

Mr. Rhodes has carried to successful achievement a very unusual change of plan in the conduct of his own personal life, and in so doing has rendered great service to American scholarship and the country.

As I cannot say these things to him myself tonight, I beg you to hand him this note.

Sincerely yours,

CHARLES W. ELIOT.

This letter from President Eliot is placed at the forefront of the record of what James Ford Rhodes was and did as a cogent statement of the occasion for that record. The work of Rhodes, resulting in his twelve published volumes on historical subjects, was a remarkable achievement. The circumstances attending the production of these volumes were no less remarkable. This is what President Eliot felt—what his letter, even unsupported by further knowledge, would cause others to realize.

President Eliot's letter, however, is more concerned with what Rhodes did than with what he was, and the record of what he was possesses an interest and value commensurate, in the relation between human beings and their work, with his achievements as a scholar and writer. The qualities of the man, hearty, generous of mind and spirit, lovable and warmly loved by persons whose affection honored any who won it, are the very qualities of modesty, directness, and fairness in sagacious judgment, that characterized all his writings. It must therefore be one of the objects of the pages that follow to set forth his personal attributes, displayed especially in the friendships that filled many of his years with a peculiar happiness. This can be accomplished perhaps better than in any other way by drawing freely upon his letters to his friends, with whom his dealings of every sort were as the apple of his eye.

The words "American Historian" in the title of this book have been chosen with a deliberately double purpose. It is not merely that Rhodes towers in that company of historians of America in which George Bancroft stood first in point of time, but that there was something about him in his own person, and something in the very nature of his career, to which the word "American" applies with a special aptness. In a peculiar degree among writers of history in the United States the very personality of Rhodes, his sharply distinctive quality as a man and a writer, were racy of his native soil. The traditional background and training of most of his fellow-historians, subjected as they have usually been to the long-continued influences of universities at home and abroad, influences inevitably rather cosmopolite than local, bore but a casual and fragmentary part in the years of his life that are counted "formative." Through these years the tendencies that surrounded Rhodes were chiefly those of American business—an active, aggressive, successful business—in the highly practical field of coal and iron. Even for fifteen years after the achievement of his somewhat desultory earlier education—that is, from twenty-two to thirty-seven—he was himself an active participant in this aggressive and successful business. From his colleagues in it he was of course differentiated by the fact that long before abandoning this occupation he must have been conscious of regarding it as a means rather than an end, a means to that economic independence which would enable him to pursue his inner bent. If the personal records of these business years were not so meagre as they unfortunately are, there is little doubt that illuminating items would come to light, points of vivid contrast between the Rhodes of outward relations with the life about him, the "Jim" Rhodes still

[6]

well remembered in the older business circles of Cleveland, and the Rhodes to whom the work of a scholar and historian was constantly beckoning.

The life with which the ensuing pages are to deal was uneventful and, except for the publication of successive volumes, essentially a private life. In books and in friendships it found its fullest expression. There was little or nothing of the dramatic in its daily course. But the two divisions into which it naturally separates itself present an inherently dramatic contrast. Let us designate these divisions "The Man of Business" and "The Man of Letters." In the first it will inevitably be seen that the second is destined and coming. In the second the traces of the first must constantly reveal themselves. In the two the full significance of "James Ford Rhodes, American Historian," should manage to reveal itself.

II

THE MAN OF BUSINESS

II

THE MAN OF BUSINESS

IN defining James Ford Rhodes as a "Man of Business" it is not enough to let it go at that. "A Cleveland Man of Business" is a more accurate definition. The word "Cleveland," in American geography, has a significance quite its own. With all the local influences implied in the name Rhodes's identification was complete, both through inheritance and through personal experience. He was born in Cleveland—May 1, 1848—only fifty years after its settlement. For more than half of that time his mother's family had played an important part in the life of the community; his father had begun more recently to count in its affairs, but counted notably in them for the first twenty-seven years of the life that now concerns us.

There is no need to recall in this place the beginnings of Cleveland and the Western Reserve, that new Connecticut, or newer New England, in the wilds— except in so far as the story relates itself to Rhodes and his forbears. This it does at the earliest possible moment. A great-grandfather of Rhodes's mother was the Hon. Sylvester Gilbert, of Hebron, Connecticut, a graduate of Dartmouth in the Class of 1775, at one time a member of Congress, and for many years a member of the Connecticut legislature, in which he served on the committee which sold the Western Reserve lands to the Connecticut Land Company, and thus provided the School Fund of the State with $1,200,000. Gilbert was, besides, a county and a probate judge, and in his law office nearly sixty young men prepared themselves for the legal profession. From just such new England progenitors good things are to be expected in later generations.

One of his daughters, Abigail by name, married Josiah Barber, of Hebron, who became the grandfather of Rhodes's mother, Sophia Lord Russell. With his brother-in-law, Richard Lord, and a considerable company of Hebron and Haddam neighbors, men, women, and children, with horses and oxen, and household goods, Barber emigrated from Connecticut to the Western Reserve in the autumn of 1818, and established himself and his band of newcomers on the west bank of the Cuyahoga River in a place called first Brooklyn, then Ohio City, and now long merged with Cleveland. He chose a beautiful spot for his log cabin, afterwards replaced by a brick dwelling house. With his brother-in-law, Lord, he built up an extensive trade in real estate. When Ohio City elected its first mayor in 1838, Barber was chosen to fill the office. As mayor at the time of "the bridge riots" in resistance to the erection of a bridge across the Cuyahoga River to replace the ferries at "The Flats," he was called out of bed at midnight to read the riot act to marauders who, despite this show of authority, succeeded in blowing up and partially destroying the new bridge.

In less turbulent fields Josiah Barber, both Mayor

and Judge—who had come to the Western Reserve from the same part of the same state at about the same time with the pioneer Ohio Bishop, Philander Chase— was an ardent supporter of the Episcopal Church. He and his family were friends and followers of Bishop Chase, and it was in Barber's house that Trinity Church, now the Cathedral in Cleveland, held its services when, through several years of early troubles, in 1820 and thereafter, it lacked both a building and a rector of its own. He was a leader also among those who established St. John's Church in Ohio City before it became a part of Cleveland; and to his descendants its continuance has been largely due.

To what extent Barber's religion modified his daily life it is possible at this late day only to guess. One circumstance is suggestive. A living descendant of this pioneer judge and man of affairs has told me that Josiah Barber, besides holding an interest in such business enterprises as the Cuyahoga Steam Furnace Company, owned and conducted the first whiskey distillery west of Pittsburgh. When his conscience began to trouble him about the effect of this enterprise upon the life of his time and place, he turned his back upon a tempting offer for the business and its plant, from which the profits were considerable, and proceeded to wreck, beyond all possibilities of future use, this source of gain. Here indeed was a Connecticut conscience at work.

Josiah Barber was twice married, and it was not till 1836 that his widowed daughter, Mrs. Robert Russell, born of his first marriage, followed him to Cleveland with her three daughters, of whom the eldest, Sophia Lord Russell, became the wife of Daniel Pomeroy Rhodes and the mother of James Ford Rhodes. The house in Hebron, Connecticut, from which they moved to the West speaks in every line for the typical New England background of many early comers to Cleveland.

This family of Russells contributed a spirited and attractive element to the life of the energetic little Ohio City. Sophia Russell, before moving West, had enjoyed the benefit of six months' teaching in singing at Hartford. Her niece, Miss Stella T. Hatch, writing of the "Pioneer Women of the West Side," has told of her being prevailed upon to sing on one occasion at a party in her mother's house, and rendering "an extremely fashionable song of the day," imported from Boston, beginning,

> Miss Myrtle is going to marry,
> What a number of hearts she will break,

and proceeding with two stanzas in a happy strain of challenge to surrounding circumstances:

> Yes, indeed, she's a charming woman,
> She studied both Latin and Greek,
> And 'tis said that she solved a problem
> In Euclid before she could speak.

> Had she been but a daughter of mine,
> I'd have taught her to knit and to sew,
> But her mother, a charming woman,
> Couldn't think of such trifles, you know.

[14]

The Man of Business

The singer of this song possessed an energy of mind and spirit, a zest for good deeds and friendly relationships, which made her in her youth anything but a "Miss Myrtle," and at the end of her long life, in 1907, caused her son, James Ford Rhodes, to write about her, "She was a woman who enjoyed doing good, and while she took pleasure in society and European travel, etc., she never seemed to be bored when in her church and charity work she was thrown among boresome people." This may seem moderate praise from a son so devoted that through many years of separation he made it his unfailing practice to write a Sunday letter to his mother; but it bears testimony to the warmth of heart that was joined in her with activity of mind and force of character. It was not strange that, in her early Cleveland days, singing of "Miss Myrtle" but embodying her opposite, she won the affections of another young emigrant from New England, Daniel Pomeroy Rhodes.

"Dan" Rhodes, as he was familiarly called in Cleveland, represented, in the general category of Yankee settlers in Northern Ohio, the masculine equivalent of his wife. The conditions of life in the new country demanded of those who were to master and direct them all the "hard-boiled" vigor—to employ an epithet of more recent years—at their command. The amenities and graces, the refinements of language and manner, were in large measure, and of necessity, entrusted to the nurture of wives and daughters. There will be occasion, a little later, to speak again of Daniel P. Rhodes. At the present moment it is enough to say that he was born in Sudbury, Vermont, in 1814, one year after his kinsman, lifelong friend, and political hero, Stephen A. Douglas, was born in the neighboring town of Brandon. A prosperous stepfather sought more than once to keep him in Vermont by offering him farm-lands of his own, but larger fields of opportunity lured him at twenty-one to the neighborhood of Cleveland, and later to Cleveland itself, where, at about the age of thirty, he took two important steps in his prosperous career. He married Sophia Lord Russell, and in 1845, in association with David Tod, of Youngstown, afterwards war-governor of Ohio, and James M. Ford, for whom he named his second son, became a pioneer in the coal-mining industry of Ohio. Beginning with the operation of a single mine near Youngstown, his business, which soon grew to include iron and lake shipping, rapidly attained proportions which established him as one of the most substantial and influential citizens of Cleveland, albeit his son James described him later as "an iconoclast in society and trade." [1] It is not surprising to learn that, living heartily and successfully, enjoying life, and dispensing enjoyment, "Dan" Rhodes used to quote with gusto the saying of his distinguished cousin Stephen A. Douglas: "Vermont is a good state to emigrate from."

Such, in brief, was the immediate and remoter ancestry of James Ford Rhodes—or enough of it to provide some apprehension of the qualities to which he would naturally fall heir. It is enough also to serve as foreground for the single bit of autobiography de-

[1] *The McKinley and Roosevelt Administrations*, p. 2.

THE PARENTS OF JAMES FORD RHODES

Daniel Pomeroy Rhodes   *Sophia Lord (Russell) Rhodes*

liberately set down by him. This was done, in 1892, when the first two volumes of his history were making their appearance, and an article intended to introduce him to the American public was in process of preparation by Dr. Frederic Bancroft. Rhodes was asked for the facts of his life, and sent to Dr. Bancroft the following statement, on which an article printed in *Harper's Weekly* December 17, 1892, was based:

Full name: James Ford Rhodes.
Born at Cleveland, Ohio, May 1st, 1848.
Parents: Daniel P. Rhodes, a Vermont man, and Sophia L. Rhodes, a Connecticut woman. I know almost nothing of their ancestry but think it was of pure New England stock.
Education: Began going to a private school before I was five years old. At seven entered the public schools, and remained in the public schools ten years, going through as they were then graded, the Intermediate, Grammar, and High schools.

If all public schools were like those that I attended, and if all public school teachers were like those whom I was fortunate in having, little but high praise could be written of the public schools between 1855 and 1865. I have a vivid remembrance of my Grammar School teacher, Charles F. Dutton, and of my High School teacher, A. G. Hopkinson. I think they were natural teachers. They did not believe in a slavish adherence to text-books; but they did believe that the true purpose of education was to teach their boys how to think. They tried to bring to bear their experience and their reading on their daily work and were prompt to encourage any tendency in their boys to investigate subjects in books outside of the school books. They laid especial stress on the writing of essays. I remember that while in the Grammar School, work of that sort came easy to me. And I have little doubt that the judicious encouragement I received from Mr. Dutton and Mr. Hopkinson induced me to devote much time to the preparation of my compositions. In my school days moral and religious teaching was considered a part of the duty of the public school teacher. Both of my teachers were ardent Congregationalists and these inculcations were tinctured by puritanical fervor. Such teaching would now be considered narrow, but I confess to thinking that it had a good side. At all events in my own case if the religious teachings were too strongly puritanical, I found a counterbalance in my own home, for my Mother was an Episcopalian and my Father a deist. But the instruction in my home was religious, being under the direction of my Grandmother. I went to church and Sunday school regularly. I acquired before I was twelve years old a great familiarity with the Bible and Episcopal prayer-book that has never left me.

I cannot remember when I did not take an interest in politics. When only a little more than four years old, I ran away from school to hear General Scott speak, then making a stumping tour as a presidential candidate. When eight, I carried a torch light in a Buchanan and Breckinridge procession. My Father was an ardent Democrat and there was no article of that party's faith in which I was not thoroughly instructed. He had an unbounded admiration for Jefferson and Jackson, and while not a man of education or reading, he was a strong original thinker and vigorous in his expressions. He was not only a Democrat in politics but he had a great respect for the people. He liked the "dinner-pail brigade" as he was fond of calling them, as well as he did the wealthy men of his city. I drank in eagerly his political opinions, and as most of my schoolmates were Republicans, I frequently had with them earnest discussions on the topics of the day. My Father was a kinsman and great admirer of Stephen A. Douglas. I was taught to revere him. After I was ten years old, I read most of his speeches, and I also took delight in reading the Congressional Globes that were sent my Father. Douglas was at my Father's house frequently and I remember well listening to his arguments and familiar conversation. I heard him make a speech in Cleveland in 1860 when he was a candidate for president. My youthful impression of his intellectual greatness still lingers in memory.

When twelve years old, in the fall of 1860, I entered the High School. The election of Lincoln, the course of President Buchanan, the varying and futile attempts at Compromise during the winter furnished food for thought and discussion among the school boys, which found vent at times in a set debate of some vital question, under the direction of the schoolmaster. I cannot praise too highly the encouragement the boys received from the master, Hopkinson, to devote their attention to an accurate comprehension of public affairs. While he was an ardent Republican and most of the boys were with him, there was always the disposition to give the handful of Democratic boys a fair opportunity for the free expression of their opinions. When the war broke out, each morning in school after prayers, it was the master's custom to have one of the boys read for a matter of fifteen minutes or more the important war news which appeared in the morning newspaper. I recollect well that it fell to the orator of the school to read the account of the firing on the Massachusetts sixth regiment in Baltimore and at the close of the reading patriotism welled from our boyish hearts and we shared that great noble feeling that then inspired the nation. Our master constantly impressed upon us that we were living in historic times, that some of the great deeds of history, to be compared with those of Greece, of Rome, of England and France, were now being done. As the war went on and after the first flush of enthusiasm was over, I began to draw my political inspiration from my Father, who remained a sturdy Democrat, and in school essay I argued against the Proclamation of Emancipation, and in school debate that Vallandigham was not a traitor but had been outrageously treated. Vivid impressions those which were acquired between the age of 12 and 17 in the midst of civil commotion! I was graduated from the High School in 1865 at 17, with a thirst for history and literature. But I had neglected my classics and mathematics and could not enter college.

My Father then sent me on a trip to the eastern cities. I saw Boston, Philadelphia, and Washington for the first time, and New York for the first time since a very young boy. I was very much interested in the historical associations connected with Boston and Philadelphia. I was taken by a friend who seemed to have the entrée of the White House to see President Johnson and heard him declaim in private against the radicalism of Stevens and Sumner and express the opinion that the great heart of the country was with him.

In the fall of 1865 I entered the University of New

York as a special student. Under Professor Benjamin N. Martin my taste for history was fostered. I was in two or three of his classes and the recitations were a delight. In one of the classes he kept us pretty closely to the text-book, which was the "General History of Civilization in Europe" of Guizot. We were so drilled in that book that the studious boys of the class, and I was one of them, could give a perfect abstract of any chapter of the work, or could write a complete abstract of the book by having for suggestions simply the titles of the chapters.

In another class our text-book was Weber's "Outlines of Universal History": but our recitation generally became a brilliant dissertation on the subject from Professor Martin in which his wealth of historical knowledge was poured out for our benefit. The lecture would end with suggestions of collateral reading. The next day was devoted to both lecture and colloquy in which a thorough discussion of the subject matter was encouraged. Professor Martin was earnest that the students should give much time to essay writing and his criticisms and praise were always highly appreciated. Martin had thoroughly mastered Macaulay, and at his suggestion I began carefully reading Macaulay's Essays, whose charm was great to a boy of 17. I also read De Tocqueville's "Democracy in America." And I read two books that mark an epoch in my intellectual life—Buckle's "History of Civilization" and Draper's "Intellectual Development of Europe." I shall never forget the interest and even excitement with which I turned the pages of Buckle's two volumes. Such purely intellectual emotion does not often fall to one. I was mastered. In my mind I became a disciple of Buckle. How I regretted his untimely death! But it seemed to me earth had no purer pleasure to offer than to be able to produce such a book; and death seemed robbed of its terror after having achieved such celebrity. The story was then current that Buckle's last words were, "Oh! my book! my book!" And under the influence excited by those two volumes no story could have been more pathetic. As I read the last words of the second volume, May 16, 1866, I resolved some day to write a history.

While at this University I took a course of lectures on Geology from Dr. John W. Draper. His great reputation gave him the close attention of his class. I do not know what scientific facts I carried away from his lectures, but I was impressed with the scientific spirit he had shown in his researches and with his great desire to get at the truth. I also took a course of lectures from Professor Henry Draper on Chemistry which were brilliant.

I do not recollect whether in either of these courses the Correlation and Conservation of Forces was touched upon. I remember, however, that was a subject of conversation in Professor Martin's classes, where discussion took a wide range. The book entitled "Correlation and Conservation of Forces," edited by Dr. Youmans, was published in 1865 and was a favorite one with reading students. I remember that the student who took the first prize in essay writing had what was considered a masterly composition on the new theory of forces.

In the fall of 1866, I did not return to the University of New York. Yielding to an expressed desire of my Father I entered the University of Chicago as a special. I was here much interested in the study of Metaphysics. We used the unabridged edition of Sir

William Hamilton's Lectures. I read at this time Mill's Examination of Sir William Hamilton's Philosophy (although the book had not been recommended by the faculty) and as an antidote to Mill, McCosh's "Defence of Fundamental Truth." I was charmed by both Hamilton and Mill but thought Mill had the better argument. Then began a profound respect for Mill that has always lasted. I carried away from Chicago a sincere love for English literature, led thereto largely by the influence of Professor William Matthews. He had a high estimation of the value of essay writing, was a severe literary critic, and chary of his words of praise. I think nothing in my whole year at Chicago gave me as much pleasure as when after having taken great pains in preparing a composition on the Reign of Louis XIV, I found written at the bottom by Professor Matthews, "a highly creditable essay." I began reading Emerson. And I commenced reading the New York *Nation,* of which since that time I have hardly missed a number. Nearly all the students at Chicago were eager to learn. The subjects of conversation in social intercourse, and in the debating societies, were books and topics of the day discussed from the would-be scholar's standpoint. On Sundays I used to go to hear Robert Collyer preach. My room-mate at Chicago read Herbert Spencer's "Social Statics" and "Illustrations of Universal Progress"; and while I do not recollect reading them, my friend exposed their doctrines so clearly and was always ready to refer to them to settle a disputed point, that in that year I got my first taste of the Spencerian philosophy.

In the summer of 1867 I went with my Father and Mother and my room-mate of Chicago to Europe. After four months my parents returned leaving me with my friend. Up to now I had the desire to pursue a journalistic and literary career, but, after being in Europe for a while, yielding to my Father's evident though not expressed wishes, I decided after my year or two in Europe to take up business. My Father had large business interests and was gratified at this decision.

The six months that I spent in Paris and France was a piece of pregnant political instruction. The empire was apparently strong and made a splendid impression on strangers. The year 1867 saw the Paris Exposition and a round of magnificent public festivities. Most of the Americans whom I met admired the emperor and the imperial policy. My own opinion would have been probably overborne by the wisdom of the elders, had not my Father, sturdy Democrat that he was, constantly declaimed against the tyranny, the evidences of which were not far to seek. Yet the beautiful, gay Paris, the clean streets, the smooth pavements, the order and the system could not fail to impress an American of 1867. I became much interested in the study of the government, and wrote some letters to the Chicago *Times,* giving the result of my investigations. While in Paris, as a farewell to my dreams of a literary career, I took a course of lectures at the Collège de France from Edouard Laboulaye on Montesquieu's *Esprit des Lois.* The lectures were interesting and brilliant. They sent me to reading Laboulaye's "History of the United States" and his "Paris en Amérique"; and to the study again of de Tocqueville.

I went to Berlin and at the School of Mines began the study of Iron Metallurgy under Dr. Wedding, whose enthusiasm inspired all. I attended his lectures and also mastered Percy's Metallurgy, then I think the most weighty English authority on the subject. But

I did not like the study and used to lay aside my books on Metallurgy to read Goethe, Schiller, and Auerbach. Yet the study left a profound impression on me, for we were then just beginning a great revolution in the iron industry. The age of puddled and rolled iron was about to give place to the age of bessemer steel. I made a tour of the iron and steel works of Western Germany, saw the bessemer process at Hoerde, which was one of the first successful working plants on the continent. I then visited the iron and steel works of South Wales, England, and Scotland and came home to Cleveland late in the summer of 1868.

In the summer of 1869 my Father desired that I should look into the coal and iron ore deposits of a part of the South. On this errand I spent considerable time in North Carolina, in northern Georgia, and eastern Tennessee. I travelled much in North Carolina by horse and buggy; then learning to ride horseback, I went on horseback in Georgia and Tennessee. I investigated coal and ore deposits, but was more interested in politics. It was the day of carpet-bag rule. In North Carolina I knew many carpet-baggers and many men who facetiously called themselves "unreconstructed rebels." My curiosity was keen. I have often regretted that I did not keep a note-book to record what I heard and saw.

In the spring of 1870, my Father started me in business with two associates of riper years. In 1874 I was able to form a better business connection with my brother, brother-in-law, and an old and valued friend of my Father. Our business was coal, iron ore and pig iron, being at the same time producers and commission merchants. In this business I remained for eleven years. We had a good measure of success in making money—due I think more to the rare business ability, energy and caution of my partners than to my own industry.

There was hardly a year in which I did not do some solid and improving reading. I hung tenaciously to my knowledge of French and read plays and novels constantly, for I regarded it as a link to that literary world to which I had with regret said farewell. Another link was the Vampire Club, instituted by John Hay, then living at Cleveland, and which was composed of twelve or fourteen congenial men, who used to dine together monthly. When Hay was present he led the conversation, and his talk was so brilliant that the rest of us were glad to listen: and we did not care to do more than to make some suggestion or inquiry that should keep flaming his interesting discourse. He took us to the literary world of New York and Paris, and to the diplomatic world of Washington, Vienna, and Madrid. My intercourse with him certainly kept alive my ambition.

One evening in 1877, while reading Hildreth's "History of the United States," I laid down my book and said to myself why should I not write a History of the United States. From that time my reading, though desultory and often interrupted by the pressure and anxieties of business and the claims of society, had this end in view. I began making notes. I resolved that as soon as I should have gained a competence, I would retire from business and devote myself to history and literature. This resolution was sometimes shaken, and sometimes lost sight of, but it would not entirely down.

In January, 1881, having the charge of the pig iron department of our business, I began writing a monthly circular, which was intended to represent the condition of the trade, and to serve as a sort of advertisement for our firm. Commencing with statements epigrammatic in form, after writing for a year I began to elaborate them and tried to apply a little philosophy to business affairs. As they attracted some attention (we distributed 800 to 1,000 of them monthly) and were published in several newspapers, I took more and more pains with them, keeping up not only with the condition of the iron trade, but with affairs of trade and finance in general. I got my facts from a diligent reading of iron trade and financial journals, and I tried to bring to bear upon these facts some reflections of a general nature. Then my desire to write history, which had slept for a while, revived in full vigor. I looked not so much on the circulars as an advertisement for our firm as my preparation for future literary work. I took pains with my style. I read a good deal and thought a good deal about each month's circular. Our business was a large one: we were brought into contact with leading business men and leading railroad men of the country; and in my intercourse with them I tried to study them from the philosophic point of view as well as from the affair of business in hand. My fifteen years of business life lost me much knowledge of books; but it gained me a great knowledge of men.

Becoming satisfied in 1884 that I could safely retire from business without doing injustice to my family, in October of that year I notified my brother and brother-in-law that I desired to give up business to pursue another line of occupation. April 1st, 1885 our firm was dissolved, and although matters connected with the settlement of affairs occupied me to some extent the rest of the year I felt December 31, 1885 that I was a free man, so far as any claims of business were concerned. I wrote my last circulars in January and February, 1885, but I hoped when devoting great care to their preparation that the time would come when I could appeal to a wider public with a larger range of ideas. I then started a systematic course of reading. I read Grote, Mommsen and Gibbon; Macaulay's Essays and History for the second or third time; nearly all the new books that were published on American history. I wrote several articles for the *Magazine of Western History* then published at Cleveland. In the spring of 1886 I went to Europe with my family where we remained thirteen months. London, Paris, and Berlin were old stories to me: yet I loved to contrast the Paris of the republic with the Paris of the empire; but Switzerland and Italy were new and brought new life. At Rome where Hawthorne says "the very dust is historic" I renewed my vows to the Muse of History.

Returning to Cleveland in 1887 I began reading for my introductory chapter and making the general plan of my book. October, 1888 I began the work of composition. November 30, 1891 I submitted the manuscript of my two first volumes to Harper and Brothers. But the whole time had been devoted to the work. I had almost nothing to distract me from it. The attention my financial affairs required was rather a genial change of occupation. I took no vacation. When I went to the mountains or sea, I took my books and manuscript and read and thought and wrote.

Literature, being a new vocation for me, I felt the need of sympathy from men who were of the craft. It was a fortunate circumstance for me that late in 1888 or early in 1889 I was introduced to Raymond S. Perrin,[2] the author of "The Religion of Philosophy," by our common friend Mr. George Stone. Perrin and I passed a large portion of the summer of 1889 together at Bar Harbor. I was constantly at work. He insisted on hearing some of my M.S. I read him then a portion of Chapter II and afterwards as I would meet him at New York, or he would be at Cleveland, other portions of the M.S. At Bar Harbor, he gave me what I most needed,—encouragement. Not that I was tempted to relinquish the task for I was not, but I was haunted by fears that my literary execution might not be up to the level of the rest of my performance. Afterwards he aided me much by suggestions and criticisms.

Domestic Life

Married Jan. 4, 1872, to Ann Card.
Have one child—a boy [3]—born Jan. 20, 1876.
Moved to Cambridge September 1891.

Thus Rhodes brings his own story, in outline, to 1891, the year of his removal from Cleveland to Cambridge, on his way to Boston, the year before the first two volumes of his History made their appearance. It will have been noticed that in writing of his parents he declared, with a frankness seldom found in a historian recording his own beginnings, "I know almost nothing

---

[2] Raymond St. James Perrin (1849-1915), who combined writing and lecturing on philosophy with the conduct of a manufacturing business in New Jersey.

[3] Daniel Pomeroy Rhodes, now living in Brookline, Mass., author of *A Pleasure-Book of Grindelwald* (1903), *The Philosophy of Change* (1909), *The Great Resolve, an Essay on the European War and the Possible Settlements Thereof* (n.d.) and *Our Immortality* (1919). On May 31, 1902, Daniel Rhodes married Bertha Harriet Johnson, of London; their seven children are living.

of their ancestry but think it was of pure New England stock." That there was something more than this to be said about them the earlier pages of this chapter have shown. In the pages that remain it will similarly appear that other points in Rhodes's record of himself are capable of fruitful elaboration. Through information drawn for this purpose from a variety of sources, I shall accordingly proceed to enlarge in order upon a number of topics to which allusion has been made in the foregoing sketch.

To what Rhodes has said about his earlier schooling and his religious training there is little to be added. One item of remembrance, provided by a somewhat younger cousin, should, however, be set down. "As a boy Mr. Rhodes was of a devout and serious turn of mind, a constant worshiper in the church of his forefathers, St. John's, now the oldest church in the city of Cleveland. Frequently after attending its services, on coming home, he would go into his mother's sitting-room, collect a dozen chairs, arrange them in rows, like the pews in the church, place a prayer-book in the hands of the imaginary congregation, and conduct a solemn church service, in a proper, dignified manner." From the same source comes another recollection, which will mean most to those who recall for themselves the deep, full, booming voice—there is hardly another word than this last for it—which Rhodes carried with him through life: it is merely that at the services in which his devout mother and grandmother saw to it that he took a regular part, his vocal contributions to the prayers and responses could be

counted upon to make themselves heard above the
united voices of the congregation. The fortunately
placed family, persons of the highest consideration in
their community, the serious-minded, quite audibly
articulate boy, addicted rather to reading and thinking
than to the more active pastimes of youth—to the eye
that searches the past they appear where it is no surprise to find them, in the old stone church on a wall of
which a rector of Rhodes's earlier years is commemo-
rated with the inscription, "He preached the comfortable gospel of Christ."

In Rhodes's own writings there are further allusions
to the influences that surrounded him as a boy. Of
the religious revival of 1858, when he was only ten
years old, he wrote: "I remember well that the revival
feeling pervaded the public schools of Cleveland and
affected profoundly many of the scholars. I have a
vivid recollection of the Congregational minister speaking to us in an earnest manner, the burden of his talk
being that we stood in jeopardy if we did not embrace
the Christian faith. Prayer-meetings were frequently
held in the school-room after school hours, and were
led by the minister and teacher." [4] How he happened,
three years later, to be in Racine, Wisconsin, in July of
1861—unless perhaps the schoolboy was enjoying a
summer trip on one of his father's lake steamers—I
do not know; but it was there, according to a footnote
in his History,[5] that he heard a sermon, a week after
the Sabbath-breaking first Battle of Bull Run, in which

[4] Vol. III, p. 455.
[5] *History,* Vol. III, p. 103 n.

he remembered well that the Confederate victory was emphatically ascribed to fighting on Sunday. Through such experiences he made an early acquaintance with certain characteristics of the Civil War mind.

For the work that lay before him the political influences of his youth were of the greatest moment. At home, as his own words have shown, the impressive figure of Stephen A. Douglas made itself felt. When Rhodes delivered his "Lecture on the American Civil War" at Oxford in 1913, he said: "As a boy I saw Douglas often at the house of my father, who was his warm personal and political friend. His great head seemed out of proportion to his short body, giving one the idea of a preponderance of intellect. But he was not a reader and I do not remember ever seeing a book in his hand. Knowing little of Europe, he had absorbed the history of his own country and used this knowledge with ready skill. His winning manner was decisive with boys and he gained a hold on young voters, which he retained until Lincoln came to appeal to their moral sense."

From a footnote in the second volume of the History [6] it appears that Rhodes's father was a delegate to the inconclusive Democratic Convention in Charleston in 1860. The failure to nominate Douglas for the presidency and his death in the ensuing year, left the elder Rhodes—who was with Douglas during his last days,[7] and became an executor under his will—with little or no interest in politics. There is a story of his

---

[6] P. 441.
[7] *History*, Vol. III, p. 415 n.

saying to Anna Dickinson after the war, when she was pleading the cause of woman suffrage with him, "Now that the niggers have the vote, the women may as well have it too."

If there was a fall in the political temperature of the Rhodes household after the death of Douglas, there was a corresponding rise in the Cleveland schools attended by James Rhodes. This has been made quite evident in the biographical sketch already cited. The eager interest of a schoolmaster and at least one schoolmate in the momentous events of the time is indicated on a page of the second volume of Rhodes's History.[8] "Among the recollections of my school-days is that of a teacher who, amazed at the encyclopedic knowledge of passing events and current topics which one of the schoolboys displayed, went to his father to learn how he kept so thoroughly informed on politics, literature and science, and was told: 'He reads the New York *Weekly Tribune.*'" Outside the schoolroom, where Rhodes may thus have begun his recognition of the value of newspapers in the study of history, there were inevitably many other provocations to sharing in the general sentiment of the city in which he lived. "I remember going when a boy of thirteen to a war meeting in Cleveland," he writes in his Oxford "Lectures on the American Civil War," "with reference to the *Trent* affair, and hearing the thunders of applause which greeted a mention of this capture as an important success." At home the saner view of the matter which soon came to prevail was probably accepted from

[8] P. 72 n.

the first. There was a further sharing of the common interest when Rhodes's elder brother, Robert Russell Rhodes, enlisted in an Ohio regiment for a hundred days in 1864. Such conflicting influences as these should be brought to notice, for no stretching of the imagination is needed to suggest that Rhodes's extraordinary fairness of mind in the weighing of historical evidence, his capacity to see both sides of a question, may well have originated in the necessity, while he was still a boy, to effect some reconciliation between the views of his Democratic father and those of his schoolmasters and companions of Republican sympathies. Perhaps this was the easier to accomplish because the Cleveland *Leader* was able to characterize Daniel P. Rhodes upon his death in 1875, as a "genial, whole-souled, and large-hearted gentleman," and to declare, "we know of no Democratic gentleman who has so many friends among Republicans as Mr. Rhodes had."

"In the fall of 1865," Rhodes has written, "I entered the University of New York as a special student." His account of his somewhat meagre college training there for one year, and for the year following at the University of Chicago, is itself meagre. But at certain points it can be supplemented with a few details. In New York, for example, it is recalled by a younger cousin, Mr. U. C. Hatch, now of Cleveland, that Rhodes lived, while a student in New York, with a German family in order to practise the speaking of German, and that, taking dinner every Sunday at the house of his aunt, Mrs. Hatch, he made himself a great favorite with her children, who delighted in the abundance and quality of the stories he habitually told them.

For his studies at the University, recent inquiry has brought from the Office of the Secretary a tabular statement of Rhodes's rating in the courses he pursued, which can mean but one of two things, either that he was a student of extraordinary brilliancy, or that it was easy at New York in 1866-67 to receive high marks. In his first term, each of his term marks in Chemistry, German, and History was 100. In the second and third terms during which he took up also Logic, English Literature, Geology, Natural Theology, and Political Economy, his highest mark was 99, his lowest 96. His average for the year was 98.5. When it is found that a biographical sketch of Professor Benjamin N. Martin describes him not only as professor of psychology and cognate subjects but as lecturing on rhetoric, belles lettres, modern history, apologetics, and natural theology, the suspicion that learning might be spread a little thin in our reputable colleges of sixty years ago may be permitted. The Drapers, father and son, had almost as wide a scope in the field of science; they, and Martin, however, were stimulating teachers of young men for whom the day of specialists had not yet dawned. Outside the classroom Rhodes found himself a member, and corresponding secretary, of the Eucleian Literary Society, and belonged to Delta Upsilon. At the end of his year he received Second Honors in the Duryea Prize Contest for the best English composition in the Junior Class. Altogether the New York year must have given the young Clevelander a taste of his own capacities. The resolve of May 16, 1866, "some day to write a history," may certainly be counted among the important fruits of this year.

In accounting for his second, and last, college year, at the University of Chicago, it is to be noted that Rhodes has prefaced his record of entering that institution, as a special student, with the words, "yielding to an expressed desire of my Father." Here may well be revealed a trace of sentiment in "Dan" Rhodes, for the old University of Chicago, quite other than the present institution of that name, was erected, in 1857, on land provided for the purpose by Stephen A. Douglas. To what other college should the son of his friend be sent? No records of the young man's work at the college are now available. A catalogue of the institution for the academic year of 1866-67, however, shows that he was enrolled as an "Elective Student," one of twenty-five out of a total undergraduate enrollment of ninety-six. The number of "Preparatory Students" was somewhat larger, and the Law School contained but forty-five. Thus the whole "University" was made up of less than three hundred students, and its library held only about four thousand volumes. The Librarian was Professor William Mathews, author in later years of a number of popular books on literary topics, and for many years before his death in 1909 a resident of Boston. Rhodes names only Mathews among his teachers at Chicago—spelling the name *Matthews,*—but it is clear that his studies in philosophy—presumably under the Rev. Dr. John C. Burroughs, the Baptist minister who was both President and "Professor of Moral and Intellectual Philosophy" —impressed him deeply. To his sojourn in Chicago, moreover, a newspaper "connection," resulting in his first known piece of published writing, was presumably due.

In describing the year of European travel and study which followed his scanty college training at home, Rhodes alludes to the letters he wrote from Paris to the Chicago *Times*. These letters are mentioned in many biographical sketches of Rhodes, but no copies of them were preserved among his papers, and up to this time no effort to disinter them seems to have been made. It would appear a simple affair to examine a file of the Chicago *Times* from October, 1867, to June, 1868, and to identify Rhodes's contributions to that journal. This, however, has proved itself no matter of plain sailing. In the first place—and here the Chicago Fire of 1871 must probably be taken into account— no complete file of the *Times* for January-March, 1868, is to be found in Chicago, though the libraries of that city have been searched for it. In the second place, the Paris correspondence of the *Times* through the months that are represented by accessible issues of the paper bears neither a signature nor any conclusive token of internal evidence identifying this correspondence unquestionably with Rhodes.

Of what does it consist? In the issues of October, November, and December, 1867, twelve pieces of "Special Correspondence of the Times," headed "From Paris," and signed "Lawrence," deal with daily happenings at the Universal Exposition then in its final days, with personal items about visitors from Chicago and other American cities, and with purely journalistic reports of Parisian sights and events. It is inconceivable that "Lawrence" could have been Rhodes. In the issues of January 21 and May 14, 1868, however, there are letters of a different tenor. These also are headed "Special Correspondence of the Times." The first of them, dated December 25, 1867, is summarized in the headlines: "France; its System of Government; the Emperor and his Ministers; The Council of State, the Legislative Body, and the Senate." The second, dated April 20, is correspondingly summarized: "French Legislation; Legislation for the Surety of the State; For the Protection of Life; With Regard to the Public Health; Industrial and Commercial Legislation; The Police of Paris—Political Police."

There is every impulse to ascribe these letters to the future historian, and to hail them as the earliest printed evidence of an eager and enlightened interest in political studies. I wish this acclaim could be made without any reservations whatever; but it cannot. The extraordinary signature, "Ferninst," under both these letters throws no light on their authorship. It may have represented a boyish attempt at mystification— and it may not. The content of the letters is no more directly helpful. They are well, if a little heavily, written; their tone is entirely mature; and they carry the conviction of a background of accurate knowledge. Certainly few such beginners as Rhodes then was could have produced them.

TWO EARLY PHOTOGRAPHS OF JAMES FORD RHODES

The Cleveland youth   *The student in Paris*

In default of positive information touching their origin, there is nevertheless this to be said—that these are the only discoverable letters to the Chicago *Times* from Paris while Rhodes was there which could be ascribed to him with any show of reason, and that his own words relating to this journalistic aspect of his Parisian experience of 1867-68 are, "I became much interested in the study of the government, and wrote some letters to the Chicago *Times,* giving the result of my investigation." It is to be remembered besides that at this very time he was attending a course of lectures by Laboulaye on Montesquieu's *Esprit des Lois,* and that his studies in New York and Chicago had lain in kindred fields. Until a more clearly accredited claimant to the authorship of the two "Ferninst" letters presents himself, I am, then, strongly disposed to look upon them as Rhodes's first venture into print as a student of politics and history. Assuming this ascription to be correct, the venture was remarkably creditable to the youth of twenty who made it.

Rhodes's own account of his first visit to Europe is the fullest that can be provided. In the letters he wrote in later life there are occasional allusions to it, as when he wrote from the Hôtel du Lion d'Or at Reims in June of 1906 to Barrett Wendell: "Mrs. Rhodes and I were here six years ago, and in 1867 I passed three weeks in Reims, making my first essay in spoken French. My chum and I had rooms on this very square, looking out on the Cathedral, and while we knew nothing about the Middle Ages architecture,

I carried away an impression of this Cathedral which has always remained with me. Our stay here is a sort of renewal of youthful experiences, yet two days has been quite enough."

Again in the summer of 1922 he wrote to Mr. Worthington C. Ford from Chamonix: "I was first in France in 1867, and the cooking, life, and good wines have always been to my liking."

The Chicago room-mate and friend who became Rhodes's chum in Europe during this first visit was John S. Buhrer, originally of Cleveland, but through most of his adult life, which continued till 1906, a resident of Chicago, where he was engaged in the iron business. A surviving sister provides the information that Rhodes and Buhrer established themselves first of all at Reims, where they lived in a French family, for the improvement of their French. Thence they proceeded to Paris and Berlin, and Buhrer continued his studies at Heidelberg. His admiration and affection for Rhodes lasted to the end of his life.

In 1868, when Rhodes returned from Europe to Cleveland, he was only twenty years old, and had learned all that the schools were to teach him. This education was obviously imperfect with respect to the laying of such solid foundations for future work in historical authorship as he might have built through more regular studies at American or European universities. Nor can it be thought to have equipped him with any distinctive qualifications for success in the business of iron and coal to which he was destined— except that he must have been early among the Americans who picked up even a casual acquaintance with the new bessemer methods which were to revolutionize the iron industry. His business prospects, however, had good fortune on their side, in that his father was in a position to start him well on a course involving large possibilities of financial success.

While Rhodes was still pursuing his college studies, his father's firm of Rhodes, Card and Co. was dissolved, and a new firm, Rhodes and Co., formed to take its place. Jonathan F. Card was the father of Miss Ann Card, who, as we have seen, became Mrs. James Ford Rhodes in 1872. Business and family relationships were closely intertwined. In the new firm of Rhodes and Co. a young and energetic member was Marcus Alonzo Hanna, who in 1864 had married James Rhodes's elder sister, Augusta. The other members of the firm were his elder brother Robert, and George H. Warmington. It was with these associates that in 1874 James Rhodes, after four years' experience in another office, became a member of the firm of Rhodes and Co.

To occupy the same office with Mark Hanna in the seventies and eighties was to be in the thick of things in Cleveland. Mr. Herbert Croly's biography of him, from one angle, and "My Story," by Tom L. Johnson, from another, produce an impression of the extraordinary vitality possessed by Mark Hanna through these, as through many later, years. To his normal business, in which his shrewdness and energy gave him a position of mastery, he added the control of a newspaper, a bank, and a theatre. It was but natural that his younger brother-in-law should be swept into the current of it all, meeting such visiting actors as Jefferson, Booth, and Barrett—with whom, for one, he established a lasting friendship—and participating in many expressions of the stirring life of a city which, between 1870 and 1890, grew in population from some 92,000 to more than 261,000. In 1850, two years after Rhodes was born, the place could claim only about 17,000 inhabitants. His father before him had thus seen it grow from hardly more than a frontier village.

In August of 1875 Daniel P. Rhodes died. In the following spring, his son James, twenty-eight years old, was enough of a personage in the coal and iron business to be the subject of an interview printed as a leading piece of news on the front page of the Cleveland *Leader* for April 18, 1876. It was headed "The Massillon Troubles—A Statement by a Gentleman Direct from the Scene of the Troubles—Not so Bad as Reported, but Bad Enough and Unworthy a Free Country." The "Troubles" were those of a coal-miners' strike in the so-called "Warmington Mine," controlled by Rhodes and Co. They resulted from a reduction of wages necessitated by the general readjustments that followed the Panic of 1873, and led to physical violence, in which Rhodes's partner, George H. Warmington, was "beaten up" by drunken miners. The incident is described in Mr. Croly's life of Hanna, with emphasis on the point that in the ensuing trial at Canton a young lawyer, William McKinley, represented the striking miners, and that here he and Hanna first met—in the character of opponents.[9] The interview with Rhodes in the *Leader* bears all the tokens of the careful, fair-minded observation which was to mark his later accounts of more momentous conflicts. The firm of Rhodes and Co., with Mark Hanna as its leading spirit, had a well-deserved reputation for square dealings with its employees, and strikes and violence were not among its constant problems. The business was nevertheless a realistic, hard-hitting affair, carried on under the conditions that prevailed at the time; and that was a time when business and social life were alike conducted on a basis involving a degree of conviviality now for many years outmoded. These conditions held dangerous possibilities for the genially and hospitably inclined—unless there was also a strong inward fibre to counteract them.

In the midst of a prosperous business career Rhodes, on his own testimony, was applying himself, even in his thirties, to the pursuits of reading and study into which his years in New York, Chicago, and Europe had initiated him. Mr. Elbert H. Baker, editor of the Cleveland *Plain Dealer,* remembers encountering Rhodes among the books of the Cleveland Public Library, asking what he was doing there, and receiving the reply, "Stealing time from Rhodes and Co."; to which the truant added, "And I don't know just where this will lead me."

The paths into which it would lead him ran through pleasant places. For a year after his marriage to Miss

---

[9] See also Rhodes, *The McKinley and Roosevelt Administrations,* p. 9.

Ann Card, the young couple lived with the parents, first of one, then of the other. Presently their own house showed its face of ruddy brick across Franklin Circle from the statelier abode of the elder Rhodeses —a typical "mansion" of Victorian America. Visited in February of 1928, it was found converted into an orphanage, with a tablet bearing the following words on a wall near the front door: "This house was once the Hospitable Residence of Daniel P. Rhodes and Sophia L. Rhodes, his wife. It was given to the Diocese of Ohio in 1909 as a Memorial, by their Children and their Grandchildren, Augusta Hanna, Robert R. Rhodes, James F. Rhodes, Philip R. McCurdy, Lucia McCurdy McBride, for an Orphanage for Girls. 'The Memory of the Just is Blessed.'" A nun-like occupant of the house exhibited to the visitor a small chapel at the left of the front door, saying, "This was Mrs. Rhodes's ball-room, and President McKinley has danced here." Thus—as the visitor was soon to learn —are myths created; but he could not dismiss as completely mythical the figure of a small boy, home from church, organizing a service of his own in his mother's drawing-room. Boy and young man of business seemed to fit into their surroundings.

It was the young man of business, probably in the later seventies, when he was about thirty, that appears in the photograph of Rhodes wearing the "side-whiskers" of the period. Of these a further word anon. In the face between them, the face that was familiar to his friends of later years, capable of illumination by the most genial of smiles, yet with something more of

JAMES FORD RHODES
At about thirty

the alertness of youth visible in its lines, is to be detected; and still, with a modicum of imagination, the hearty, reverberating voice that issued from the shaven lips may be heard. There was no pursuit of athletic pastimes to keep the large frame from giving finally the impression, through shoulders and carriage, of the physical relaxation that marks the indoors man. It is indeed related that in these Cleveland business days Rhodes joined a fishing club, which he visited once, and once only. To his books he had begun turning for pleasure, as he continued to do through life.

In his immediate circle the interests of business were naturally paramount. The paper on Edwin Lawrence Godkin in his "Historical Essays" touches with a certain wistfulness on the plight of "the man who lived in the Middle West for the twenty-five years between 1865 and 1890," and on the New England, New York and Philadelphia circles in which "literary criticism was evolved by social contact in clubs and other gatherings." Rhodes proceeds, "We had nothing of the sort in Cleveland, where a writer of books walking down Euclid Avenue would have been stared at as a somewhat remarkable personage."

One such figure there was, for the decade beginning in 1875, in the person of John Hay, who in this very period wrote his vastly popular anonymous and unacknowledged story, "The Breadwinners," with its scene laid in a Cleveland represented by a nabob so sophisticated, and "bobs," and their social inferiors, so simple—to employ the local terms for residents of the two sides of Euclid Avenue—as to give the book today a pervasive effect of unreality. Most American novels of that post-heroic, pre-modern period produce, to be sure, a similar impression; but John Hay and the Vampire Club, a small dinner club organized by him and including Rhodes and his brother Robert in its membership, made amends for some of the lacks in provocative human intercourse of which Rhodes was apparently beginning to feel conscious. Hay's witty talk, ranging far afield, through America and Europe, doubtless served to make one of his dinner companions restless.[10] It is significant that in direct sequence to the words in Rhodes's autobiographical sketch about Hay and the Vampire Club he records his final resolution to take up the writing of history.

One of the anomalies in Rhodes's preparation for his task of writing is found in his attitude towards the monthly trade circulars which he wrote for Rhodes and Co. between 1881 and 1885. At that time "trade letters" were not the familiar messages they have since become, and there was an element of pioneering in Rhodes's production of his firm's communications to customers. What appears to be the last of them—for it is dated February 26, 1885—lies before me. Its four pages of generous italic type discuss conditions in the iron trade with an intelligent simplicity and hopefulness, though with at least one indication—not to be ignored when the circulars are counted exercises in style as well as in business—that the split infinitive had not become a thing to shun. The important point

---

is that the circulars were received with warm appreciation, and therein some incentive to more ambitious writing may well have lurked.

Even after more than forty years Mr. Samuel Mather, of Cleveland, in a private letter of April 9, 1928, records the definite recollection of Rhodes in business, "that he was in the habit of writing, and distributing to the trade circulars—monthly circulars—of a distinctly original and literary quality, which it was a delight to receive and peruse."

In 1885, as the reader has learned from Rhodes himself, came his retirement from active business. The firm of M. A. Hanna and Co. took over the business of Rhodes and Co. The junior partner, thus enabled to retire with a fortune considered substantial more than forty years ago, has not set down what Professor Albert Bushnell Hart remembers being told by Rhodes himself—that before his final abandonment of business he had twice increased, as his goal, the amount of accumulated principal which seemed to him adequate for his future needs. Having placed himself at thirty-seven in command of what he deemed sufficient, he shut the door of his office, opened that of his library, and set about the task which won him his place among the historians of America.

A few of the points touched upon in the autobiographical sketch which has been serving so long as text for amplification remain to be considered. But, since they have to do with the Man of Letters rather than the Man of Business, their consideration appears proper to the ensuing chapter.

III

THE MAN OF LETTERS

III

THE MAN OF LETTERS

I

From Business to History
1885–1892

It was while Rhodes was still a Cleveland man of
business that his methods as a man of letters began to
take definite form. A significant piece of apparatus for
writing is found in a substantial quarto volume, with
all but a few of its pages originally blank, on the fly-
leaf of which the words "James F. Rhodes, 1878," are
written both in pencil and in ink. On an opposite
blank page is the scribbled sum in subtraction:

$$\begin{array}{r} 1878 \\ \underline{1848} \\ 30, \end{array}$$

indicating clearly enough that, presumably in some
later year, Rhodes indulged his curiosity to
learn at precisely what age he began his elaborate
system of note-taking, and found it to be thirty.
Below the signatures on the fly-leaf he copied
a quotation from Keats, found in the *Nation*, and a
passage from the "Editor's Easy Chair" of *Harper's
Magazine*, each printed in 1890, while he was still
working in Cleveland on his first and second volumes.

[51]

The passage from Keats is this: "I find I can have no enjoyment in the world but continual drinking of knowledge. I find there is no worthy pursuit but the idea of doing some good to the world." The sentence from the "Easy Chair"—which George William Curtis was soon to quit—read: "In writing history the vital necessity is the historic sense, the ability to conceive the spirit of a time and to interpret it with candor." What was the notebook in which Rhodes, early in his endeavor to make himself a writer, gave to these fragments, above a multitude of others, a special place of honor?

The title-page of the volume will answer this question: "Index Rerum;/or,/Index of Subjects;/Intended as a Manual/to aid the/Student and the Professional Man/in Preparing himself for Usefulness./ With/an Introduction,/Illustrating its Utility and Method of Use./ By John Todd, D.D./ *Nocturna versate manu, versate diurna.*/Hor. Northampton, Mass./Bridgman & Childs." This book was copyrighted in 1833 and again in 1861. A second volume, filled with notes by Rhodes, is inscribed on its title-page, "James F. Rhodes, 1888." This was a copy of the "Semi-Centennial Edition," copyrighted and published in 1883. A third and a fourth volume, equally filled by Rhodes, but undated by him, were of the "Semi-Centennial Edition."

It would be interesting to know how many other scholars of the nineteenth century used John Todd's "Index Rerum." Obviously it passed into several editions and enjoyed a long life. What Todd did to convert it from a mere blank book into a tool of scholarship was to alphabetize the pages, in their upper corners, and to rule their margins, after a fashion which contributed simply and considerably to their convenience for the entry and later finding of references to one's reading; and to provide an Introduction for the guidance of those who would use the book. One paragraph in this Introduction might well have attracted the attention of Rhodes at thirty, working at his iron business, yet with thoughts that were forever straying elsewhere:

Let a young man when he begins life be in the habit of making an index to all that he reads which is truly valuable, (and he ought to read nothing else,) and at the age of thirty-five or forty he has something of his own, and which no price could purchase. Many would think hundreds of dollars well spent, could they purchase what they have thrown away; and what each one might most easily save for himself, and to aid in saving which, this book is prepared.

A further word may have been reassuring to a student of thirty: "I feel confident that the plan is as well adapted to those who have lived past their youth as to any other class." Certain it is that the four "Index Rerum" volumes which Rhodes began to fill in 1878 bear witness to the remarkable range of his reading in history, of all times and peoples, in biography and general literature. If self-education is indeed the only true education, here is the record of an elaborate and abundant course in it, early begun and long continued. There will be later occasions to refer to specific items in the curriculum of this private university.

It was not long after the termination of Rhodes's active business life that his reading and his leisure began to bear fruit in the form of published writings. He has already been seen at the work of producing "trade letters," which he valued especially for their training in worthier expression. By sheer good fortune a monthly *Magazine of Western History*, edited by William W. Williams, began to be published in Cleveland in November, 1884. This afforded an ideal outlet for Rhodes's new activities. The issue for August, 1885, contained his first contribution to the magazine—an article, "The Coal and Iron Industry of Cleveland," largely historical and statistical, and thus bearing some relation to his trade letters. It dealt with the pioneer work of his father in the Ohio coal regions, and with the astonishing developments of the forty years that followed. Touching in its final paragraph on the educational and artistic uses to which the rich men of Cleveland were already devoting their fortunes, it ended on a note quite foreign to the trade letters, but bearing clear witness to the reading and thinking which were already engrossing Rhodes's attention. The concluding words of the article, amplifying the statement, apropos of Cleveland, that "something besides great wealth is needed to make the influence of a city enduring," are these:

Of the ancient peoples, the Phœnicians were the keenest money-getters; their commercial and maritime enterprise was admirable; their cities of Tyre and Sidon were renowned for wealth and splendor; but their riches were used in magnificent and luxurious living; nothing was done for literature, philosophy or art; no advance was made in the science of government and towards the wellbeing of the masses. Their civilization perished with their cities and is only interesting as one of the many human failures. The Athenians were likewise traders, skillful and adventurous on the sea, successful in commerce and prosperous from the growth of industry. Much of their gain was used to beautify the city with works of art; poetry, philosophy and literature were encouraged; political advances were made and a system of justice between man and man was established to a degree sufficient to term Athens preeminently the Democratic City. The old Greek civilization is gone, but its influence, its language, literature, philosophy, art and Democratic ideas abide, have been of weighty influence in our intellectual development and are not without their lessons to the enlightened nineteenth century. Phœnicians and Greeks both knew how to make money; the Greeks only knew how to spend it so as to leave for their successors in human progress lasting monuments and enduring examples.

The next contribution of Rhodes to the *Magazine of Western History* is found only a month later, in the issue of September, 1885, and consists of an eleven-page review of the second volume of McMaster's "History of the United States." In this it appears that Rhodes is beginning to study not only the content of such a book, but the manner in which it is written. "This," he declares of McMaster's habit of making his own opinions clearly known, "is the proper way to write history." In November, 1885, appeared a careful study of Woodrow Wilson's "Congressional Government," revealing the writer's own familiarity with Bagehot and Matthew Arnold, and the possession of definite opinions differing at important points from those of Wilson, in whose book nevertheless he found much to admire. From a brief memoir of Rhodes by Dr. Harvey Cushing it may be learned that this article was submitted to the *Atlantic Monthly,* then edited by Thomas Bailey Aldrich, who might have found a place for it had he not been provided—for his February 1886 issue—with a review of the same book by a young Boston lawyer and student of government, Mr. A. Lawrence Lowell.[1] About ten years later the two reviewers, quite unknown each to each in 1885, began the formation of a long and cordial friendship.

Two more articles by Rhodes in the *Magazine of Western History*—"Some Lessons of History," December, 1885, and "Samuel S. Cox's Three Decades of Federal Legislation," February 1886—give evidence of his continued concentration upon historical reading and writing. In the second of these papers there is a brief passage pointing directly to the reviewer's preoccupation with the question of form: "It was once the fashion of writers to express their ideas in long involved sentences and attach to their main clause a number of correlative phrases, so that it was no small

---

[1] See *Later Years of the Saturday Club,* p. 351.

labor for the reader to understand what was intended to be conveyed. But under the guidance of the best masters of English, and from the study of the artistic methods of the French, it has become the aim of a writer to indicate his meaning in the clearest manner possible, and thus the use of short sentences has come into vogue. This was not, however, accomplished without some opposition by the adherents of the old method, for Macaulay somewhere mentions that there are people who do not believe that anything which is clear can be profound." Add to the implications of this passage the number of notes in Rhodes's "Index Rerum" on points of style in writing, and it is manifest that he was thinking early and late about his own efforts towards a mastery of expression.

If the magazine papers at which we have been looking are not intrinsically of the first importance, they have a biographical significance which cannot be ignored. It is to be remembered, moreover, that they appeared in Cleveland as the first tokens of the new employment to which Rhodes had turned from the business of coal and iron. In some remarks before the Massachusetts Historical Society immediately after the death of Rhodes, Judge Robert Grant quoted an observation of an industrial magnate visiting the "North Shore" of Massachusetts long after the historian's fame was established: "I knew Mr. Rhodes very well in the old days. He was highly thought of. What a pity he dropped out, for he would have made his reputation." The early magazine articles must indeed have seemed to this observer—probably by no means solitary—an unpromising start in the pursuit of fame.

A year of Europe at this time with his wife and boy, ten years old in 1886, could hardly have looked more auspicious to some of Rhodes's former associates in business. Nothing can be added to the brief mention of this excursion in the autobiographical sketch. There it appears that he went abroad in the spring of 1886, and returned to Cleveland thirteen months later. Yet the first appearance of Rhodes's name on the title-page of any book may fairly be related to this visit, in the course of which he could hardly have escaped an acquaintance with Ernest Renan's play, "L'Abbesse de Jouarre," published in Paris in 1886. Its daring plot, as many will remember, concerned a young patrician abbess and the high-born lover she had refused to marry before she entered upon the religious life, their reunion in a prison of the French Revolution on the eve of their expected execution, the tragic reprieve of the abbess when her lover was led to his death, and the complications arising from the birth of her father-less child. The play, a philosophic drama, had an immense vogue off the stage, and passed rapidly into twenty-five editions. An Italian version of it was prepared in 1896 for Eleanora Duse and acted by her at about that time. An English rendering of it, "translated from the French by Georges Delon and James F. Rhodes," a translation "authorized by Monsieur E. Renan," was published in New York, with the copyright date of 1888, by "G. W. Dillingham, Publisher, Successor to G. W. Carleton & Co.

London: S. Low, Son & Co." A translated "Preface to
the Twenty-first Edition," not found in the eighteenth
French Edition which lies before me, consists of an
alleged extract from an ancient Life of Plato, an
imaginary conversation in which Plato refutes the
charge of impurity in his writings, and declares, "I
write for the pure." This sentence is printed on the
title-page of the American translation.

Rhodes's collaborator in this work, Georges Delon,
was a teacher of French in Cleveland. It cannot be
said that a translation in which such an expression, in
the stage directions, as "*à demi-voix*" is rendered "at
low voice" represents the highest vigilance in matters
of idiom. Indeed a certain stiffness at a number of
points in the translation suggests the hand of a Frenchman not entirely at ease in English. It would appear
that his American collaborator might have helped
him more than he did. But for Rhodes, with his face
now set definitely towards more ambitious undertakings, the whole episode of "The Abbess of Jouarre"—a
mildly surprising interlude in his work as an historian
—had at least the advantage of providing an initial
bit of training in the processes relating to the production of a book.

Near the end of the very year of this publication,
namely in October, 1888, Rhodes has told us that he
began the composition of his History; also that at the
end of November, 1891, he offered the first and second
volumes to the publishers, Harper and Brothers, who
produced them in 1892. It will be worth the reader's
while to turn back to the few words Rhodes has

written about the labors of these three years.[2] The
two volumes covered the decade ending with 1860, and
bore on their title-pages no general definition but "History of the United States from the Compromise of
1850," a designation that remained unchanged through
the first five volumes.

It requires no special gift of insight to perceive that
the labor involved in the preparation of Volumes I
and II was prodigious, and the more noteworthy as the
first sustained effort of a business man turned writer.
For all this it would have been quite unlike Rhodes
to claim a particle more of credit than he deserved.
A footnote in the first volume[3] repeats the acknowledgment of indebtedness to his friend Raymond S.
Perrin, mentioned in the autobiographical sketch, and
contains these further words: "And I wish to mention
the assistance received from my friend Professor
Bourne, of Adelbert College, who read carefully the
whole manuscript, and gave me the benefit of his historical knowledge and literary criticism."

Edward Gaylord Bourne, who went from Adelbert
to Yale as Professor of History in 1895, died in 1908,
with a secure reputation for historical work of the first
importance. At the March meeting of the Massachusetts Historical Society in that year Rhodes read a
paper about him, included in his "Historical Essays"
(1909), which specifies in more detail the nature of
the older historian's obligations to the younger.
Bourne, it appears, came to Cleveland in 1888, and

[2] See *ante*, p. 28.
[3] P. 383.

the acquaintance with Rhodes which soon followed grew quickly into a friendship between the two men. Once or twice a month Bourne would dine with Rhodes. For a month in the summer of 1889 he went to Boston at Rhodes's instance and gathered material from the newspapers of the early fifties found in the Boston Athenæum. Then he visited Rhodes at Bar Harbor, where they discussed this material and Rhodes's task in general. "Bourne was a good critic," wrote Rhodes after his death, "and, to set him entirely at ease, as he was twelve years younger, I told him to lay aside any respect on account of age, and to speak out frankly, no matter how hard it hit, adding that I had better hear disagreeable things from him than to have them said by critics after the volumes were printed."

Rhodes and Bourne are both recorded as members of the American Historical Association who attended its annual meeting at Washington in 1889. Entirely unknown at that time to his fellow-students of history, Rhodes is recalled by Dr. Frederic Bancroft, then Librarian of the State Department Library, as visiting this collection, asking an attendant to show him certain papers, and then expressing a desire to meet the Librarian. This was readily accomplished, and Dr. Bancroft, regarding his visitor at first as merely a side-whiskered business man, was amazed to discover his interest in history as a thing not merely to be read but also to be written. From this chance meeting a long and valued friendship resulted.

The widow of Professor Bourne has recently characterized the relation between Rhodes and her husband in the words, "Interested in each other's work and stimulating to each other." From Mrs. Bourne also comes the intelligence—so typical of Rhodes's human relationships as to demand a word of record—that for many years after her husband's death their children received gifts every Christmas from the unforgetting friend in Boston.

On returning from Europe to Cleveland in 1887 Rhodes had left the house near his mother's on Franklin Circle, and established himself in a pleasant abode at 901, Euclid Avenue—albeit on the "bob side" of that famous thoroughfare. To this house—as I learned first from the memoir by Dr. Harvey Cushing already quoted [4] came daily a barber, now for many years a familiar figure in Cleveland, not only as the proprietor of the famous barber-shop of the Hollenden House, but as a factor of influence in the Republican politics of his city and state, especially with respect to his fellow-members of the negro race. If the ministrations of Mr. George A. Myers were constantly needed by Rhodes at the time of his wearing the "Piccadilly weepers" that preceded the Van Dyke beard of his later years, Myers on the other hand was indebted to Rhodes, together with a few other substantial men of Cleveland, including Mark Hanna, for setting him up in business in 1888. The bearing of all this on Rhodes the historian, and not the barber's client, appears in Dr. Cushing's anecdote of his first meeting with Rhodes at a chair in the Myers barber-shop,

---

[4] See *Later Years of the Saturday Club.*

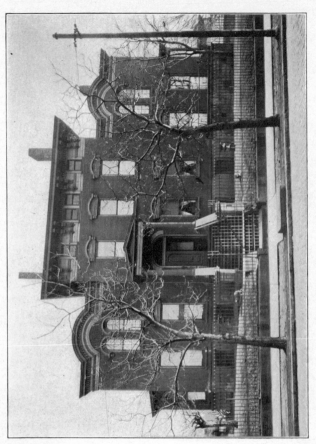

Home of James Ford Rhodes's Parents, Franklin Avenue, Cleveland

when its proprietor declared of the historian's books: "He did the easy work on 'em and I did the heavy. Every morning when I went out to his house on Euclid Avenue to shave him I had to stop at the Case Library so's to tote a big bundle of things he wanted. I did the heavy work on those histories." The ways of collaboration are indeed various.

If this reminiscence of the historian and his barber were all, it would be hardly worth recounting; but the last words in Rhodes's last book, "The McKinley and Roosevelt Administrations," concluding a footnote on the final page, are, "I am indebted to George A. Myers of Cleveland for useful suggestions," and thereby hangs a tale. Rhodes and Myers conducted a correspondence covering many years, rich especially at the time when Rhodes was working on the Mc-Kinley and Hanna régime at Washington, in questions and intelligent, amply informed answers in the field of Ohio politics. The barber knew whereof he spoke, and Rhodes, knowing that he knew, drew considerably on a valuable source of information. When Rhodes in 1900 gave to his fellow-members of the Massachusetts His-torical Society "Some Recent Impressions of England," and declared, "The American barber is the aristocrat of the profession," it is hard to believe that George Myers was quite absent from his mind. The personal keepsakes that went to him upon the death of his dis-tinguished friend bear witness that he was remembered to the end.

When Rhodes sent to Dr. Frederic Bancroft the autographical sketch to which so many references have been made, he wrote two letters about it, the second of which read as follows:

To Frederic Bancroft

> Reservoir Street, Cambridge,
> March 26, [1892].

One thing I meant to add that I forgot.

The only credit that I take to myself is that I withdrew from business when I was making money fast, for the reason that I thought I ought to devote myself to something higher.

The other is that after having withdrawn from business I did not become an intellectual dawdler or a European sojourner.

"A man's worst difficulties begin when he is able to do as he likes," says Huxley.

My aim is what Lowell wrote of Quincy.

"We are glad to have the biography of one who though beginning as a gentleman, kept himself such to the end—who with no necessity of labor, left behind him an amount of thoroughly done work such as few have accomplished with the mighty help of hunger. Some kind of pace may be got out of the veriest jade by the near prospect of oats; but the thoroughbred has the spur in his blood."

I rejoice to say that I never worked as hard in the pursuit of gain, as I have worked on this book the last 3½ years.

It would be superfluous, even if it were possible, to add to the implications of this letter any details of

Rhodes's daily labors, chiefly in Cleveland, upon the opening volumes of his History.

In 1891 he took the step affecting more than any other the outward circumstances of the remainder of his life, and moved, with his family, from Cleveland to Cambridge, Massachusetts. One reason for this change of residence was that his son, at an uncommonly early age, was on the point of entering Harvard College. There was, moreover, a natural desire on Rhodes's part to place himself in closer proximity to libraries and collections in which the materials for his work were to be found, and also to create a personal association with the men of his late-adopted craft.

Like other typical Clevelanders of his time and kind, Rhodes knew the East as an habitual visitor—to New York in the winter, to the New England coast in the summer. For several seasons, indeed, he had occupied a house of his own at Hyannisport on Cape Cod. But it was quite a different thing to come, unheralded as a scholar and without academic or social affiliations, to such a community as Cambridge, and there to set up his abode. In that city, however, he established himself and his family in the autumn of 1891, occupying a house on Reservoir Street belonging to Professor Adams Sherman Hill of Harvard, the author of "Hill's Rhetoric." This shrewd and stimulating teacher of English had been a Washington correspondent of the New York *Tribune* during the Civil War, and footnotes in the fourth volume of Rhodes's History bear testimony to profitable intercourse between landlord and tenant. But the circle in which Rhodes moved at first was both restricted and somewhat fortuitous.

There was a Cleveland association with the first callers on the Rhodeses in their new surroundings, Professor and Mrs. Albert Bushnell Hart. Justin Winsor was then Librarian of Harvard College, and as Rhodes is seen—again through the medium of a footnote—to have used the College Library before his first volume went to press, it was most natural for him and Winsor to have met within its walls. Yet there is the well-accredited story that when Winsor received the first and second volumes of the History as a gift on their publication in the autumn of 1892, and saw the name Rhodes on the title-page he experienced surprise that a Cambridge printer of that name whom he happened to know should have produced such a work.

There is not much to show for the preliminaries to the appearance of these volumes. In a letter of December 3, 1891, to Dr. Frederic Bancroft—from whose name the prefix of "Mr." was soon to be dropped in the frequent communications from Rhodes —these words are found: "I was in N. Y. Monday and left my M. S. with Harpers'. I presume in about three weeks I shall have it returned, then try another publisher, and finally publish it on my own account. However, a business life of fifteen years has habituated me to disappointments. I have enough M. S. to make three small volumes." Of the actual reception of the work in the Harpers' office there is no record, but the nature of it is made manifest through a letter, dated Cleveland, February 16, 1892, from Professor E. G. Bourne to Rhodes: "I had heard from Mrs.

Zerbe of the very gratifying result of offering the History to Harper Bros., and was waiting to hear directly from you. The news gave very great pleasure and I feel sure that once published the work will win its way solidly with the students of American history. I was struck in reading Mr. Alden's [5] remarks about history being unreadable if not set out with the greatest literary power. I had just been reading Seeley's 'Expansion of England' and he has not a little to say about the past sacrifice of historical science to 'mere literature.' Considering the frankness with which the readers expressed their opinion the verdict is a most encouraging one for the future of the book. I am very glad you thought of sending me the reports, which I enclose."

Of Rhodes's state of mind at this time there is a clear indication in a letter which he wrote nearly eight years later to Dr. Bancroft: "It is not very pleasant for me to think what a fool I was when Harpers took my first two volumes to give them an option of all the rest. I would not have done that in pig iron. But I was too eager to get a good publisher and to get before the public." This was written in 1900, when, owing to financial difficulties in the Harper firm, the four volumes of the History then published were transferred to the Macmillans, whose London house had published the English edition from the first.

When the first two volumes, covering, respectively, the years 1850-1854 and 1854-1860, appeared—in 1892—Rhodes could have felt nothing but satisfaction

---

[5] Henry M. Alden, long editor of *Harper's Magazine.*

in the fruits of his labors. By the professional historians, by the critics at large, and by the "general reader," the work was instantly recognized and acclaimed as a production of the first importance. Craving especially the approval of scholars in his own field, the author had good reason to be pleased when their recognized organ, the *American Historical Review*, declared of him, "He is writing a political and social history with rare judgment, accuracy, and patience, with good literary skill, and with sincerity and honesty of purpose."

Thus Rhodes as a writer stepped at once into a place which did not essentially change through the remainder of his life.[6] As volume after volume appeared that place grew constantly larger, both through the natural growth of his fame, and through the extension of his circle of congenial acquaintances and friends, of whom the number became legion. But of outward events there was in store for him nothing of a dramatic interest comparable with the change of his estate from that of the Cleveland man of business to that of the New England, and national, man of letters. Henceforth he is to be seen either at work in his study, pursuing historical reading and writing with an unflagging zest and industry, or in the world of human

---

[6] The lively interest with which private persons were reading his first volumes is recalled by the following passage from a note of Rufus Choate's daughter, Mrs. Bell, to the late Theodore F. Dwight: "The account of Sumner's experience in the Senate [in Vol. II] excels all novels for interest. What an extraordinary power distance has of intensifying! I remember being calmer the morning I read of that scene, though he was my father's friend, than I was to-day reading about it."

companionship which meant hardly less to him, as host, and guest, and happy participant in social contacts of many forms.

To follow him, not too minutely, through these experiences of some thirty-five years, there seems no better plan than to take them up in chronological sequence, with such breaks in the narrative as will be seen to be dictated by circumstances, and to treat at appropriate points, and with frequent light from his own letters, the methods and results of his labors, his friendships, his recognitions and rewards, and the value of his individual contribution to the life of his country.

2

Past the Beginnings
1892–1899

Since it is purposed to follow Rhodes "not too minutely" through his experiences as a man of letters and of society in its broader sense, the outward circumstances of his life through the final years of the nineteenth century may best be summarized at this point. It was late in 1899 that he took up his life at 392, Beacon Street, Boston, the scene of much of his work and many of the pleasures of that hospitality of which he made so fine an art; only a little later, after spending a summer at Seal Harbor, Mount Desert, the house, "Ravenscleft," to which he and Mrs. Rhodes became deeply attached, was bought. A characteristic note from President Eliot in August of 1901 testifies to the place the Rhodeses promptly made for themselves there: "I hope Mrs. Rhodes will secure the piece of rock she has become attached to. That kind of attachment seems to me to add considerably to the satisfactions of life. We should have been glad to have you as a nearer neighbor; we shall be highly content if you become a summer resident of Mount Desert on any part of the shore." But this is anticipating the sequence of domestic events.

After three years in the Cambridge house occupied in 1891, Rhodes and his family spent a year in Europe. While there he decided to move from Cambridge to Boston—which he had defined to Dr. Bancroft in 1893 as the "most difficult place in the world to get acquainted"—and on his return in the autumn of 1895 established himself at 176, Newbury Street. Here—if a personal digression may be permitted—I first met him. The meeting is to be recorded only because two of its circumstances illustrate so clearly certain characteristics of the man. I happened to be interested at the time, about 1897, in launching a series of brief biographies, on which, at the suggestion of Barrett Wendell, I wished to consult with Rhodes, hoping indeed that he might possibly be persuaded to write one of them. In an old letter-file I find a note from him, undated as to year, evidently responding to a request for an interview, and declaring, with a modesty almost appalling to one so much his junior, and still ignorant that this modesty was a fixed habit, "I shall be glad to give you any ideas I possess, but you know more about biographies than I do, and

I shall ask you to give me some of your knowledge."
I remember well the heartiness with which he received
me, and—I hardly need add—my own inability to
impart the instruction his note had suggested. Besides
the modesty revealed, another characteristic of Rhodes
appeared: he was not to be deflected for an instant by
any piece of minor work from his History. The files
of his general correspondence make it plain that
editors of every degree and applicants for all manner
of writing, either for print or for oral delivery, learned
again and again from Rhodes himself what I learned
at a relatively early day—that the writing of his History was his sole and central task, and that nothing
could beguile him from it.

Through the years of transition from his coming to
Cambridge till his settlement in the Boston house which
was longest his home, some letters illustrate passing
events and thoughts, some remembrances of friends
add touches to the picture. Rhodes was a fairly
prolific, though not a brilliant, letter-writer. He re-
sorted but rarely to dictation, that bunker in which so
many strokes of individual expression are commonly
lost; yet his manuscript letters are not marked by any
special felicity of phrase, nor with many of those
tokens of insight and humorous apprehension which
ensure an element of liveliness in the best correspondence. The qualities of his published writings are,
however, present in abundance—sagacity in comment
upon affairs and persons, fair-mindedness and modesty
in judgment. The nature revealed by these letters is
obviously one of greater simplicity than subtlety—and

no less clearly one in which the essentials of satisfying friendship were sure to be found.

Of the letters he wrote during the nineties the largest number now available were written to Dr. Frederic Bancroft of Washington, that younger friend to whom, as a previous chapter has shown, Rhodes sent the material on which the biographical sketch introducing him to American readers was based. Evidently Dr. Bancroft was planning to call the work of Rhodes to the attention of influential readers, among whom Carl Schurz was counted, for on March 21, 1892, Rhodes was writing: "But the greatest of all of whom you have spoken is Schurz. I am well satisfied that if he would read the book, he would find in it matter to commend. For I have tried to write in the same spirit in which he wrote H. Clay—a spirit of impartiality, which, however, does not go so far as to emasculate the judgment and which prompts one to speak plainly when plain-speaking is necessary."

A few weeks later, on April 7, another letter to Dr. Bancroft revealed something of the education of James Ford Rhodes: "After my four or five hours of composition daily I try to read two or three for style— Shakespeare, the Bible, Burke, Webster, Lowell, and Hawthorne are just now my guides; and I am reading Frederick the Great for method. What good things books are to be sure! And how faithful we should be to the Muse of History! She is not a strumpet, and I think not a fickle jade."

To this passage it should be added that throughout his life the Bible and Shakespeare remained his daily companions. The careful reader of his History will detect many traces of his familiarity both with the Bible and with the Book of Common Prayer; and the direct quotations from Shakespeare so far outnumber those from any other writer as to prompt the wish, in academic terms, that more of "distribution" had been added to his "concentration."

The reception to which Rhodes's work was destined meant much to him in 1892, but he did not sit idle awaiting it. In the summer of that year Mrs. Rhodes, who left him so infrequently that letters between them are rare, went to Colorado, and two letters in August speak for the ways of industry in which he was habitually walking.

To Mrs. J. F. Rhodes

Cambridge, August 3, [1892].

. . . Don't worry about me being here alone. I am doing very well. The atmosphere of my library is conducive to work and since I have got buckled down to it I am having a fairly agreeable time. Of course the house is far from what it would [be] were its mistress and the rest of the family here; but I am very comfortable; and while I am lonely at meal times and in the evening, yet I am much better contented here than I was at Plymouth. Next to my family I do believe I love to study better than any thing else; and I have the satisfaction each night of thinking what I have accomplished during the day. If I stay here until the 29th or 30th I shall have done a great deal of reading towards my next chapter. I had thought I could do the reading in two months, but as I get into

[73]

it the subject grows on me and I think I shall have to read, read nearly three months before beginning to write. I presume I shall be at work all winter on this chapter and then we shall only be to the firing on Sumter.

I read the best speech of Douglas yesterday I ever read of his. It was made January 3, 1861, after South Carolina had seceded and the other states were threatening secession. It is wonderful what a power of expression that man had, considering his limited education and the fact that he never read any literature. I think the *Congressional Globe* of that session of Congress will engage me all this week and next, for the print is so fine I only read one hour and a half a day on it.

I have read over all but 100 pages of my vol. 2, and only found one trivial mistake. Other errors must be there but they have escaped me. I shall probably be like Longfellow who had three persons read the proof of his Dante, and when he finally received the book at his breakfast table, he opened at once to a very serious misprint.

I am pretty well satisfied with the 2nd volume. If some good critic will say as that gushing female did, that it is "vivid" I shall be delighted. But I can make the third volume better in point of style. I expect vols. 3 and 4 will be my chef d'œuvres: then after those I shall be old and grow prolix. . . .

To the same

Cambridge, August 19 [1892].
. . . I finished the French Revolution yesterday. As a history proper—as a work from which to get a

full and complete account of the times I cannot rank it as high as Macaulay's or Lecky's. It may be said perhaps that Carlyle has not the historic sense as have the other two. But he has the poetical gift which is a rarer endowment. It is fitter to compare the French Revolution with the Iliad and the historical plays of Shakespeare than with a formal history; though I take it Carlyle is more accurate and impartial than Shakespeare. Yet as Macaulay said, the historical plays of Shakespeare have superseded history. Everybody's idea of Henry V and Richard III is that derived from S's graphic portrayal of their characters.

Macaulay's History of England, I think, brought him $100,000 and more. After the French Revolution had been published a year there came to Carlyle £150 from America, the first money he had received for the work. Yet I think I would rather have written the French Revolution than the History of England. It would be rash to say that one would live longer than the other, for both have great merit. Of course Macaulay has had 100 readers where Carlyle had one; but that proves nothing as Dickens in his lifetime had many more readers than Thackeray. Macaulay was much more popular in his lifetime. Carlyle has probably the more enduring influence.

But what is literary renown? In the formation of the new cabinet Gladstone submitted the name of James Bryce as one of its members, and the Queen did not know who he was: had never heard of him. . . .

To Dr. Bancroft Rhodes owed one of the first acquaintances of the kind to which he frankly hoped that his authorship would open the door, and the pleasure he took in his meeting with Carl Schurz is worthy of record:

To Frederic Bancroft

New York, November 27, 1892.

I wrote you in such a hurry the other evening, it occurred to me afterwards that I forgot to say how pleased I was with the biographical sketch, barring some parts of undeserved eulogy, and in a way I was of course pleased with those.

Thanksgiving morning I received a note from Mr. Schurz saying Friday would be agreeable to him to receive my call, and asking me to stay to his midday meal. This I replied I could not do, having an engagement for dinner early in the evening. I left on the early train Friday, arriving at Pocantico Hills at 10 o'clock. Mr. Schurz met me at the station. Before we had arrived at his house he had put me entirely at my ease and I felt that I knew him well. We went into his library—and what a delightful room it is—and we talked for three solid hours of books, of men, of American history and politics. To say that it was a delightful visit does not express it. When you spoke of him as "the great Carl," you never said a truer word. He has a great mind and pure and honest purposes. Since 1868 I have learned much from him, and my pleasure in meeting him was of a high order. I did regret I could not stay longer. We talked of you. . . .

I cannot tell you how much obliged I am to you for having introduced me to Mr. Schurz. The acquaintance so auspiciously begun will be kept up. I met two sons and a daughter. Is he a widower?

After all we had dinner at 12.30 and I broke bread and drank vin du Rhin with "the great Carl."

The second election of Cleveland, in 1892, over his Republican opponent, Harrison, brought forth the following comment:

To Frederic Bancroft

Cambridge, November 11, 1892.

. . . Mrs. Rhodes says à propos of your letter of yesterday that it was breezy and jaunty and must have come from a man overflowing with spirits. Naturally you feel very happy over the result of the election. I have been living so much in the past for the past four years that I do not get quite so much excited over election as I used to. Have tried to study this canvass from a philosophical point of view. Two men of integrity and executive ability were running. The canvass has been decently conducted and has turned on a question of principle, as all agree that the tariff has overshadowed all else. The campaign has been remarkable for its quiet, and I shall look with interest to see what was the total vote. For two years it has seemed to me that the Republicans were wrong on the tariff and Southern questions and I should have voted for Cleveland, but, while he is all right on the silver question, I am afraid of the party. In the House last winter 130 Democrats and 10 Republicans. But after Cleveland what? Hill they say. And were I an enthusiastic mugwump like yourself my joy would be mixed with regret that Cleveland, as it is commonly reported, was forced to make a deal with Tammany for its support. And he didn't need it. . . .

Before the year was out Rhodes had made another congenial acquaintance in John Fiske, of whom he wrote to Dr. Bancroft, "His Discovery of America is a great book; it is the greatest historical work I have ever read by an American except The Rise of the Dutch Republic," and, at the house of Justin Winsor, he had met Sumner's biographer, Edward L. Pierce, with whom he soon found himself on terms of a delightful friendship recorded more than ten years later in a memoir written for the Massachusetts Historical Society.[1] The circle was rapidly extending. When Carl Schurz came to Boston and was asked by his host, Charles Francis Adams, whom he would like to meet at dinner, Rhodes was named—and began the friendship with Adams which became one of those that he valued most highly. Falling in a little later with Barrett Wendell in Egypt, he laid the foundations of an intimacy which ended only with Wendell's death in 1921, when Rhodes wrote about him to Mr. Worthington C. Ford, "I regarded him almost a brother." The first meeting with Wendell must have occurred not far from the end of 1894 [2]—slightly beyond the time we have been considering; but it bears so directly on a bit of record typical of these early years of Rhodes's establishment in New England that

---

[1] See *Proceedings*, June, 1904.

[2] It was not as strangers that they first met, for Wendell had been one of Rhodes's teachers in his course of self-schooling. On October 29, 1909, he wrote to Wendell: "I am glad that you mentioned your book on 'English Composition.' I have told you more than once its immense value to me when I made a thorough and repeated study of it when revising my first two volumes."

the rigors of chronology may be remitted for a moment. "He had come to the East as a complete stranger," writes Mr. John T. Morse, Jr.,[3] whose distinction as a biographer and as editor of the "American States Series" had made him well known to Rhodes before they met; "he had been here only a very few short years before his circle had expanded so that it was equalled by that of few even among those who had been born to inherited local alliances. I well recall my first meeting with him—at a dinner at Barrett Wendell's house. After dinner we sat all the evening on a sofa, talking together; it was very uncivil, but for my part I found the temptation so strong that no sensible man would think of resisting it merely to avoid the indignation of a host who should have felt some gratification at seeing one of his guests enjoying himself so much. When I said my good-night I excused myself by saying that I had been making a new and very valuable friend. In this instinct I was quite right. Ordinarily I should only have been making an acquaintance; but where other men made acquaintances Rhodes made friends."

In the year 1893 Rhodes, like most of his civilized fellow-citizens, visited the Columbian Exposition in Chicago. A letter written soon after his return to Cambridge bears its testimony to his having carried with him the historical and personal interests that were his chief concern.

---

[3] See "Memoir of James Ford Rhodes," *Proceedings* of Massachusetts Historical Society, March, 1927.

To Frederic Bancroft

Cambridge, October 5, 1893.

Yours of the 7th ult. was forwarded to me at Chicago, and yours of the 14th I received while there. I did not, much to my regret, see your brother. The beautiful city was so fascinating that I hated to go to the dingy and dirty city at all. I was obliged to go twice but got away as soon as I could. I went to see Von Holst on your letter and had a delightful visit of two hours with him. Reading his book in the translation I have perhaps not found it as interesting as you and others who have read it in the original, although of course I have been profoundly influenced by it. But after my visit of two hours I can well understand yours and Hart's enthusiasm for him. He is a real typical German scholar, and I am glad to have made his acquaintance. He is coming to Boston next February to deliver a course of lectures before the Lowell Institute, when I expect to see much of him. He reviewed Woodrow Wilson's book in the *Educational Review;* some number of this year. In that I think you will find an answer to your suggestion of the 14th.

Von Holst frankly confessed he had not read my book, but he had read the *Nation's* and Burgess's criticisms. Having read Burgess he felt that we had a common cause in our treatment of John Brown, and that put us in sympathy at once. Touching your hit at me for my treatment of John Brown you must fight that out with your old teacher, Von Holst, who is more of a John Brown man than I am. I find, too, I have lost all power of controversy and argument, but I have reviewed very carefully in my own mind my treatment of Webster and John Brown and have paid attention to all criticisms and yet if I were to make a thorough revision of my volumes today I should make no change in my general conceptions of their characters. I should probably condense the characterization of Webster and the account of John Brown somewhat.

You will have no great trouble in getting Nicolay and Hay's "Lincoln" badly snarled. Their conception is that Lincoln made no mistake, but that the mistakes were made by Seward, Chase, and the other fellows. If you have not already done so I hope you will read Charles Francis Adams's address on Seward. That is an example of an effort to make Seward great by belittling Lincoln.

You and Schurz are quite right in saying that Von Holst's material was thin in some places; but consider the difficulties he labored under and consider the advantages you and I have with the great libraries about us. . . .

Agreeable as it was to have the value of his work recognized by individual readers and critics, the note which Justin Winsor, as Corresponding Secretary of the Massachusetts Historical Society, wrote him on December 14, 1893, announcing his election as a resident member of the Society, had a significance which Rhodes was quick to appreciate. Witness his note of acknowledgment:

Nothing could have given me greater pleasure than your announcement that I had been chosen a resident member of the Massachusetts Historical Society. This I have always thought the highest honor a historical scholar can receive in this country, and that it has been conferred upon me so soon in my career of author I believe is due as much to your kindness as to my merit. I therefore thank you heartily and also your fellow members who have given me an earlier recognition than I could have dared to hope for.

It is indicative of his own estimate of the meaning of this election that on the title-pages of his fifth volume, published in 1904, and of the sixth and seventh, published in 1906, his name appeared with no embellishment, beyond the honorary degrees he had received, but the words, "Member of the Massachusetts Historical Society." To the work of this body he contributed much, both with writings for its meetings and Proceedings and by active participation in the conduct of its affairs. He held in later life the post of Vice-President, and it was but through his own determined modesty that he did not step into the only higher office.

While recognition that he valued was beginning to come to Rhodes, he himself was reaching out towards such extensions of his own horizon as his new surroundings would permit. Related neither to business nor, directly, to history was his visit, in the summer of 1894, to Plymouth, Massachusetts, where he attended the Summer School of Ethics. A course of lectures on Plato by Bernard Bosanquet of England was the bait that specially attracted him. But he turned the occasion to other than philosophical uses,

James Ford Rhodes

March 1892

for here he first met Woodrow Wilson, then a professor
of government at Princeton, with whom he formed the
relations out of which his confident voting for Wilson
as President in 1912 naturally grew; and here he began
his friendship with Professor Crawford H. Toy, the
Biblical scholar of Harvard, and with Mrs. Toy, to
whom both Wilson and Rhodes were to write many
letters that have furthered the work of their biogra-
phers.   To Mrs. Toy I am indebted for the following
bit of reminiscence:

I do not recall our meeting, but it must have been
soon after he came that Mr. Toy said to me, "Mr.
Rhodes is a remarkable man.   He is an historian, is
not particularly interested in the objects of the School,
and has come to hear Mr. Bosanquet lecture on Plato."
Later he told me that Mr. Rhodes had just published
two volumes of American history; and I remember
Mr. Toy's saying, "I think he has the historical mind."
At another time my husband said, "I have had a long
talk with Mr. Rhodes.   I wanted to talk about his
History and the West, but he got me talking about
the Old Testament and how it was put together."
Many years afterwards, and more than once, Mr. Toy
commented on the courtesy of Mr. Rhodes in bringing
out his interlocutor, and always with the manner of
eager interest—not, like President Eliot, in order to
gain information, but with the definite purpose of putting the other fellow at his ease and making him have
a good time!   I personally have not known man or
woman with such unfailing tact.   He never insisted on
his own point of view.   It was always, "You think
so and so?   Well, you know more about it than I do."

And it never sounded ironical.—Accuracy in statement about unimportant as well as important things, an unprejudiced view of persons and affairs, an historical background for opinions on current happenings, an incredible modesty for a man who had accomplished so much, and, above all, the best of *bons camarades*—these all stand out in my memory as I think of Mr. Rhodes.

To such remarks may well be joined two others: one by Rhodes himself, that the historian "must be a man of the world, but equally well a man of the academy"; the second by John Hay—and since Rhodes quotes it from "a private letter," [4] it is not an unsafe guess that it was a direct personal reference to the historian whose acquaintance we are making—"No man can be a great historian who is not a good fellow."

Again a few of the many letters to Dr. Bancroft afford passages that will serve as Rhodes's own record of the years now more immediately under consideration. It should be said that for approximately a year from September 8, 1894, he and his family were abroad.

To Frederic Bancroft

Cambridge, January 27, 1894.
. . . I am delighted to hear all that you say against Webster. I deem it the bounden duty of a historian who has a pet hero or a pet theory to hear all that possibly can be said against him and it. I am going to

---

[4] See *The McKinley and Roosevelt Administrations*, p. 123.

revise my two volumes some day and unlike Mézeray [5] who wrote the history of Rhodes (the island) I am always open to conviction. There is enough to be said against Webster—and not a month goes by that I don't hear much of it—but my characterization was arrived at by striking a fair balance, I thought. At all events I have not changed my opinion yet and I hope it is not from obstinacy. . . .

To the same

Cambridge, March 6, 1894.

. . . We had a good time at the dinner, Von Holst, Winsor and Judge Chamberlain were the stars and they made it very interesting. As Dr. Winsor said to me when leaving: "We had a very breezy time of it." The discussions you would have enjoyed very much. Von Holst is a most agreeable man at a dinner. I wonder he has not been entertained more here. He and I are going to dine together Wednesday evening and go to the opera. I have got a great deal of good out of my intercourse with him since he has been here. I am glad to think that I owe to you the benefit and pleasure of his acquaintance.

You remark you think Schurz, Von Holst and I would agree with you that Seward was our greatest statesman since those of the revolutionary period except Lincoln. Count me out of your imaginary quartette *decidedly*. But you have the proper biographical spirit and I rejoice at it. [6] You will not be oppressed therefore with the weight of authority against you.

[5] This appears to be a trace of Rhodes's reading of Sainte-Beuve, two of whose *Causeries,* in his eighth volume, deal with the French historian Mézeray.

[6] Dr. Bancroft was then writing his biography of Seward.

For we may be wrong. If you can construe the facts honestly and plausibly to establish that proposition it will add to the interest of your book. But you must let me keep my private opinion. I will promise not to review your book in print and also agree not to get mad should you criticise my vol. III with the savagery of the ideal biographer who growls furiously when his idol is shaken. I do not think we four would disagree at all about the facts. It is only in the inferences we draw from them. From the way I have heard you talk you will be the most candid biographer I know of, except Mr. Pierce, who has written from the subjective point of view, and candor is the main thing. It is refreshing that you neither deny nor ignore the ugly facts. Keep your admiration for Seward. He was genial and amiable and we should have been glad to dine with him even if he did toast his bare feet before the fire before dinner.

To the same

Cambridge, June 26, 1894.

. . . I do not want to be an officer of the American Historical Society. That means to get in the line of presidential succession, which makes a point of going to the meetings and also involves some work as well as time. I cannot make a speech. I would be a poor presiding officer. "Shoemaker, stick to your last." My tastes are essentially those of the student. The best work I do is that in the library. Of course I have an advantage in having the experience of fifteen years to draw upon. Now it is foolish for me to leave that which I do tolerably well to do that which I should do very ill. . . .

To the same

Stratford-on-Avon, September 18, 1894.

. . . I am ashamed that having been in England twice before I have not until now visited the home of Shakespeare. For since 17 I have been a reader, a hearer and admirer of the great dramatist. Yet as the love and appreciation has been growing on me I do not think I could before have been so interested and satisfied as I have been this afternoon. It always amuses my wife when I tell her that Shakespeare was a great historian but to me he and Homer are the greatest. Often have I thought of the remark of Macaulay's that Shakespeare's historical plays have superseded history. Today in coming from Chester when we passed Shrewsbury, the battle of Shrewsbury was to me Shakespeare's battle and it would be spoiled for me could I not think of John Falstaff's bearing a part in it. I presume you have been here. Indeed I know not whether you are a lover of Shakespeare. You criticised my falling into Shakespearean and Biblical phrases, and deeming your criticism for the most part well taken I have in the main avoided that defect in vol. III; and though rhetorically your criticism was probably just yet I think, did you love in the very fibres of soul Shakespeare and the English bible, you would not have made it; for you would have said to yourself, the poor fellow has affectations but they are affectations with a good backing. The miracles of the bible are insignificant affairs to the miracle of Shakespeare, growing up in what was then a dirty and malarious village. The beautiful pastoral scenes of his plays, one can see the suggestion of in this beautiful garden of England, but how did Shakespeare recreate Rome, Egypt, and Italy of the Middle Ages and the Renaissance? More Rome than Roman, more Egypt than Egyptian I think someone has said. This is the thought that comes to me on my way to Rome and Egypt. The English historians have an immense advantage over us in the wealth of historic suggestion they have all around them. . . .

To the same

On The Nile, December 13, 1894.

. . . I take it you have never been to Egypt and I wish I might infuse into this some of the enthusiasm of the Egyptologist, but so far I have not been able to rise to the height. It is useless to speak in the way of a judgment after a fortnight's experience merely, but so far Egyptian sight-seeing does not take hold of me as does that of Florence and Rome, which are, unless I should admit into the class London with some qualifying phrase, the most interesting cities I have visited. "Egypt," wrote Herodotus, "is a land of many wonders"; and the same may apply still, but the artistic beauty of what you see at Florence and Rome is lacking. The historical aspect of sight-seeing interests me more than the artistic, and as I am glad to devote the rest of my life to American history so it is a pleasure to contemplate for a while the story of the oldest civilization. It is possible I may be able to take a more correct measure of the space our civil war should occupy in the world's great drama, and I may gratify my friends by being less prolix and in boiling down my material more than I should have done were it not for this year's vacation I have laid out for myself.

With interest I have been reading Herodotus's account of Egypt in Rawlinson's translation which is enriched with his and Wilkinson's notes; and it is a sensation worth having to look at the Pyramids and the site of Memphis and the colossal statue of Rameses II and then go over again the accounts of them by that charming and popular Greek writer. In reading some of the mass of literature which Egypt has called forth, it is pleasant to see how often the Father of History is referred to and what just importance is attributed to his description and relation, and with what charity his errors are viewed. For I take it Herodotus is one of the historians we all take off our hats to in that he was sincere, honest, and readable. Strabo and Diodorus and Pliny I have yet to go through, for the modern literature on Egypt must necessarily claim the larger share of attention. The climate is worthy of all praise. Herodotus found it so, and so may the modern man. We were ten days in Cairo. The coldest part of the morning the mercury would be at 55° and the warmest part of the day at 70°. We now sit out all day on the steamer's deck and in the evening until too sleepy to sit out longer. The air of the desert is wholesome and agreeable. I want to bottle up a lot of this Egyptian sunshine in my system and spread it over my M.S. next fall and winter when I shall have got to work again. . . .

To the same

Vienna, April 6, 1895.

. . . From your talk of the criticism attracting purchasers I hope there is nothing at all sensational in the whole volume. I have been in many cases positive but have only expressed my heartfelt convictions. My estimate of Lee is wholly sincere and I shall be sorry if it shocks many of my old friends who bore the brunt and burden of the war and to whom Lee's "traitorous conduct" obliterated in their minds all his virtues. But an historian cannot be partisan. One large element in the impartiality of Thucydides is that, Athenian though he was, he treated the Spartans with fairness and respect. You and I are far enough away from the Civil War to look upon the actors without bitterness, convinced though we may be that in the grand balance of right and wrong, the right was on the side of the North. Agreement on such a main point will make up for any differences we may have as to Webster, Seward and J. Brown. . . .

In the year of Rhodes's return from Europe, 1895, the third volume of his History, covering 1860–1862, made its appearance. In 1899 came the fourth volume, 1862–1864. These were received in America and England with all the tokens of approval that an author could desire. In New York the *Nation*, which had so appreciably affected Rhodes's political thinking, avowed its belief that "here we have something very near to what time will prove to be the accepted story of the nation's great struggle for self-preservation." Professor W. A. Dunning of Columbia wrote in the *American Historical Review*, "Mr. Rhodes has now attained that agreeable position in which a new volume of his history is distinctly an 'event.' The position has its responsibilities; but the present volume offers abundant evidence that the author is quite capable of sustaining them. In guiding us through the central heat of the Civil War, he never loses the clearness of head and the calmness of spirit with which he brought us up to the conflagration." In a word his arrival as an historian was complete: it could hardly have been more rapid.

In the summer of 1895 he had written from Scotland to Dr. Bancroft, telling of five weeks in London, where he had enjoyed a half hour's conversation with Samuel R. Gardiner, had lunched with Lecky, and breakfasted with Bryce. "Thus," he said, "I met the three men whom of all others I wished to see in England." Back at home, he applied himself vigorously to his work. "I do not allow myself to be diverted from my fourth volume," he wrote to Dr. J. F. Jameson in declining an invitation to contribute to the *American Historical Review;* and went on, "I am really sorry I cannot do something for you besides good wishes in words! words! words! but I will explain to you some day what abundance of material one has offered him who deals with a recent period of American history. The fact of it is, I am working *almost* as hard as a college professor, and am not making very rapid progress." There was little or no let-up in the summers. On August 28, 1896, he wrote to Dr. Bancroft from Beverly Farms, "All my summer I have sat on the piazza and read, read, read. I must now write." The summer of 1898 he passed at Willard, Ohio, on the shore of Lake Erie, in order to be near his son, then employed in the Cleveland office of his uncle, Mark Hanna. From Willard he wrote to Mr. Worthington C. Ford on August 8, that he was "enjoying the summer, and as the spirit is on me on my native heath I am doing a good stroke of work." Nothing else was so sure to take him away from his work in winter as the annual Christmas-week meetings of the American Historical Association, at which he became a familiar figure. In the spring of 1897 he projected a more adventurous outing, by inviting Dr. Bancroft to accompany him on a trip from Washington to Chancellorsville, up through the Shenandoah Valley to Gettysburg. "Three or four days," he wrote, "ought to do it, and we should live over again the defeat of Hooker, the advance of Lee into Pennsylvania, and the victory of Meade. . . . We can discuss history to our heart's content, and may learn something one from the other." This journey was not accomplished, as planned, with Dr. Bancroft as a companion. That this would have been in some measure a sentimental journey may be inferred from an anecdote related by President Lowell. Once, when Rhodes and he happened to be in Richmond together, they visited the church, St. Paul's, from which Jefferson Davis was summoned, during the Sunday morning service of April 2, 1865, by the news that Lee's army could no longer prevent Grant's from entering the capital of the Confederacy. The sexton pointed out the seat which Davis had quitted,[7] whereupon Rhodes, with much solemnity, sat himself down in it for a few moments of silence. Slender as this incident may seem, it suggests something of the sympathy with which he sought to enter into the personal elements of every scene he had to depict.

---

[7] See *History*, Vol. V, p. 118.

If significant letters from Rhodes to his friends were written in the closing years of the nineteenth century, few of them have come to light. Among his papers, however, a truly significant letter to him is found. It was written by Lord Acton, December 19, 1896, and, coming to Rhodes only four years after his first appearance among the historians, must indeed have seemed to justify all the hopes with which he had begun his work. He was invited to write all or a part of the seventh, the American, volume of the Cambridge Modern History. "To myself," wrote Lord Acton, "this is a matter of high importance, knowing you as I do for the best and the most impartial of American writers, and supported as I am in that conviction by Bryce, and Lecky, and all who, over here, are any way competent to speak." A draft of Rhodes's reply shows how amply he recognized the honor of the proposal and the force of the temptation to accept it. But even this did not cause him to swerve from his constant course. "To complete my own history," he wrote, "will require twenty years more, and as I cannot hope for intellectual vigor longer, it would not be right for me to make any further engagements. . . . I have the consolation, however, of believing that other American historians will do the work better than I could. Indeed I am far from being certain that I should be able to make an interesting story out of so compressed a narrative."

Among his recovered letters here is one, foreshadowing the view of the McKinley Administration set forth in his final volume:

James Ford Rhodes

To Frederic Bancroft

Boston, January 10, 1898.

. . . I think with you that the President is doing admirably. I know of no country in the world that has as good a lot of men at the head of it as we have now in our national government. Of course I cannot subscribe to every article of the Republican faith, but of the sincerity, honesty and integrity of the President and his cabinet I have absolutely no question. It is very desirable for the good of the country, in so far as it is dependent on correct financial legislation this session, that Mr. Hanna should be sent back to the Senate. I have a reasonable degree of faith that he will win, for the reason that he is backed by the popular sentiment of his state, party orthodoxy and the earnest support of the independent mugwump element of the party.

Later in 1898, on August 25, Rhodes was writing from Willard, Ohio, again to Dr. Bancroft, in significant terms. "Please the élite: the rest will follow," he said; and proceeded, if half humorously, yet surely with another half of seriousness: "The puff in the *Critic* which you suggest does not attract me now, nor would any puff of the sort. I have changed from what I was five years ago. Supplementing my Shakespearean and Homeric studies with Goethe's Conversations and the Goethe-Schiller correspondence, I am aspiring for culture and wish to be a scholar. Ephemeral popularity I care nothing for. If I can live twenty years more and continue my studies and produce a volume every five years, I shall be satisfied with whatever notices the good gods send me with my friends or I striving for them."

Of the work that lay ahead of him (in his Volume VII) there is an indication also in a note to John C. Ropes, March 19, 1899, acknowledging a bit of material to be filed in his scrap-book for future use and saying, "While I did not think so at the time, I now believe that Hayes made a better President than Bristow would have made, but he was handicapped badly by the moral cloud, so to speak, over his title."

Relating to a piece of work more immediately at hand is a letter of December 4, 1899:

To John T. Morse, Jr.

Boston, December 4, 1899.
I was highly gratified to get yours of November 18. Nothing is so pleasant as to have appreciation from those who are working in the same vineyard. It is always an incentive to better work.

In the presidential address that I am preparing for the meeting of the American Historical Association December 27 in this city I am endeavoring to show that the writing of history impartially within a generation of your own time is not as difficult as it has been thought to be. The exigencies of the address do not permit me to elaborate the subject or to illustrate it as copiously as I might have done.

If you do me the honor to read the address—I think it may be published in the *Atlantic Monthly* for February [8]—you will see how high I rate the power of

---

[8] This address was printed not only in the *Atlantic* but also in the opening pages of Rhodes's *Historical Essays* (1909).

compression and how I have fallen short of my own ideal. It is a pity that I have not your power of expression and compression; it would have shone so well in my study of such a mass of original materials.

We were sorry Mrs. Morse and you could not come to dinner but it was a case "without Hamlet." Senator Hanna could not come to Boston on account of the Vice-President's death and funeral and Mrs. Hanna felt obliged to leave us for the same reason.

It has been seen that no longer before this time than June of 1894 Rhodes had written to Dr. Bancroft in a *nolo episcopari* vein with regard to holding office in the American Historical Association. Here, in 1899, he is entering upon the presidency of that body. In the interval he had come to occupy a place which rendered his election almost inevitable, and his Presidential Address, designated simply "History" in his volume of Essays, may be read today as a vital portion of the historian's *credo*. The articles of his faith were supplemented a year later by an Address, "Concerning the Writing of History," which he read at the 1900 meeting of the American Historical Association, when called upon at the last moment to appear in the stead of Edward Eggleston, who was absent through illness. Calling this paper "a continuance of my inaugural address," Rhodes took up the subject of his craft, and his own methods, both here and twice again—in 1908, in a lecture on "The Profession of Historian" read before students of history at Harvard, Yale, Columbia, and Western Reserve; and later in the same year in a paper, "Newspapers as Historical Sources," read at the annual meeting of the American Historical Association. All of these papers, like the first, are to be found in his "Historical Essays."

In intimating what a man has done it is always desirable to consider what he tried to do. The four papers just mentioned provide the basis for such a consideration. It is characteristic of Rhodes, in the first place, that he made no claim for the writing of history as "the highest form of intellectual endeavor; let us at once agree," he declared, "that it were better that all the histories ever written were burned than for the world to lose Homer and Shakespeare." [9] These are the two authors, he said again, who helped him most in his study of human character. To Molière, Balzac, Goethe, and Sainte-Beuve, he avowed the further indebtedness of an historian. His models for the writing of history may be inferred from the statement that follows: "If the English, German, and American historical scholars should vote as to who were the two best historians, I have little doubt that Thucydides and Tacitus would have a pretty large majority. If they were asked to name a third choice, it would undoubtedly lie between Herodotus and Gibbon." [10] In Rhodes's advice to future historians, moreover, there is abundant evidence that he had given careful study to the methods and results of such modern writers as Carlyle, Macaulay, Green, and Gardiner.

The uses by which Rhodes himself sought to turn

---

[9] *Historical Essays*, p. 1.
[10] *Ibid.*, p. 5.

all such study to account may be summarized in his own words: "Natural ability being presupposed, the qualities necessary for an historian are diligence, accuracy, love of truth, impartiality, the thorough digestion of his materials by careful suggestion and long meditating, and the compression of his narrative into the smallest compass consistent with the life of his story. He must also have a power of expression suitable for his purpose." [11] And there was, in his view, yet another essential: "A historian, to make a mark, must show some originality somewhere in his work. The originality may be in a method of investigation; it may be in the use of some hitherto inaccessible or unprinted material; it may be in the employment of some sources of information open to everybody, but not before used, or it may be in a fresh combination of well-known and well-elaborated facts." [12] In a word of warning to others he expressed, besides, one of his own constantly guiding principles: "Beware of hasty, strained, and imperfect generalizations. A historian should always remember that he is a sort of trustee for his readers." [13]

Rhodes himself was acutely conscious of the historian's need of an attractive style in writing, and did his best to cultivate it. Many notes in his "Index Rerum" volumes—from such simple guideposts as a rhyme embodying the proper uses of "will" and "shall" to passages from masters of English copied evidently as

---

[11] *Historical Essays*, p. 20.
[12] *Ibid.*, p. 27.
[13] *Ibid.*, p. 32.

examples of felicitous expression—speak for his self-
schooling in this respect. In spite of these efforts his
pages exhibit comparatively little of grace, ease, and
beauty, though much of the clear and cogent statement proper to his sound, impartial judgment, and his
sense of justice equally intellectual and moral in its
quality. In the matter of form there is also the orderly arrangement to be expected of one trained first
in the conduct of affairs.

He esteemed "a knowledge of Latin and French of
the highest importance," and deplored his own lack of
classical training. "When doubtful as to the use of
words," he wrote, "I should have been helped by a
better knowledge of Latin and enabled very often to
write with a surer touch." [14] Such an avowal disarms
criticism, which might be extended from Rhodes's use
of words to the construction, now and then, of sentences which an early drilling in Latin and Greek
grammar would have rendered impossible. Though
obliged to read the classics in translations, he was
completely at ease in the reading of French and fluent
in speaking it, though with anything but a Parisian
accent. In speaking his own tongue he sometimes revealed a lack of familiarity with the sound of words
which he knew perfectly well by sight. An allusion in
one of his letters to Barrett Wendell to "my intrepid
French" relates itself amusingly to a fragment copied
in the first volume of his "Index Rerum". "When
someone asked Talleyrand how the Duke of Welling-
ton spoke French, the courteous diplomat replied,

[14] *Historical Essays,* p. 54.

'With the utmost intrepidity, as he does everything else.'" With Rhodes the act of utterance, whether in the speaking of French, or in the speaking and writing of English, was conducted without a trace of affectation. He employed what he possessed, without self-consciousness, but effectually to the end at which he was aiming. This represented the same simple acceptance of conditions that is revealed in his statement: "For myself, I have never found any royal road to learning, have been a slow reader, and needed a re-reading, sometimes more than one, to acquire any degree of mastery of a book." [15]

A like simplicity is found in another statement in his paper on "The Profession of Historian": "In intellectual development I believe that in general an important advantage lies in accepting the dicta of specialists." [16] In this remark both the historian and the man are revealed. In his writings and in his human relationships alike he showed a respect, sometimes almost naïve in its humility, for the opinions of those to whom he felt that respect, on grounds of whatever real or imagined superiority, was due. Mrs. Toy, who travelled in Europe with Mr. and Mrs. Rhodes in 1903, remembers that "in the galleries of London, Berlin, Dresden, etc., Mr. Rhodes determinedly looked at only those pictures double-starred by Baedeker. Mrs. Rhodes asked, 'Why not choose for yourself?' 'I know nothing about pictures,' was his firm reply; 'I bow to authority, and waste no time

[15] *Historical Essays,* p. 69.
[16] *Ibid.,* p. 58.

or strength in looking at any but the best.' " In his last book, "The McKinley and Roosevelt Administrations," a single sentence, relating to Roosevelt's position with regard to the fixing of railroad rates,[17] indicates a habit of mind which probably grew upon him with advancing years: "I would not venture to differ with so great a man as Roosevelt were I not buttressed by the opinion of Henry Cabot Lodge, Roosevelt's intimate and faithful personal and political friend." It was so natural for Rhodes, in direct intercourse, to defer to the opinions of others that his tendency towards "accepting the dicta of specialists" was inevitably the stronger when these specialists were his personal friends. It is an engaging quality in all his writings, however, that, once satisfied with the competence of an authority in any mooted matter —and there are countless evidences of the pains he took to get at the true relative weight of conflicting testimony—he gave this authority his confidence ungrudging and entire.

The four essays which shed so much light upon Rhodes's aims and methods touch upon many details besides those already named—his system of note-taking, his use and sliding valuation of newspapers as such and in comparison with other sources of material, his view of the financial expectations to be entertained by historians. To illustrate this point he relates an anecdote, which was something of a favorite with him: "A young friend of mine, at the outset of his career and with his living in part to be earned, went for

[17] Pp. 325-326.

advice to Carl Schurz, who was very fond of him. 'What is your aim?' asked Mr. Schurz. 'I purpose being a historian,' was his reply. 'Aha!' laughed Schurz, 'you are adopting an aristocratic profession, one which requires a rent-roll.' " [18] To Rhodes himself the ability to secure the most competent assistance was an important element in the successful outcome of his work, and so recognized by him.

It has already been seen how greatly he relied, in his first and second volumes, upon the help he received from Professor Edward G. Bourne. This scholar's surviving brother, Professor Henry E. Bourne of Western Reserve University, also conducted investigations for Rhodes in the earlier years of his authorship, and has preserved many of the notes of instructions by which his work, covering the years 1856-59, was guided. As one turns them over they are found to indicate beyond a question that Rhodes was issuing no blanket demand for information on a merely trouble-saving basis, but rather that he knew precisely what he wanted, and, legitimately applying the principle of *qui facit per alium facit per se,* was furthering his own work. A manuscript memorandum, headed "For Mr. Bourne," and filling some twenty pages, begins, "Your work may be called a search for historical material not ordinarily found," and proceeds with many directions both general and detailed. A number of brief letters from Rhodes, in Manchester, Vermont, to Professor Bourne, in Boston, followed upon the broader sailing orders. A paragraph

---

[18] *Historical Essays,* p. 78.

from one of them illustrates the character of the investigations: "In Von Holst, vol. 1854-56, on p. 34, Note 1, you will find cited private letter taken from *Tribune* June 10/54. Will you please transcribe for me all that Von Holst does not quote. Is there a signature to the letter? Does the paper indicate in any way who the letter is from or what sort of man the writer is, or give any particulars? Kindly let me have this by return mail, as I am on that subject now." As Professor Bourne warmed to his task, it is not surprising that Rhodes supplemented his long list of specific points with the words, "Now that your enthusiasm is awakened cover the ground as if you were gathering material for yourself, and if you do not get through the years I outlined in the month it will not matter."

Two other helpers must surely be mentioned. One of them, Miss Alice Wyman, receives a word of acknowledgment through a footnote in Rhodes's third volume, expressing indebtedness for "her intelligent aid" in the Boston Athenæum, to which she was then attached. Again and again in later volumes her help as his secretary is cordially recognized. At times indeed she was a member of his household, in Boston and Seal Harbor, and even travelled abroad with Mr. and Mrs. Rhodes, often exercising for their benefit, wherever they were, her excellent gift of reading aloud. It is strange that one of Rhodes's business training never—except apparently for one brief period—employed a secretary who used a typewriting machine. The great bulk of his correspondence was in his own handwriting, with occasional excursions into the clear script of Miss Wyman. Her death, shortly before his, deprived his biographer of a source of enlightenment on many points. He is nevertheless bound to record her remarkable helpfulness to the employer who was also her friend.

Another helper, who has survived him, is Mr. D. M. Matteson of Cambridge, Massachusetts, who from about 1900, when Rhodes was working on his fifth volume, to the end of his years of production, not only performed the functions of research which the Messrs. Bourne had provided at an earlier stage, but gave a critical reading to successive volumes in manuscript, and made the indexes for them in print. Mr. Matteson has kindly placed at my disposal many memoranda bearing on this work—letters of instruction from Rhodes, together with short and long reports from himself on specific points and larger subjects. These are supplemented by a letter of Mr. Matteson's, explaining details in the material, and containing a passage which must be quoted here: "Certainly, so far as my work for him was concerned, his mind as well as his soul was his own. Except when he deliberately quoted from me, there was in all the volumes but a single phrase that I could claim as mine. He was not in the least afraid of criticism or of having ideas suggested to him; several times he asked me to read such and such volumes, and suggest whether he should amend any statements in his work. . . . Whatever went into the melting-pot, the gold that came out— and it was gold—was all Rhodes."

For all such assistance, paid and unpaid, including the valued "literary revision" which his son contributed to most of his later volumes, Rhodes was prodigal of acknowledgment in his prefaces and footnotes. Having adopted "an aristocratic profession," he was scrupulous to follow it like a gentleman.

From these considerations of his aims and methods, adopted early and pursued to the end, it is time to turn again to the progress of passing events, illustrated chiefly by his letters.

3

ACHIEVING THE MAIN DESIGN
1900-1906

In 1904 Rhodes published the fifth volume of his History (1864-1866), and in 1906 the sixth (1866-1872) and the seventh (1872-1877). On the title pages of the first five the scope of this "History of the United States" was limited by nothing more than the words, "From the Compromise of 1850." In the sixth and seventh volumes he added to this definition of a beginning the definition of an end, in the words, "To The Final Restoration of Home Rule at The South in 1877." The first sentence in the first chapter of his first volume had read, "My design is to write the history of the United States from the introduction of the compromise measures of 1850 down to the inauguration of Grover Cleveland, thirty-five years later." In the Preface to his sixth volume he explained to his readers that as his work proceeded it had become clear to him that 1877 and the restoration of Southern home rule provided a more logical terminus for the writing he began in 1888 than the year 1885 and the inauguration of the first Democratic president after Buchanan. He intimated clearly, however, that further writing might follow after he had broadened his vision of more recent tendencies by "a systematic study of the history of Europe during the eighteenth and nineteenth centuries, especially the histories of England, France, and Germany." We shall see that in due time this intimation was fulfilled. But his sixth and seventh volumes, published in the same year, 1906, represent substantially the completion of the main design with which he began. The years devoted to this achievement, and to the production also of his fifth volume, may be counted among the most important in all his historical writing. His letters of this period speak for many of his interests. The familiar superscription, "392 Beacon Street," is found henceforth for more than twenty years on all his Boston letters. The first of them has to do with the American Historical Association presidential address already touched upon.

To William Roscoe Thayer

Boston, February 14, 1900.
I am very much gratified to get your letter of the 28th ultimo. Appreciation from a fellow historian and scholar is the dearest of all.

I have thought for many years on the subject of my historical address, and in spite of some friendly criticism on it which I have received, I see no occasion whatever for changing the views therein expressed. I have been pleased that the article, though dealing with an old subject, has attracted attention.

It seems to me that our scientific historians have done a good deal of good by their methods of teaching history, but in their eagerness to get at original material and make a comprehensive search, they have overlooked the importance of digesting materials, of accurate generalizations and method of expression. As Morse Stephens [1] says, when he reads over a sentence of his that seems particularly good, he scratches it out and rewrites it, for fear someone will think he is aiming at fine writing. Still I think the basis is industry in the search for materials and critical power in sifting them. I have always thought, however, that there ought to be one lecturer at Harvard presenting the other side—what Mr. Winsor called the ornamental part and what he was in favor of having presented. . . .

To Frederic Bancroft

Boston, October 10, 1900.

. . . In Mr. Schurz's speech in New York a fortnight ago I do not think he showed his usual candor. Some of his opponents have pointed out errors in his premises and mistakes in his facts. I have not

---

[1] H. Morse Stephens, of Scottish birth and English education, was professor of modern European and English history at Cornell in 1900, and from 1902 until his death in 1910 professor of history at the University of California. Rhodes valued him highly as a congenial friend, and took much pleasure in the annual Christmas visit of Stephens to Boston and to the meetings of the American Historical Association. Efforts to recover the many letters which Rhodes must have written to him have been unavailing.

time to go into the matter to see who is right. I did not read the whole of the speech, but I read all of it which was published in the Boston *Herald*, and from point of view of orderly arrangement and unfolding of his theme, it seemed to me equal to his best efforts in the past. But it is really mournful to see a champion of sound money and civil service reform like Mr. Schurz using his influence indirectly for Bryan. What twists do get into the brains of good people! Your candidate has not, I think, helped his cause since he started on his stumping tour. But truly the ordeal is a hard one, and he would be more than human if in his many speeches, travelling about with loss of sleep, he did not say silly and injudicious things. But I think many reflecting people have come to the conclusion that he has not the ability and judgment together which we should have in a president. President McKinley and all the members of his cabinet have shown great dignity during the canvass. I suppose that you have heard that Mr. Olney and Moorfield Storey have both come out for Bryan. Mr. Olney is, I believe, the only member of Cleveland's cabinet who has so declared himself. Carlisle, McVeagh, and Morton are for McKinley. The strong probability at this writing is that McKinley will be elected. I suppose you will be glad of it, because then you can maintain your critical attitude for the next four years, but if Bryan had been elected you would have been on the defence. . . .

To Frederic Harrison

Boston, May 8, 1901.
I received your kind notes of 20 and 23 ult., the extract and the book. I am glad to be able to use

[108]

your words exactly as you wrote them, and although my next volume will not be published for a matter of four years, I am glad to have my quotations right as I go on.[2]

I note all that you say about your South African war, but you will soon be at the end of it and you will not go to war again for a generation. The more I study war the more I detest it and I think that most wars nowadays might be avoided; however, as human nature is what it is, it seems to me that the cause of peace will advance slowly. All honor, however, to gentlemen like yourselves who advocate peace without ceasing.

Our President, his cabinet and his intimate friends were opposed to the Spanish War but were forced into it by Congress and I suppose Congress was backed by popular sentiment; at all events the senators and representatives thought that they had a popular backing. We have had our war and I hope that we shall never have another and I feel pretty sure that the inclination of your generation is towards peace decidedly.

I omitted to say that I read the whole of your essay. I found it very excellent reading. You were harder on your Tories than I was; but in one respect you are quite right—it was a great pity your governing classes had not sympathized with the North. It would have made the position of the present friends of England here stronger. But you will soon be through with your present troubles and no one can wish so more strongly than do I.

---

[2] Rhodes quoted Harrison's characterization of Lincoln in his Vol. V, p. 144 n.

James Ford Rhodes

To Frederic Bancroft

Boston, May 20 [1901].

Your valued favor of 8 at hand. I read Barrett Wendell's book [3] immediately after it came out. I neglected one Sunday all my classical reading, all my French and German, and stuck to Wendell's book with avidity. I was enthralled and read it for five hours consecutively. It seemed to me then and seems to me now a fresh and original treatment. Naturally all original men meet adverse criticism and Wendell has had a lot of it, much of it ill-natured. Your criticism is admirable in its tone; of course it ends with a joke which you mean only as a joke. I wish as a friend of his some things were not in Mr. Wendell's book; but then there are matters in all of our books which our best friends wish that we might have omitted. . . .

To Charles W. Eliot

Boston, February 7, 1902.

. . . I wish to repeat what I said about Mr. Rockefeller the other evening, adding an additional consideration. I knew him somewhat but my knowledge of him comes from a more intimate acquaintance with his school-fellows and business associates than with himself.

I attribute Mr. Rockefeller's success first to his rare executive ability. This was displayed markedly by his power of organization and his judgment of men. As I look back over the men who have been connected

---

[3] *A Literary History of America,* by Barrett Wendell, appeared in 1900.

with the Standard Oil Co. I marvel at his selection of men before they had to the rest of us displayed business ability. I would not say that he was never influenced by sectarian prejudice (being as you know a strong Baptist) or by matter of family relationship, but the main question was, Has the man brains and will he be steady and diligent? It is amazing the fortunes which have been made by his subordinates who started with nothing in the way of money. A trait I have admired in Mr. Rockefeller is that he never showed the slightest jealousy of his subordinates or associates. If they were very able, so much the better. I have known captains of industry whose success has been impaired by such jealousy. I presume that Mr. Rockefeller with his keen judgment of men has felt that no matter how able such or such an one was, he himself knew a great deal more.

Another circumstance to which I attribute Mr. Rockefeller's success is his absolute honesty towards his associates and stockholders. However remorseless he may have been in crushing his competitors, a widow or an orphan or anyone who owned one share of Standard Oil Co. has always received the same rate of dividend which he himself has. There have been no inside deals in which he and a favored few have participated; no "wheels within wheels" as we used to say. This does not seem now a great business virtue, for the tendency of railroad and industrial corporations has been for the last twenty years in that direction, but it was not so when the Standard Oil Co. was formed. Inside arrangements were then common. I esteem it very sagacious on Mr. Rockefeller's part that he adopted at once a different method from that which had been pursued by a number of rich men in New

York and Cleveland and of course all over the country.

I also count it as a contribution to Mr. Rockefeller's success that he has never been an operator in the street—a speculator. He has invested his money in properties and looked after them with ability.

I beg pardon for having inflicted on you this long note but I wanted to answer your question to what did I attribute Mr. Rockefeller's success and a little reflection has enabled me to do it better than I could upon the spur of the moment.

The observant reader will have noticed that the foregoing letter was written in answer to one of those characteristic inquiries of President Eliot which signified a genuine desire for information, and it is not surprising to find that at just about the time of his making it the General Education Board, of which he became a member a few years later, was established by Mr. Rockefeller. To the President of the United States Rhodes was writing a little later.

To Theodore Roosevelt

Boston, April 22, 1902.

MY DEAR MR. PRESIDENT:

Home again and thinking of the fruitful, interesting and enjoyable visit I had at the White House I must give expression to the sense I have of your kind hospitality. With my satisfaction at being entertained by the President I had the delight of talking *à cœur ouvert* with a distinguished member of the republic of letters, but I shall say no more for fear of indulging in superlatives which we agreed in decrying.

May I present my kind regards to Mrs. Roosevelt and Miss Roosevelt?

With the expression of my very high esteem, I am

Very truly yours,

JAMES FORD RHODES.

This first visit of Rhodes to the White House during Roosevelt's presidency was, as we shall see, not the last. A side-light upon it is found in a letter which Rhodes received from his sister Mrs. Hanna at about the time of the 1902 visit. She reported the President's high opinion of the historian and his work, adding, "The only criticism he had to make was, he thought it would be better for you to get out of that dreadful mugwump district." And here a brief digression may be permitted.

In Rhodes's fifth volume,[4] he quoted a declaration of the Richmond *Dispatch* on March 21, 1865: "Failure will compel us to drink the cup of humiliation even to the bitter dregs of having the history of our struggle written by New England historians." Was Rhodes himself a New England historian? Roosevelt's remark about his "mugwump district" half jokingly implies as much. Professor Dunning of Columbia detected in Rhodes's later volumes a certain loss of the "Western refraction" which marked the first and second, and clearly raised a question when he wrote: "The seekers after a Western interpretation of our national life must be content with speculation whether, if Dr. Rhodes's taste had led him to transfer

---

[4] P. 81.

his home to Chicago or St. Louis, rather than to Boston, the contents of his last volumes would have been any different." [5]   But back to Roosevelt this digression brings us, though the medium of a letter to Rhodes from Professor William E. Dodd of Chicago telling how Roosevelt's interest in his life of Jefferson Davis (published in 1907) had brought him an invitation to the White House "to lunch and to 'talk Davis,'" and proceeding: "It is a sign that our country, which even historical students may be permitted to love, is really getting past the time when the differences of 1861-65 serve as red rags.   May I say that I believe your masterly History has done more than any other historical agency—perhaps any other agency of any sort—to bring about this state of feeling?"

If Rhodes is to be rated, through the accident of residence, as a "New England historian," such a statement from another historian, Southern in birth and sympathies, must betoken some sweetening of the dregs of that cup of humiliation so dreaded at Richmond in 1865.

Another letter from Rhodes to Roosevelt, dated Boston, November 15, 1904, expressed a hope—"when you get through your job as President I desire to spend at least a day with you or have you spend one with me in order to have a long talk on history and literature, which I hope may be followed by many others"—and announced that his fifth volume, then just published, "should go to you tomorrow."   Evidently it went, for a letter in Bishop's "Theodore

---

[5] *Educational Review,* Vol. XXXIV, p. 114.

Roosevelt and His Time," dated November 29, 1904, informed Rhodes that Roosevelt had just read this volume with high approval, and expressed some difference of opinion about the responsibility for our Civil War. It must have been this letter that Mrs. Robinson had in mind when she related in "My Brother Theodore Roosevelt" a feat of her hero's in the small hours of the night following an exhausting day at the St. Louis Fair—a feat so nearly incredible that the reader receives due, if unconscious, warning through finding these introductory words ascribed to Roosevelt himself: "I am going to do something that is very interesting. William [*sic*] Rhodes has asked me to review his second and third volumes of the 'History of the United States.' You may have noticed I was reading those volumes on the way from Washington. I feel just like doing it now. The stenographer is rested, and, as for you, it will do you a great deal of good, because you don't know as much as you should about American history." The review, completed, according to Mrs. Robinson, by 5 A. M., seems to have been entirely satisfactory to both Roosevelt and his sister, who has unfortunately omitted to inform the reader where it may be found in print; and nothing in the little episode is less credible than that, even if Rhodes had strayed so far from his customary modesty as to ask the President of the United States to review his history, a book-review so produced should have escaped publication. But the letter printed by Bishop was well worth preserving.

That Senator Lodge was also an early and appre-

ciative reader of Rhodes's fifth volume the following
letter indicates.

To Henry Cabot Lodge

Boston, January 4, 1905.

I was gratified beyond measure to receive your kind
and appreciative letter of December 20. A few days
previous your ears must have burned as Mr. John
T. Morse and I were talking about you and saying
what a loss history and literature had incurred when
you forsook them in part for politics and statesmanship. Mr. Morse said if you had selected my period
I must naturally have chosen some other, and, while I
deny that a historian can appropriate any one period,
such would likely have been the result. But you chose
the more difficult and the more glorious part. I was
just today reading in John Morley's Voltaire that
"though Voltaire was perhaps the most puissant man
of letters that ever lived, he rated literature as it ought
to be rated below action."

I like all the good things you say about my volume
and I rejoice that we agree so well. It is to me un-
thinkable that Lincoln would have broken with his
party on Reconstruction. So far as one can divine he
would have been obliged to defer in some degree to the
radical Republicans, and while I do not believe he and
Sumner would ever have agreed on negro suffrage and
might have remained on that one point politically apart,
I feel sure that the President and the senator would
have remained friends as they did after the Louisiana
debate in January or February, 1865. And I like
one of your criticisms where you assert the "world
glory" of Lincoln. I hope that you are right, and I

am quite willing to believe that you are, for you have had a large intercourse with European men of action. I believe you cited in your Cambridge speech last summer the opinion of Sir Spencer Walpole that "perhaps of all the men born to the Anglo-Saxon race in the nineteenth century Mr. Lincoln deserves the highest place in history." The two great men are, as you say, Lincoln and Bismarck, and I quite agree with you that Lincoln was the greater.

Your other criticism I shall bear carefully and constantly in mind. I am always glad to have your criticisms, as indeed I ought to like suggestions from one who bore an honorable part in the Republic of Letters before he went upon the larger stage. I rejoice that the President and you have shown that bookish men can be successful men of affairs. We are proud of you that you furnish us a comparison with English public men; and I cannot help thinking of Mr. Bryce and Mr. John Morley of whom I saw a good deal while they were in Boston. . . .

Among the other letters of 1905 there is more than one to Theodore Roosevelt, to whom Rhodes, on November 19, addressed what he called a "conventional bread-and-butter letter" after a second visit to the White House.

. . . I returned to my desk yesterday [he wrote] with renewed zest which I think is due to what the biologists call anabolism, arising in this case I am sure, from contact with a vigorous personality, who is rendering an immense service in the cause of political righteousness.

I hardly expected to see in my own day a President
who would so thoroughly carry out the ideas that I
have embraced from my life of affairs and study. I am
confident that in this I speak the thought of a large
number of men whose life is passed at the universities
and in libraries. To evolve these ideas from solitary
thought in a library is not difficult. To carry them
out as you are doing with physical and moral courage
and with persistence requires rare qualities of the highest order. I think that I appreciate these fully as I
see plainly where I myself would fail as indeed would
most men given to contemplation.

This tremendous energy, this power of doing things
falls so often to men of low political ideals that it
is a constant cause for rejoicing that one of our own
kind possesses it, who is in a position to give it full
exercise.

But, rejoicing as I do, I am not nevertheless going
to say nunc dimittis. . . .

The evidences of Rhodes's hearty and long-sustained
admiration for President Roosevelt are many. In one
of his "Index Rerum" volumes there is something more
than that—an example of his practice of recording
talk that might be of use to a writer of history. In
1906 he was probably innocent of any purpose to
produce in 1922 "The McKinley and Roosevelt Administrations," yet the footnotes of that volume give
clear evidence that when he came to write it he had
helpful recourse to the extensive memorandum of conversation during the visit that called for the "bread-
and-butter letter" of which the larger part has just
been quoted. Both as a piece of "material" and for

its intrinsic interest this memorandum, informal as it is, may be printed almost entire:

Nov. 16, 1905. Dined at the White House with President and Mrs. Roosevelt. Among others who were present were Secretary and Mrs. Root, Secretary and Mrs. Taft. I remained over night, leaving the White House at 9.35 Friday morning Nov. 17. The President had invited me in order that I might hear an account of his trip to the South.

South.—Description of his rebuke to Gov. Jefferson Davis of Arkansas who had attempted a quasi defence of lynching. The retort was not immediate, although he was mad and made up his mind that what he said ought to be rebuked. He spoke on other topics until he got the crowd in sympathy and then he marched up to the Governor, looked him in the eye, made his gestures towards him until the Governor and the crowd seemed to think that he was going to strike him. The cheering was enthusiastic and genuine. Jones, a political opponent of Davis, applauded vociferously. At Chapel Hill, N. C., a splendid reception. There a professor had taken a manly stand in regard to the B. Washington kind of negroes. He spoke of the blue and gray always taking care to put first, the blue. He paid sincere tributes to Lee and Jackson. Always had some regard as to how his speeches would read at the North. He would not say in one section what he would not in another. A Confederate badge was pinned on him. "I accept this," he said, "in the spirit in which it is tendered as signifying that no section is now more loyal to the Union and would do more to preserve the flag than the South."

"The XV Amendment very unjust and bad policy."

Was much struck with the first part of my chapter on Reconstruction, with my suggestion of what Lincoln would have done, how he would have worked up to negro suffrage gradually, based on the negroes' winning intelligence and property. Spoke of the way the negroes had gone back in the Yazoo district of Arkansas and Mississippi. . . . The negroes, the President said, are 200,000 years behind (I suggested a million, an amendment which he accepted). Still it is not pleasant to think that John Sharp Williams represents one vote to a representative of Massachusetts four.

I said I instanced the election of 1874 and 1890. I inferred that the President had no intention of tackling the question. Root drew a parallel of interfering with the Jews. Any pressure on the South, and pressure on Russia would make fate of negroes and Jews worse. On the whole the President well satisfied with his trip South. Taft thought at the expiration of the time of the grandfather's clause the thing would work out all right. The President spoke of two negro letter carriers who had stood the best examinations in Williams's district, but the white men threatened them and they would not pursue their occupation. Finding not so [much] prejudice against them in Memphis there they were transferred.

England.—Present government, a set of split carrot-heads—answer perfectly well for a pink tea. Not up to the work of a governing body.

The President thought more of England than of any other foreign country, more sincerely our friend; detests the Anglophobists. Sometimes when in contact with the Irish he is tempted to become an Anglomaniac. We are a different people from the English. We are thoroughly democratic. They are not. M—— made a mistake in sending his boys to Oxford. Men who are going to live in America should be educated in American universities. Does not believe in marrying foreigners. All right for a son to marry an English woman and bring her here to live, but he should dislike exceedingly to have one of his daughters marry a foreigner.

Alaska Boundary.—Out of friendship did not want to press it during Boer war. English wanted it settled. The President in no hurry. Let it rest. But if gold was discovered there he intended to occupy the boundary. All of our ministers to England pro-English except Bob Lincoln. Tendency of cultivated people to take the side of the English. Choate for arbitration. The President said No, not a question for arbitration. Letter the President wrote in 1903 to Justice Holmes. English objections to Lodge and Root because their opinions were known. The President said Canada [had] no more right to that territory than it has to Nantucket. "If the Commission fails to settle the question, I shall move troops into the territory." He asked Justice Holmes to impart this to Chamberlain. Holmes showed Chamberlain the letter. He wrote substantially the same thing to Henry White to be imparted to Balfour. The English Government, he thinks, tipped the wink to the Chief Justice. In the Atlas of the English Case. In all the differing maps from 1830 on, no claim made to the disputed territory, until 1884. Map after map shows the American line. Our case established by the volume of maps entitled the *British Case*.

Russo-Japanese Treaty.—Hay largely incapacitated for business for year and a half, so much of the State Department work fell to him. He conducted the

Russo-Japanese negotiations. Japan made the first move by requesting in writing his mediation. Japan was getting to the end of her tether. A decided falling-off in the quality of her recruits—best men, men of education needed at home, workers in the field. Japan insisted on indemnity. Roosevelt saw they would not get it. Take Moscow and St. Petersburg and then you will be in a position to demand it. (German-France precedent.) But they bluffed to the last, bluffing Roosevelt. Good work of Meyer. Meyer has a higher opinion of the Czar than has the President. The question in regard to that Island, Sakhalin. Russia would not cede a foot of territory. Finally settled by her letting Japan reoccupy what once was hers. Japanese minister wanted to withdraw first part of the correspondence. No, says the President. Surprised that the President was going to make no mention of the matter in his message.

Part the German Emperor played. A regular fuss-cat. Wanted to have a hand in it and was willing to accept other people's ideas if he could call them his own, even if they were diametrically opposed to his first pronouncement. Witte much impressed with this country. The great prosperity and wealth, the industries, this barbaric strength were what appealed to him. He was surprised to hear so much talk about corruption. "Why all this talk about corruption?" he says. "I ask what is this corruption and they tell me that Croker or Murphy the boss of New York help great financiers in their enterprises and then accept presents from them. Why shouldn't they?" he asked. Witte thoroughly selfish, everything for Witte, country second. The Japanese thoroughly patriotic, easy to work with. Delcassé's underhand game. Wanted the negotiations to fail so that England and France might step in and bring the two warring nations together.

Tariff Question.—Two-thirds of the members of the House opposed to touching the tariff. He himself, if he could do it by a ukase, would revise the tariff. Would put hides on the free list and make general reductions. But he could only do it by breaking with his party. People blame him for working with Penrose, Platt, and Depew. He has to. He did not make them senators; if he had had the power he would have sent very different men from Pennsylvania and New York, but those states elect them.

The President is determined on his rate revision. Spoke of me as a great historian who understood practical affairs. In such wise superior to Lecky.

Odell corrupt. McClellan personally honest, but does what Murphy tells him. Tom Johnson. The President suspects. Taft does not think him honest. He says to the crowd, "I know how these people have made their money. I know their crooked ways because I have been in the same business." The President and Taft have no admiration for Steffens. Taft said he would not record an actual fact told him by Cox lest it should hurt his antithetical sensation.

Root on newspaper criticism: even that which is untrue, unjust and harsh, a necessary step in our political evolution. Immense admiration of the President for Root. He accepts, the President said, the conditions of the game.

Root and Taft.—That Akron speech may make Taft President. No, says Taft, I want Root President, so that he will appoint me Chief Justice.

Anthracite Coal Strike.—Bacon and Perkins. Five, not seven. No labor man would accept an eminent sociologist. I shall then appoint a labor man and call him an eminent sociologist. Appointed the head of a conductors' Union. Catholic Bishop. Cleveland urged him to take possession of the mines by the right of eminent domain. The President intended to take possession of the mines. Had General Schofield in full sympathy and he was going to represent the government of the State. Root and Knox opposed to his action, but supported him loyally.

With the advent of 1906 the completion of Rhodes's seventh volume—and so, with some deliberate abridgment, of the task he had set himself almost twenty years before—was clearly in sight. On the 8th of May he wrote to President Roosevelt, "I have finished my history, stopping at 1877 instead of 1885 (the reason whereof I explain in the preface) and Mrs. Rhodes and I are going to Europe in a fortnight for an indefinite absence. I shall for awhile take a rest from 'scribbling' and devote my time to a study of modern European history as a fitting preparation for the continuation at some future day of the history of the United States from 1877 on." The letter, containing expressions of admiring confidence in Roosevelt's recent course in the presidency, brought forth a cordial offer of notes of introduction to officials in Europe, to which Rhodes replied, on May 11, that the Secretary of State was attending to his needs of this sort, and added, "Mrs. Rhodes and I expect to stay in Europe for a year if we can content ourselves that long. When we go to London in the spring of 1907 it is just possible that I may want a word of introduction from you. But we are not going to Berlin, and outside of Germany there is no emperor or king I care to take the trouble to meet." Thus it was altogether a delightful and well-earned holiday on which Rhodes and his wife set forth. But for one sentence in a letter to Charles Francis Adams from Interlaken, August 11, 1906—"I am reading proof—and, for needed relaxation, Balzac and Voltaire"—there is every indication that he carried out his intention of leaving his work quite behind him.

In the years through which he had just passed there had been no lack of the honors that crown the labors of a scholar. The first of these had come to him even as early as 1893, when he received the honorary degree of LL.D. from Western Reserve University in his native Cleveland. In 1901 both Yale and Harvard conferred the same degree upon him. In that year also he received from the Berlin Academy of Science the Loubat Prize in recognition of his work in history. In 1903 a second Ohio college, Kenyon, made him a Doctor of Letters, and in 1904 his third honorary LL.D. came from the University of Wisconsin. On the occasion of receiving his Harvard degree he was unexpectedly called upon for an exhibition of the composure that rarely failed him. Through some mishandling of memoranda President Eliot, having conferred the degree which appeared to be the last on his list, sat down while cheers for the new honorary alumnus were still ringing through the hall. Fortunately Dr. Henry P. Walcott, of the Harvard Corporation, was close at hand to twitch the President's

gown and whisper "Rhodes," whereupon the belated
ceremony was duly performed. "How did you feel?"
Rhodes was afterwards asked. "I was wondering,"
said he, "why the Corporation changed their minds." [6]
The terms in which President Eliot bestowed the degree may well have compensated its recipient for any
temporary distress.

Besides his academic honors Rhodes had been enjoying in Boston an intercourse with congenial spirits
that was quite as much after his own heart as any
of his success as historian. Professor Bliss Perry
summed it up at the beginning of a newspaper article [7]
written immediately upon Rhodes's death: "No man
who ever became a Bostonian in middle life conquered
that difficult city more easily and completely than
James Ford Rhodes. His habits were sedentary. A
singularly modest scholar, he hated publicity, and was
not one of the men who liked to be seated on the
platform. Yet for nearly thirty years, and up to the
period of his final invalidism, he was despite of himself a very well-known personage. His heavy figure,
shrewd, kindly face, and loud cheerful voice were familiar to all residents of that inner Boston which begins, let us say, at the Athenæum on Beacon Hill and
ends at the Historical Society's building in the Fenway.
That is not all of Boston, but it gives plenty of room
for a triumphal procession."

The "inner Boston" to which Professor Perry refers
is embodied in what I have called in another place its

---

[6] This incident is recalled by Mrs. Toy.
[7] See Boston *Evening Transcript*, January 29, 1927.

"subcutaneous clubs." It is not necessary to enumerate the organizations of this essentially private order with which Rhodes was identified, or to expatiate upon the pleasure he found in them and added to their meetings. At least two of them he held so sacred that at the beginning of each winter he would record in his book of engagements the dates of all their dinners and inform his wife that he must be involved in nothing else on any of those evenings. They were what he most missed when he went to Europe.

The pleasures of hospitality, extended and accepted in a measure equally profuse, were indeed real pleasures to Rhodes, whether at home or abroad; and in these, as in all the affairs of his life and work the sympathy and coöperation of Mrs. Rhodes were unfailing. Except for his "Index Rerum" volumes, containing occasional words of dinner-table conversations of historical significance, Rhodes, never addicted to the diary habit, left no such chronicle of his daily life as may be found in five leather-bound "Dinner Books." In these it was his practice to enter the names of guests at luncheon or dinner at his own board—generally with the addition of the variety and number of bottles of wine consumed—and of his fellow-guests at the houses of friends or at clubs. If one were writing a social history of his time and place, the mere names, local, national, and foreign, which appear in these countless entries would furnish a complete index of the persons, and personages, constituting what may be regarded as the most interesting "society" of the first quarter of the twentieth century. His notes suggest—but unhappily do not record in detail—the wealth of talk on many matters of more than passing moment in which he bore a part. On the occasion of a small luncheon which he gave to John Morley (November 20, 1904) one of his guests made a record of the talk that took place, and Rhodes—jotting only in his notebook, "A very jolly luncheon, with witty and interesting conversation; Mr. Morley at his best"—preserved it as a keepsake of the day. A single passage from it may be copied here as a specimen of the table talk in which so human a being as Rhodes delighted:

Mr. Morley told with gusto an incident of his visit to Harvard the day before with President Eliot as cicerone. It seems that after showing his guest the larger, more expensive dormitories Mr. Eliot had said: "Now you must see how our poorer men live," and had knocked at random on a door in Stoughton Hall. An undergraduate opened the door. He was without collar and cravat and in his shirtsleeves. When he saw the President of the College with a stranger, he looked abashed. Mr. Eliot very suavely explained that he was showing the college to Mr. John Morley. "Fancy my surprise," said Mr. M., "when the man seized my hand, burst into laughter and said, 'You are welcome, Sir. I am just writing an account of your visit to America for a newspaper.' And when we entered the room," continued Mr. M., "we found it barely furnished, a bed, a chest of drawers, two chairs and a table. On the table was a few scattered sheets of paper and the man held up one for me to see the title:

'The Honorable John Morley's Visit to America.' By it lay a copy of *Les Chansons de Roland*. I sat down and asked the man to tell me something about himself. He had been a conductor on some railway and was now making his way through Harvard by writing for the newspaper. If you have many such young men in America," here Mr. M. turned to Mr. Lowell,[8] "you will go ahead of us in England."

A reporter with ghostly legs under the many tables at which Rhodes rejoiced to sit, and with invisible fingers recording the talk that filled the air, might have produced an intimate chronicle in which an editor of 1975 would be sure to find enlightening matter for future students of the past. Even as late as 1920 Rhodes copied into the last of his "Index Rerum" volumes a quotation from the *Spectator*, in which his own philosophy of hospitality doubtless found satisfying expression: "Is it necessary to what in our higher moods we call civilization that meals should be attractive, that meal-times should be intervals for recreating and not only pauses for the stoking of the human machine? The dining-table has been for very long the centre of family life and the emblem of friendship. It is there that we have eaten one another's salt, acknowledged one another's equality, and entered into a tacit pact not to treat one another as enemies."

The holiday on which Rhodes entered in the spring of 1906 consisted in large measure, both directly and

---

[8] A. Lawrence Lowell, not yet President of Harvard, was a guest at this luncheon.

indirectly, in preparation for the years still to come, and the letters that bear upon it belong to the next division of this narrative.

4

FRUITS OF LABOR AND LEISURE
1906-1922

Rhodes's European holiday which began in May of 1906 did not end till the early summer of 1907. Before leaving home he wrote to Dr. Bancroft (May 1, 1906), "I have been at this job nineteen years, and am glad to be through with it. . . . I am really sighing for Europe and rest and a chance to get a little culture." Thus frankly he was wont to look upon Europe as a means for repairing some of the deficiencies of his earlier years. Specifically at this time he planned, as we have seen, to apply himself to the study of European history, for the enrichment of his own later dealings with the history of the United States. But the opportunities of leisurely reading in general, of travel, with all its answers to an inquiring mind, and of meeting the scholars and others to whom his own work afforded a valid introduction beckoned him overseas again and again. There has been, and will be, no attempt to record his European travels in detail, and readers may take heart from the knowledge that merely descriptive letters of travel are forming no part of this volume. From this point forward, however, it will be more practicable than it has been in the pages that have gone before to commit the chief burden of the narrative to passages from Rhodes's letters, written on either side of the Atlantic.

Let us draw first upon some of the letters of that year and more of travel on which we have seen Rhodes about to embark.

To Dr. Frederic Bancroft

Rheims, June 10, 1906.

I received your kind letter shortly before leaving home and I can in some degree appreciate your grief at the loss of Mr. Schurz who was such a good friend and genial companion. My acquaintance with him I owe to you, and it turned out one of pleasure and benefit. As a public man I renewed my knowledge of him in writing my last two volumes, and it seems to me that on the whole his senatorial career was the brightest and most useful part of his very useful and interesting life. Do you remember when he was visiting you in '96 and '97 how he gave us an account one night at dinner at the Arlington of the battle of Gettysburg? I hope that your voluminous notes have a record of it. It was great talk and a great description. It was a pity that Mr. Schurz could not have been constantly senator. I suppose many tributes will be paid him at the meeting of the Massachusetts Historical Society this week. I wish I might have been there to read some personal recollections. I wrote Mr. Adams that next to himself you knew Mr. Schurz better than any other man in the Society. I wonder if you will be going on to the meeting to pay your tribute. I am glad to know that you think of writing a biography of Mr. Schurz eventually. It will be a case of a good subject and a good author.

[131]

You must not think that champagne has attracted Mrs. Rhodes and me here. It is the Cathedral. We are getting to be a bit knowing on Cathedrals, and this is our second joint visit here, where we have remained three days. But in 1867 my chum and I were here for three weeks: and here began my knowledge of spoken French. Our rooms (which were on the cheap lay) were right near this hotel and I have identified the place, so that I am doing something in the sentimental way of reviving youthful recollections. We (i.e., Mrs. R. and I.) were in London nine days and came to Amiens four days ago, making our second visit to that beautiful cathedral. It makes one think to see these stately edifices and read the brief history of them we get in the guide-books. How one does wish for knowledge, and how I wish Haskins or Gross or Merriman were here for a day so that I could get from them what they know of the subject! Tomorrow we shall be going to Paris and I wish that I was going to find you there as I did in 1900 and that we were going to eat déjeuner, and drink bordeaux and eau de vie together. . . .

To Barrett Wendell

Geneva, July 8, 1906.
. . . I will not weary you with a detailed account of our doings, but I wish to give you an instance showing that the impressions of youth are not always vain delusions. Thirty-nine years ago I travelled through that country with a chum, walking sometimes and sometimes travelling third class. I remember how we were impressed with the comfort and good cheer of Angers and, indulging in an extravagance twice; on

two separate days we had a bottle of Vin d'Anjou
which I am quite sure cost 3 francs. We motored to
Angers one day and at luncheon had a bottle of this
same wine at 3 francs. It was so good that we had
a second and I give you my word it tasted as good as
it did thirty-nine years ago. I think there is nothing
like it except the "Sunshine" (I think is the brand)
in the Marble Faun. . . .

To Mrs. C. H. Toy

Interlaken, August 7, 1906.
. . . Not to lose my five weeks wholly while here I
set myself diligently to the study of French and was
fortunate in securing Dr. Béguin to come and take
coffee with me in the morning and talk for an hour.
So I am all for French. I think I wrote you from
Geneva that, led to it by a book of Brunetière, I have
taken to reading Balzac. Brunetière lays stress on the
historic value of the works of the great novelist. You
have, he says a perfect *histoire de mœurs* from 1815
to 1850. Now as in the preface to my VI volume I have
promised my future readers a study of English, French,
and German history of the XVIII and XIX centuries
before I bother them with more American history, I
said to myself here is my chance for summer reading
—history and story together. I began with *Eugénie
Grandet*, then *César Birotteau*, and was delighted with
the history. With *Un Ménage de Garçon* I felt that
something was gaining on history and, with *La Cousine
Bette*, Lubricity drove the Muse into a dark corner. I
am going to read the Life of Balzac in order to pene-
trate the thoughts of the man who believes *La Cousine
Bette* a high moral treatise. Still he does some good

preaching. I wish the Prince of Wales might take this to heart and not follow in the vicious footsteps of his father but rather emulate his grandfather, whom our friend Morfill called "a royal Tupper"; "En voyant ce que doivent avoir coûté les maitresses des rois, on mesure l'étendue des obligations des peuples envers ses souverains quand ils donnent l'exemple des bonnes mœurs et de la vie de famille." Brunetière tells me, "La monarchie de Juillet revit dans *La Cousine Bette*." If that story is a true picture of the state of society in the "good old times of L. Phillipe" (spelled wrongly I fear, try Philippe) what an advance in morals has been made during the Republic! Therefore how democratic-Republican institutions conduce to morality, as Bryan might say if he were reading Balzac. I cannot elaborate this further, but, tested by any true historic judgment, Brunetière and Henry James have said a lot of nonsense about Balzac. But I am going on with my study and may end up by adopting their opinions, although I shall never think Balzac equal to Shakespeare, as both these men seem to intimate. . . .

To the same

Château d'Oex, Switzerland,
August 27, 1906.

. . . Dr. Gordon was bound of course to protest against Mr. Santayana's book if the book denied the existence of God. It is his métier and, if there be no God, his church has little reason for existence and much of his work must be without meaning. But the professors of a university should have absolute freedom of speech and no book should affect a man's

[134]

standing or promotion, provided his views are expressed with decorum; and as Mr. Toy has a high standard of decorum, and, as I understand it, likes the book, that would settle the matter for me. Of course I know little about philosophy but I supposed that, for two or three centuries at least, philosophies had been doubting the existence of a personal God. If that is Mr. Santayana's whole offense, it does not seem to me a grave one, and if the book is, as Dr. James says, the most notable book published since Emerson, Mr. Santayana not only deserves promotion but the highest honors of the University. I cannot believe that he will be asked to resign and I should think that he will have a stanch supporter in Dr. James. Of course you know Dr. James a thousand times better than I do, but I suspect that when he talks with intimate friends he is sometimes thinking aloud.

I cannot see the force of Mr. Schiff's remark. The hopeless failure of Judge Parker made Bryan the next Democratic candidate if he would accept the candidacy. The war of President Roosevelt against trusts makes Bryan's chances for election less than they otherwise would have been. He cannot now conduct his campaign on the basis of regulation of trusts and railroads, but I think he must logically stand for government ownership of the railroads and telegraphs and this, it seems to me, makes his success less certain. I believe Mr. Roosevelt would beat Bryan, but the President is estopped from running again by his election day declaration and the prejudice against a third term. It is a pity Mr. Root or Mr. Taft cannot succeed him so as to carry on the Roosevelt policies. I quite agree with Norman Hapgood that no President since Lincoln has, on the whole, been so great a benefactor to the country. I am glad that Norman has a vacation for six weeks. Colliers ought to give him one for six months. He looked dreadfully when last I saw him, and he is too valuable a man for the Colliers to let him break down when with their immense profits they can make it so easy for him. I wish Norman might be in this air for two months, not to see a newspaper except the Paris *Herald,* and do nothing but walk over these hills one day and motor the next.

If Bryan is to be our next President, it will in my judgment be a calamity, but not so great a one as in 1896 and 1900. Mr. Bryce wrote to me that Bryan made a favorable impression in London; and his peace speech was certainly splendid. I believe him honest and good, but he is unsound on the fundamentals and the President is sound to the core. Still there will be compensations. It will be entertaining to hear Wall Street and State Street, the mugwumps, and the *Nation* finding more fault with Bryan than they have with Roosevelt. The representatives of the *haute finance* will see how silly they have been in saying that the President was worse than Bryan, and they will perhaps appreciate that Roosevelt has been the best of friends to honest wealth. . . .

To Barrett Wendell

Château d'Oex,
September 1, 1906.

. . . A week ago when we were motoring through Vevey on the way to Montreux, as a little day excursion, I caught a glimpse of Russell Sullivan. He invited Mrs. Rhodes and me to take luncheon with Mrs. Sullivan and himself yesterday. It was too much of an undertaking for Mrs. Rhodes but I went and was well paid for my four hours' trolley ride. Mr. and Mrs. Luce and Mr. and Mrs. Dwight were there. The conversation in some way fell upon your visit to Vevey last year and the Fête des vignerons, so that I spoke of your letter and your hard summer's work, and afterwards in a little tête-à-tête with Mrs. Luce told of your dining with Senator and Mrs. Lodge and your admiration for the Senator, an admiration which I share with you. Mrs. Luce [1] was well pleased to hear a good and kind word for the Senator from your social circle, among which she intimated the Senator was not without honor save in his own country. One runs up against a sentiment in Boston concerning Senator Lodge which seems to me essentially unjust. I have never been able to find out exactly why, for when I question and question I get nothing but generalities. I think it very largely due to his support of Blaine in 1884. . . .

To the same

Nice, November 4, 1906.

. . . I am very glad that you went over to see the President. The opportunity you had is one not to be missed. I think a great deal about the President and my life here in Europe, seeing practically nobody socially since the summer, is an aid to reflection. I count the President a very able man, one who has constantly grown since he has been in office. No country in Europe has three such able men at the head of affairs as are the President and Secretaries Root and Taft. I like often to think of the evening I passed

[1] A sister of Mrs. Henry Cabot Lodge.

with the three last autumn. All three, too, are men of such high character. The mugwump and *haute finance* criticism of the President has seemed to me essentially unjust. . . .

While in Paris we went on a Sunday to Lourdes, when many pilgrims were there humbugging themselves and being humbugged. The evidences of sincere piety and the desire of relief, if it be God's voice, we saw at the Grotto were in striking contrast with the mercenary demeanor of the shop-keepers, who pressed upon you their pious wares. The landlord of the hotel where we took luncheon was a good and honest man. It was cold and wet and we asked for a private room with a fire, which he gave us for our luncheon and made for them not the charge of a sou. The two bottles of Burgundy he furnished us had not been diluted with water from the miraculous spring. The fire and the wine gave us a contented spirit as we reflected on the immense investment at Lourdes in churches, shops and merchandise, and hotels, all based on the silly story. I had read Zola's book and racked my brains to remember all I could of it, which helped to make the day eventful. . . .

To the same

Rome, December 2, 1906.
Yours of 18th ult. came two or three days ago. I thank you heartily for your kind words about my last two volumes and in regard to my history in general. It is very pleasant to receive such praise.

All the news that you sent was read with avidity. Since the winter social season has begun, I miss Boston keenly. The Lord knows how I would like to drop into the Wednesday Evening Club and the Historical Society; at the same time we are here for the winter, and if I enjoy it all as I have enjoyed the first ten days of our stay I shall in the long run be recompensed for giving up for a winter the society in Boston which I prize so highly.

I am not at all surprised at the success of your Lowell lectures. What I heard of them at Cambridge prepared me for the gratifying encore. . . .

Between reading a lot about pre-Raphaelite art in Florence (where we spent eleven pleasant days) and Roman history here, I read your book;[2] and it is the book I have long been looking for. I wanted to see the case of the United States presented in a well-bred way with refinement of style, by someone who knew his England and France. In the international debate in literature these two countries get the better of us, not that they have the better case, but, from their mastery of language, they present it better; and our replies are apt to be brutal or chauvinistic or spread-eagle and make our case worse with all sensible men. Hence I am delighted with your quiet exposition, which is in the best English or French manner. The people of America are as far from anarchical as any in the world; our country in occasions of actual stress has never characteristically striven for the destruction of public order; America is only superficially material; it has high political ideals; our hands cannot help becoming gnarled and horny; we do not like abrupt breaches of historical continuity (a failure to appreciate this was one of Münsterberg's mistakes); the native Americans have a deep conservative impulse;

2 *Liberty, Union, and Democracy, The National Ideals of America* (1916).

Americans have a reverence for a college education, a reverence for demonstrated excellence—all this, and a good deal more, I call profound thinking expressed in a happy manner. I think that you strike high-water mark in the essay on Democracy, and it seems to me the best thing I have ever read. I rejoice too that we are in agreement about the historical meaning of the French Revolution.

Unfortunately Lawrence Lowell left here before we arrived, but we had some correspondence and his last letter was an exceedingly thoughtful one in which, among many other things, he said that he agreed with Morse Stephens that the French Revolution was rather the end of an era than the beginning of one. Lowell and Stephens know a thousand times more about European history than I do, but I cannot receive that notion of theirs, and it is pleasant to have my notion supported by your book and by your letter. Your pages from p. 317 to the close are very serious and are indeed the highest thought.

I am no critic but were I one, the only criticism I should make on your book would be in the words used by Gaston Boissier in criticism of the "History" of Tacitus. After remarking that the work was introduced to the public in "les lectures publiques" he writes: "Les Lectures publiques avaient ce défaut que l'auteur, pour se faire écouter d'un auditoire de gens du monde souvent ennuyés et distraits, était porté à multiplier les phrases à effet, les pensées brillantes (sententiæ) les cliquetis de mots et d'idées, les artifices ne manquent pas dans les premiers livres des *Histoires;* ils sont visibles surtout à la fin des paragraphes, on dirait que l'auteur tient à terminer ses développements, ses discours, ses récits, par quelque trait qui reveille l'assemblée; et ce trait est ordinairement si heureux, si frappant, qu'avec un peu de complaisance il semble qu'on entende à chaque fois les applaudissements éclater." But I recognize the thorough digestion of your material which could have been had only by the process that you used. I wish that I could talk to an audience as you do. I would like to work these phrases as Boissier imagines Tacitus did. . . .

To Charles Francis Adams

Rome, December 9, 1906.

I was glad to get two days ago your kind letter of 21st ult. I am gratified at your report of the sale of my new volumes by Lauriat, as I am democratic enough to rejoice at a large sale and circulation. I have little doubt that the money balance sheet would be substantially what you divine. I suppose that I spend what money I receive from the work on it, as I have endeavoured to spare myself all possible drudgery as I have grown older and my eye-sight poorer; but, on reflection, it may be that since Macmillan took the work I have something to the good. When, however, I put upon the other side of the account the acquaintances I have made and the friends I have gained by my History, when I reckon my friendship with you and my connection with the Massachusetts Historical Society, my book has a large amount to its credit. Had I continued in business, I should have been rich by this time and I should be roaming around Europe in a fast automobile, restless, living high, drinking '89 champagne, while now I am leading the simple life and having a delightful time, studying Roman history in some new books I have lighted upon,

[141]

and going about during the pleasant time of the day
to the actual spots, vivifying the knowledge I am getting from the works of Boissier and Ferrero. I have
been reviving my Tacitus and reading from time to
time the letters of Cicero. It is a far cry from Cicero
to Goethe, but I am reading also Goethe's letters from
Rome, and I am trying to get myself into his mood
and say, "I am living a new youth," and "Here one
must become solid."

Society in Boston, New York, Washington, and London was yours whether you wrote books or not, but
your books must have given you a friendly feeling
with literary men; and you must have a sentiment of
satisfaction that, although your method is not academic, you have compelled a hearing from the experts
in history—the professors and advanced students—because you have told essential things without which
certain eras cannot be understood. . . .

To Frederic Bancroft

Rome, December 13, 1906.
. . . I am trying to get as much good as possible
out of Rome, and Mrs. Rhodes and I are enjoying our
stay here very much indeed. I am impressed in my
different visits to Rome how the authority of the contemporary Roman historians is growing. Tacitus, with
the exception of perhaps two brief periods, has always
stood high; but it is interesting to me how the progress
of the excavations is supporting many assertions of
Livy that the Niebuhr-Arnold school denied. Significant too is the reverence paid by everybody to
Mommsen. That is a matter of course with German,
English, and American students; but the Italians and

the French vie with the others in homage to this great
historian. With such an example before one it is well
worth while to devote one's self to the study.

With my other wanderings I have been to the Church
on the ruins of the Capitol where, in hearing Vespers,
Gibbon conceived the idea of writing the "Decline
and Fall." Last September I went for the third time
to the garden in Lausanne where he finished his great
work, so that I have in mind the beginning and the end.

We have been here three weeks and shall spend the
rest of the winter in Rome and I want to spend one
or two more winters here before I die. Bliss Perry and
his wife, Mr. and Mrs. W. R. Thayer, Professor Morgan (Latin) of Harvard and Professor Lounsbury of
Yale are here, and at one time or another we see a
good deal of them. It has been very nice for us to
meet such pleasant and intelligent people. . . .

To Henry Cabot Lodge

Rome, January 7, 1907.
 . . . I have no satisfaction in my differences in my
VI and VII volumes from what I think must be your
own views. I can readily conceive that were you to
give the same study to Reconstruction that I gave you
would arrive at a different conclusion. I have derived
instruction and advantage from your books and
speeches, and it would have been agreeable, could I
have remained as near in accord with you as in my
earlier volumes. In the "Eternal City" where for
the past seven weeks I have read nothing but Roman
history, I am impressed with the different attitudes
honest men take towards these well-threshed historical
events. Scholars who are partisans of Cæsar or Cicero

grow hot as they press the merits of their respective heroes. And whether Tacitus and Suetonius were fair to Tiberius is another burning question. Carter, the brilliant director of the American School here, told us this morning that one learned German had written three volumes to show that the aim of Augustus was to restore the Republic; another had made him out a greater man than Julius Cæsar; while Mommsen considered him a little man masquerading under the greater Cæsar's name and reputation.

I have now been in Europe nearly eight months, looking at America through European spectacles. Naturally President Roosevelt's career is most interesting, and he loses nothing from this point of view. That he makes mistakes I am ready to admit, but the essential thing is that in his weighty policies and well-matured acts he is (in my judgment) absolutely right. I hope that he is careful in regard to exposing himself to danger, as anarchy is in the air and it is most important that he shall live to complete his term. If happily peace is preserved with all foreign nations we shall have, I believe, in his terms of office the country's greatest benefaction since Lincoln's. . . .

To Charles Francis Adams

Rome, February 2, 1907.

I received yesterday your address on General Lee and have read it with interest and pleasure. How well you have considered the charge against him that he was a renegade from the flag and a traitor to the nation! Nothing could be better than the way in which you name the "respectable company" who accompany him at the bar of History. Your insistence on his high character, shown in peace as well as in war, is exceedingly well put. I am delighted with the address; but you have gone fully over the ground I expected to cover in a future treatment of the same subject. But you have left me nothing to say. I rejoice, however, that you have done it. Your historic name, your long citizenship of Massachusetts, your four years' service in the Union army give to your clear and cogent words an especial force.

In cordial agreement as we are regarding the life and character of Lee, I am glad that we are equally at one touching the Reconstruction Policy of Congress. Of course this Address will appear later in a more permanent form. It should be preserved. I think you have said the last word to those who would fain regard Lee as a traitor. James Russell Lowell, despite his broad way of looking at things, could not rid himself of the idea.

I should be without vanity were I not especially pleased at the graceful footnote reference you make to myself. . . .

To Theodore Roosevelt [3]

Florence, March 16, 1907.

MY DEAR MR. PRESIDENT:—Reading your speech at the Harvard Union [4] as reported fully in the *Transcript* suggests that I give you some account of some of my thinking during my ten months' sojourn abroad. It's an old saying that the judgment of foreigners fre-

---

[3] This is one of a limited number of letters in this volume copied not from the originals but from pencilled notes preserved with Rhodes's papers.

[4] February 13, 1907.

quently anticipates that of posterity, and the American who has been abroad nearly a year may get some of that detachment which naturally resides in the European.

I have thought much of you and your administration, and I believe that among and in addition to the achievements of ten years you reckoned in your Cambridge speech three things are going to impress posterity.

I. He whom his critics had called the champion of war has turned out a great minister of peace. I am treading on delicate ground with insufficient information, but I believe that the historian will have to look for examples of "shirt-sleeve diplomacy" under Cleveland's and McKinley's administrations and not under your own.

II. You have erected a high standard for honesty and straightforwardness in public life, which is felt in every state and municipal government in the country. Your career and your example are being an incentive and inspiration to young men of good family and education to take part in politics. It is true that this is an incidental benefit, but a student of history comes to rate high the unconscious and indirect influence of governors of men.

III. I think you have emphasized the position of our government as being neither a government for the rich nor for the poor, but an arbiter endeavoring to deal out exact justice to both. Until the XIX century most governments were apt to be under the sway of one class or the other, more generally the rich, because the men who got the government and got their hands into the public till and the power to force tribute obtained the money. In the immense communities of nations now it is disastrous to have the rich and the government synonymous, for resentment and indignation at their selfishness is apt to turn into an attack on the nation's life. I consider therefore the policy you have identified yourself with a boon for the country; and those who are eager that we shall deal properly with the different questions that arise must congratulate themselves that a man sound in fundamental economic doctrines who is not a socialist should have the opportunity to grapple with this grave issue. It is yet impossible to measure the result of your policy, but it seems so essentially just and right that I believe its benefits must be enduring.

During my stay abroad I have come to a higher opinion of our rich men. I have never heard their selfishness better characterized than by you during my first visit to you at the White House, and I am quite willing to agree to the general dictum that few large fortunes are made honestly. But that will apply to Europe and to ancient Rome as well as to our own country, and comes from a defect in human nature and not from an American failing. But where in my judgment our rich men are the best rich men who have ever lived is that when they get this immense amount of money they do not give themselves up to a life of calculated luxury and unbridled sensuality. Being in Rome three months I read little but Roman history, and as I contrast the rich men of the last century of the Republic and the first of the Empire with our own I feel that there has been an improvement.

Lucullus dying of an overwrought sensual life, and Marius of the delirium tremens, Sulla (one of the master minds) of luxurious eating and drinking make me think how much superior the men are who give their surplus to universities, to education and to libraries and to the relief of the sick and unfortunate, and who lead simple lives.

It is a pretty good country, I think, where popular sentiment exacts such results. I know you are proud of being our President, and that you feel you have the support and confidence of so many thinking men and of the "plain people" must enable you to bear with equanimity the rather trenchant criticisms I feel some of your acts during the past few months have called forth.

Mrs. Rhodes and I shall be sorry not to see Mr. and Mrs. Bryce in London, but I am glad Mr. Bryce is Ambassador. We are returning home during the summer. After doing a few odd jobs I think I shall continue my History from 1877 on. . . .

To Charles Francis Adams

Florence, March, 1907.

A longer stop at Florence than I purposed gives me an opportunity to send some reply to your very interesting letter of February 20. The correspondence excited by your address on Lee must have been significant. I take it that most of it was complimentary, written by persons in substantial agreement with you, although you may not have escaped criticism by some disciple of Sanborn et al. It was a noble address and I know that it attracted much attention. It ought to have and will have much influence on Northern sentiment.

You owe me no apology whatever for saying that "no well and philosophically considered narrative of

[148]

the struggle has yet appeared," as the remark did not disturb me in the least. For a philosophical narrative was not my aim. There is use for the philosophy of history, and it will ever have an attraction for busy and profound thinkers, and addiction to it does not necessarily preclude good narrative work. Lecky did little but philosophize in his "History of Morals," but that did not prevent his writing a good narrative of the XVIII Century. You yourself who are given to philosophy wrote a gem of a biography in the Life of your Father: and that and your essay based on the Fish papers show that you need yield to no American historian in the matter of narrative style. But a purely narrative historian should, so far as he can, put all philosophic conditions aside. His aim is to tell a story and leave philosophy to others. One great merit of Macaulay, said Justin Winsor, is that his narrative carries his philosophy along with it. This was not strictly true of Macaulay in all cases, nor is it of my volumes, but such was my aim, and what little philosophizing I have indulged in has diminished as my volumes have grown.

A concrete case will show why one with my method should avoid if possible all philosophic theory. Did I believe with you (which I do not) that the "blockade was the controlling condition of Union success," that "the blockade was the determining factor, as cotton was the dynamic factor of the struggle" I would not have "woven the narrative over this philosophical skeleton." For had I done so, such is the constitution of the human mind, or at any rate my own, that as I went through the mass of my material I would have seized upon all the facts that made for my theory and marshalled them in its support while those that told against it I would have unconsciously and undoubtedly quite honestly neglected. As William James said of H. Spencer, he has a great avidity for facts that support his theory and amasses them in a surprising manner; but has no eye for the others. My aim therefore was to get rid so far as possible of all preconceived notions and theories.

But your aim is different. You might quote Pasteur: "One can do nothing without preconceived notions, but he must not let them run away with him." I do not think you let yours run away with you, for in thinking as intently and as restlessly as you do you serve as an acute critic for yourself as you do for others.

Now for your criticism on my Fifth Volume,[5] which I have taken the opportunity to re-read. All the facts touched on by you except two are in my volumes. The story of the blockade, of cotton, of the evasion of the blockade, of its gradual closing in around the Confederacy, of the immense trade carried on between the

---

[5] In the Massachusetts Historical Society *Proceedings* for October, 1905, and reprinted as a separate pamphlet, appeared "Some Phases of the Civil War, an Appreciation and Criticism of Mr. James Ford Rhodes's Fifth Volume," by Charles Francis Adams. The spirit in which it was written is indicated in a paragraph near its beginning: "Mr. Rhodes approaches his subject in a general way. Neither a politician nor a soldier, he is unskilled in practical diplomacy as he is innocent of any study of international law, nor can he be classed as a publicist. Once, indeed, a man of affairs, he is now a judicially minded general investigator, bringing much hard common-sense to bear, always modestly, on the complex problems of a troubled and eventful period. Now it so chances that as a participant in the earlier time, and, more recently, through the study of historical material as yet unpublished, I have looked upon the same problems from other points of view. In what I now have to say, therefore, I propose to discuss, in a spirit of criticism wholly friendly, what from those points of view seem to me deficiencies and shortcomings in Mr. Rhodes's treatment."

lines of the armies are there. A detailed account of the work of the Navy is indeed lacking, but when I wrote my History of the War the Naval Records were not published and I was quite right not to write it from second hand material. The great effect of the taking of New Orleans on European sentiment, the influence of Farragut's victory on the election of 1864 are there; (the great importance of Lincoln's election in 1864 was, if I remember rightly, most effectively stated in a paper you read before the Historical Society in 1896).

Many considerations of military strategy are indeed lacking but that was from incompetence. I own my work is not consistent, for McClellan is criticised; but Ropes justified me in that by saying, "Any fool can criticise McClellan."

The question of the Sea Power I cannot grapple with. I have not the basic knowledge.

Your air pump illustration I have never seen; from your point of view it is striking.

With regard to your theory I will only put a few questions. If McClellan had been elected in 1864, what would have been the result? If Hood had beaten Thomas at Nashville, if Lee had got away from Grant and made the junction with Johnston, might not your blockade have gone on to the crack of doom without the subjugation of the Confederacy? Had the material development of the South been equal to that of the North, would she not have laughed at your blockade? She could raise enough food; she had cotton for clothes; she had iron ore and coking coal in abundance. Before 1848 armies fought without anæsthetics for the wounded, and it's not more than one or two hundred years I believe that they have had quinine; these were two deprivations from which the South suffered severely by the blockade.

In your letter you put in a most graphic way our military incapacity during the first two years of the War. Had we not developed some better military talent I fear the blockade would not have won the game for us.

Your letter is very effective. I do not see why the elimination of one swear word and perhaps a more general characterization of Hooker's Headquarters it should not be read before the Society, published in the *Proceedings* and eventually in another book of Essays.

I have had to write this without a book, not even one of my own volumes, so I pray you be merciful to the errors and omissions.

To Barrett Wendell

Fontainebleau, April 7, 1907.

I was very glad to get your interesting letter of March 3 with its graphic account of one Longfellow celebration. I have read much about the other which took place across the river. I did not know that Mr. Aldrich was ill until I saw that he could not read his poem. I was sorry about his death. The first time I ever had much conversation with him was when you gave a play at the Tavern Club and invited me as a guest. That was before March 4, 1897, as I remember well it was before McKinley was inaugurated and after he had been elected. I sat between Charles Eliot Norton and Russell Sullivan. Norton was expansive and I enjoyed his talk exceedingly. When with the others I went to the theatre, I found that I was seated next to Aldrich and during the first wait and others we had much conversation. I remember two other long talks with him, and I think there must have been others as I knew from him direct how he sorrowed over the loss of his son. I have always been a great admirer of the finish of his work although it never came pat for me to tell him so.

By the way, his admiration for your play that night was unbounded. . . .

The cooking and food at our hotel are excellent (Hôtel de France et Angleterre), and the Bordeaux and Burgundy red wines in the cellar are delicious. I have two huge volumes of Jaurès's "Histoire Socialiste" of the French Revolution and I am reasonably happy. I should be entirely so, were I not homesick. Until I had completed the eight months of my sojourn in Europe I was interested, eager, and happy, but then a change came over me and I have been longing since for Boston, its duties and pleasures. Tom Perry (who is living in Paris) and I were dining together the other evening at Paillard's when the waiter brought a card to me. I thought it came from a disagreeable individual in the restaurant pretty nearly opposite me who had tried to "scrape acquaintance" with me at the Excelsior Hotel, Rome, and I said to the waiter "bye and bye." But something in his manner induced me to put on my glasses and read the card. It was from Guy Lowell, expressing surprise, etc., to see a Taverner there. Lowell afterwards came over and had a little chat with us. He brought vividly to my mind the Tavern Club and all the other good things of Boston. Well, I wish that I were home, but I think (in fact I am sure) that we shall not sail until the end of May. I hope that we shall get away then. . . .

To the same

London, May 7, 1907.

. . . You are quite right to place Booker Washington and me in the same category, although I know of course it was unwittingly done. We are equally impossible. If Booker had my complexion, facial angle and lips, he would do. My complexion is all right, but I know nothing of education, lack executive ability, am indolent when it comes to active exertion, and cannot make a speech. Booker possesses these qualities and has not these defects. I want to spend the rest of my life reading and writing, going to Boston clubs and societies, with an occasional dinner, and I shall be quite happy enough. . . .

To Charles Francis Adams

Boscombe, Bournemouth, May 10, 1907.

I was very glad to receive your interesting and kind letter of April 18. It is pleasant to know that your opinions agree so well with my own judgments but I differ from you in this, that some of my historical conclusions are at variance with my contemporary opinions. Like you, however, I have been profoundly influenced by the *Nation;* and in a less degree by Carl Schurz. Like you on a vital question I did not follow them at the time nor do I now believe they were right —that is in regard to the imposition of negro suffrage on the South. This policy was advocated earnestly by Godkin and Schurz, and to his dying day I am convinced that Mr. Schurz believed that there was no alternative policy.

The two facts you state which prevented your father

obtaining the Cincinnati nomination in 1872 were new to me; also that the reported remark of John Q. Adams, "This is the last of earth," is mythical.

As you detect a weariness and haste to get done in my last two volumes, they are undoubtedly there, although I was not conscious of them. An author, however, is not a good judge in such a case. It shows that I was wise to treasure up and act on your chance remark that 1877 was a more logical termination for my History than 1885; and also that it was worth while to break away from American History and life for a full year.

I am very much obliged to you for your list of corrections. It is real friendship to take the trouble to transcribe such annotations. When I get back to my Boston library next autumn, with all my books and authorities about me, I shall make a careful study of your emendations and undoubtedly end by adopting many of them.

I spent nine days in London but saw only two of our common friends. Frederic Harrison was passing through London on his way to the Continent and came one day and took luncheon with Mrs. Rhodes and me. He is as ever interested in everything, says he is nearer 80 than 70 (he is 76), and is an unwearied and delightful talker. I met personally Sir Spencer Walpole for the first time, although we have been correspondents for some years. I passed last Sunday with him at his Sussex place and had a very enjoyable day, finding him a charming host and companion. He told me that you had sent him the *Nation* review of his last book; and this led to our discussion of your address on Lee and two of your printed volumes; and our remarks were complimentary.

We are sailing from Southampton on May 29 and should reach New York June 4. . . .

To Mrs. C. H. Toy

Boscombe, Bournemouth, May 13, 1907.
. . . Now I have your delightful letter of April 24. It is flattering to know that a "gentle reader" has read your book a second time; and when you add that two chapters are kept for constant reference for comfort and consolation—well, nothing could be more complimentary. It is lucky that I had a talk with my London publisher the same day or I should have been puffed up with pride. No one is green enough to expect that a ponderous history like mine should have much of a sale in England, but one does like to have it attract a little attention, and while my Vols. I, II, and III received a great deal of notice from the English newspapers and reviews the subsequent volumes have been more or less neglected; Mr. George Macmillan explained in the most courteous way why all this should be so. I happened to remark that counting friends and acquaintances and a further rough estimate I thought that I had a hundred readers in England. "Well, you couldn't expect more," was the reply. Most Englishmen look upon a seven-volume history of the United States as we would upon a seven-volume history of Brazil. But as it was what I expected, I am not disappointed, as, if I were an Englishman, I should probably be a good Tory and with the majority, entirely incapable of the broad views of Mr. Bryce, Mr. Dicey, and Mr. Firth, and, if I speak of the dead, of Mr. Gardiner, Mr. Lecky and Leslie Stephen (whose **Life and Letters** I am just now reading). . . .

Your pessimistic mood is not unnatural. The pessimists in the United States are people of large intelligence and high ideals and they are pessimistic because the country falls short of their aspirations for it. For a cure of it, I know nothing better than to spend twelve months in Europe; and if one be generally pessimistic in regarding the XIX and XX centuries, let him study the history of the past, I care not of what past, and he will have cause to rejoice that his lot is cast in the present.

As you have derived all the consolation you can from those two chapters I am going to transcribe something from Lord Acton from his Lectures between 1899 and 1901: "The Federal Constitution, by the development of the principle of Federalism, has produced a community more powerful, more prosperous, more intelligent, and more free than any other which the world has seen." To cheer you up about your native state I am going to give you this, also from Lord Acton: "The cavaliers of Virginia, who went out under James I surpassed the fugitives of the *Mayflower*. They produced the Declaration of Independence and bequeathed to America religious liberty and the political function of the Supreme Court." If you quote this to any of your Cambridge friends, who are to the manner born, do add this opinion of Leslie Stephen: "The best Yankee is about the best of mankind."

Recurring to pessimism, I met in Paris a very intelligent Frenchman, a member of the Chamber of the Deputies, and withal a cheerful and affable man, who spoke in terms more pessimistic of the present condition of France than I have ever heard a Cambridge or Boston mugwump speak of our own state. And I get

it at second hand, that in the army and navy circles of
Great Britain the feeling about the future is very
gloomy; not so much from the troubles in the East
as from the overpowering greatness and competition
of Germany. And a war with Germany is strongly
advocated with a view to smash the navy and merchant
marine of this great rival. If I may believe half what
the English newspapers say, the feeling of Germany
toward England is very bitter and she is ready for the
fight. But I shall not believe in this much predicted
war until it comes. . . .

To Charles Eliot Norton

Seal Harbor, Maine, July 28, 1907.
. . . From questions that have been asked me from
time to time by correspondents, I infer that a reaction
of sentiment in favor of Douglas is going on among
some of the younger historical students and writers.
Whether the desire to say something novel and sensational is at the bottom of it I cannot say; but I was
glad to see that, while Rothschild [6] appreciated fully
the mental force of Douglas, he characterized him on
the old lines: from which I do not believe there will be
any lasting change in historical sentiment, unless our
young men prove their thesis that slavery was not
the cause of our civil war. I am myself glad to be
with the old-fashioned thinkers in history, and in
literature as well. In literature, the new gospel of
Bernard Shaw, which I have been dipping into during
the last eight days does not incline me favorably to

---

[6] This letter followed promptly on Rhodes's reading of *Lincoln,
Master of Men,* by Alonzo Rothschild, which Norton had called to
his notice.

the new points of view of many young English writers, some of whom write history. . . .

To Charles Francis Adams

Seal Harbor, Maine, August 11, 1907.

. . . I have re-read *A College Fetich* and have read for the first time *Some Modern College Tendencies*. It is unnecessary to say that I have been interested in both. I know almost nothing about education, and the opinion that I shall express I fear you will regard as infantile. But I look upon President Eliot as a great man, great in character and intellect and, as he has devoted his time almost exclusively for thirty-six years to the College and University, I must believe that his work of reconstruction has been of merit. I doubt whether the English plan could have been grafted on to Harvard and the best thing that was open to him was the German with American modifications. Three or four years ago President Hadley was visiting President Eliot and five of us took him for a day's excursion up Green Mountain. President Eliot was not of the party. Over our frugal luncheon we talked and under the influence of our bright skies and bracing air Mr. Hadley was unusually brilliant. "What are the great Universities?" was asked. "Paris, Berlin, and Harvard," was his prompt reply. "Why will you not include Oxford-Cambridge?" I asked. "Oxford-Cambridge is not a university," he replied. "They have an atmosphere, just as we have at Yale." Now, it is difficult to create an atmosphere. You can a university; as Berlin and Chicago bear witness.

Two of my friends at Oxford—both professors—are not at all backward in criticizing the Oxford system, pointing out merits in the German and American systems which it does not possess.

The criticism of an Overseer of twenty-four years' standing cannot be ignored. I am glad to have read it. I shall ponder it, but perhaps my basic knowledge is not sufficient to duly weigh it. . . .

To William James

August, 1907.

Your book on Pragmatism begins to be attractive on its dedicatory page. No dedication can be better than to the memory of J. S. Mill. In days gone by I used to read some of Mill's philosophy and I am struck by the resemblance between his and your own —in their sanity and in their making abstruse ideas comprehensible to those who are not students of philosophy. I always knew that Mill in the sphere of politics had much influence on Godkin and the remembrance of this influence has been emphasized by reading the life of Godkin; and since I got some of my political ideas at the time when Mill was the most important teacher of young men, I thought of my indebtedness last October while at Avignon when I paid a visit to the grave of Mill; so that it was a real delight to read your recognition of him.

I think all laymen must thank you for the saneness and serenity of your book. I have read it with care and interest and I feel sure at least that the lecture on the Nature of Truth will have an abiding influence and be a constant companion. I think President Eliot has read your book: at all events we discussed it the other day and he told me that it was splendid.

I am going to show you how different the common

mind is from the philosophic. I am wrong I know, but I do not see the difference between your "I myself believe that the evidence for God lies primarily in inner personal experiences" and Sir William Hamilton's knowing the existence of God from the testimony of his own consciousness. But I feel sure that as between Hamilton and Mill you are with Mill.

I have a concrete example which properly raises a doubt whether there is much of anything in the Christian religion. My mother is eighty-six years old and has always been a religious woman, but, being an Episcopalian, has enjoyed the innocent pleasures of the world. She has been kind, amiable and good, and during the whole course of her life I do not believe she has ever done anything herself which has caused her bitter regret. My thought suggests an experience so foreign to hers that I don't believe she would understand it. Now she is failing fast physically and while up and about, is physically uncomfortable a good deal of the time. She cannot possibly live much longer and that fact must be apparent to her. Now here is a case when the person should welcome death, when she should be so sure of the eternal bliss awaiting her that she should be ready and anxious to go. On the contrary her clinging to life and her desire to live is positively painful and could not be greater in an infidel or agnostic.

To Barrett Wendell

Seal Harbor, August 30, 1907.

. . . I appreciate your sympathy on account of my mother's death, and it is a real pleasure to know that you remember her so well from your meeting her in

Cairo and Athens, when she was in her seventy-sixth year. Had she lived until next Tuesday, she would have been 86. She led a happy, useful life. Sincerely religious, she liked nevertheless the innocent pleasures of the world, and in her church, the Episcopalian, she could harmonize the two sentiments. She went abroad with my wife and me twice, once in 1886 and again in 1894, and I do not believe anyone ever got more pleasure out of such travels than she did. Two years ago she spent most of the summer with us here and I am glad to have been the means of giving her so much enjoyment in the later years of her life. I passed six painful days with her last June, devoting all my time in Cleveland to her. It was pitiful to see her so weak and trying to struggle against the end which everyone saw was near. I arrived in Cleveland two days before her death, saw her, and she recognized me; her death was painless and peaceful, and it is better so than to have had her live on as she was last June.

A mass of business details and correspondence consequent on my year's absence in Europe and my mother's death have prevented me from reading as much this summer as I had expected to. Three professors from McGill College and their wives, who have passed the summer on Greenings (Thorp's Island) have been very agreeable and I had two enjoyable walks with them. I frequently say that walking is the only manly thing I do in the shape of physical exercise. I had rather of a notable walk yesterday with President Eliot, Jacob Schiff (of Kuhn, Loeb & Co.), Toy, and Hapgood (Father of Norman). As a good part of my investments have of late years naturally worked into securities bought and sold on the New York Stock Market, I wanted to talk with Schiff about the financial outlook, while he preferred to talk of the unique walk we were taking amongst rocks and trees. Being somewhat persistent and seeming very much so, because Schiff is deaf and I had to shout as loud as Darius's Egyptian, I received a mild rebuke when we reached the top of Gorham Mountain whence the outlook was fine. My mind being on my stocks and bonds, I said, "Mr. Schiff, this is a more pleasing outlook than Wall Street." "Well," was the reply, "I guess you have Wall Street more on the brain than I have." After that I talked scenery! I had never met Mr. Schiff before and I was much entertained with his deference to and admiration of Mr. Eliot. He always addressed him as Mr. President and seemed to want to cling to him and not lose one of his winged words. It was otherwise than Shakespeare put it, for here the man of gold bowed to the learned pate. . . .

The ensuing letter to Morley, like the foregoing letter to James, is copied from pencilled notes preserved among Rhodes's papers. The letter to Morley may be introduced by a few words about Rhodes's reading habits. It appears from the first sentence of this letter that he had previously read Morley's "Gladstone." Fortunately his method of dealing with such a book can be illustrated by turning to the very volumes which he read in September of 1907 at Seal Harbor. On October 8, 1924, he presented them to Mr. C. K. Bolton, Librarian of the Boston Athenæum, who has kindly called them to my notice. On page after page there are marginal lines, single, double, and triple, obviously indicating degrees of approval and interest. On the fly-leaves at the end and beginning of each volume there is a long succession of pencilled page references to phrases and topics—a sort of supplementary index—spilling over in one of the volumes into the opening page of text. How many of these notes were written on the first reading, recorded as of December, 1903, and how many on the second, noted as having begun on September 4 and ended on September 20, 1907, it is impossible to say; but they show clearly that Rhodes observed the honored injunction to read "pencil in hand," and employed the books he possessed as a scholar should—as tools for more than a single use. The phrases that attracted his attention, the expressions of approval, dissent, and, occasionally, of correction, all throw a light on the workings of his mind. One may even come upon a bit of autobiography not discoverable elsewhere, as on page 519 of Morley's third volume, opposite a paragraph of Gladstone's on his content in retirement (September 13, 1894); for here Rhodes pencilled in the margin, "This is about the time I saw Gladstone at Hawarden." If his library in Beacon Street were still a unit, there can be little doubt that many illuminating bits could be brought to light.

To John Morley

September, 1907.

Taking advantage of the abundant leisure of the summer and early autumn I have re-read your volumes on Gladstone. I remember on the first reading that I compared notes with the President and Mr. Olney and we all three agreed that we rose from our perusal with a higher opinion of Gladstone than before. This time I have been struck with the high historic value of the book as giving an intimate account of the working of parliamentary and cabinet government in England such as I have never found elsewhere. The book was only possible by a man who himself knew the life, and I am impressed by the candid exposition of the machinery as well as the strength of the system. The balance struck will confirm the general American and Continental opinion that parliamentary and cabinet government in England has been very successful. From your volumes I perceive more clearly than ever the immense indirect influence of the Queen, and I can hardly think that parliamentary government would be equally successful without royalty and the respect of the common people for the sovereign. Very weighty is Gladstone's remark on "the dangerous isolation in which the monarchy will find itself if the hereditary principle goes down in the House of Lords; 'it will stand bare, naked, with no shelter or shield, only endured as the better of two evils.' " (III. 470.) Your expression on the note of our generation, "Men are disenchanted" (page 475) is one that tells the whole story.

Among the letters of 1908 there is one to President Eliot, dated February 28, recalling his request, several years before, that Rhodes should deliver a course of lectures to Harvard students of American history. Rhodes had declined the invitation on account, as he said, of his "utter deficiency in the art of lecturing." Urged by friends meanwhile to reconsider this decision, he wrote, "I have now written the three discourses (on Gibbon, Godkin, and the Profession of Historian) which are yours if you care for them. It is perhaps unnecessary to add that I do not desire any compensation for them, as, whatever they may be worth, I am glad to offer them in partial return for the indirect benefits I have received from Harvard University." These lectures, now to be read in Rhodes's "Historical Essays," were delivered in the following April, to audiences recorded, in his social memoranda, as "appreciative" if not of extensive proportions. For some years Rhodes served as chairman of the committee appointed by the Board of Overseers to visit the Department of History—a position which led Professor Dunning, enumerating his New England affiliations,[7] to write of him, erroneously, as "a member of the governing body of Harvard University." Lecturing, whether near at home or far afield, he never enjoyed, but the opportunities to be of use to his university by adoption were unfailingly welcome.

So too were the opportunities for meetings with President Roosevelt, two of which occurred during his final year in the White House. Of the first of these, in May of 1908, there is a full record in one of the "Index Rerum" volumes:

Visit to the White House on May 15, 1908, written directly after my return to Boston from notes made on the 16th and from memory.

Arriving at 9.45 A.M. I drove directly to the White House. The convention of governors was in session— a convention called by the President for the purpose of

---

[7] See *ante,* pp. 113-114.

consultation as to the best manner of the conservation of the national resources of the country. I was much interested in hearing the speeches of a number of the Southern governors. They seemed to enjoy speaking of the President as a man of large brain and great heart, wide views, generous ideas. Great enthusiasm over the President. I also heard Wm. J. Bryan who was received with much enthusiasm. I append here a remark by Bryan and an impromptu quasi answer from the President.

[Here follow two clippings from the *Washington Post* of May 16, 1908, containing, respectively, Bryan's remarks on his belief that "there is no twilight zone between the nation and the State in which exploiting interests can take refuge from both," and Roosevelt's rejoinder that his primary aim had been to eliminate such a zone.]

The Southern governors referred often to the indissoluble Union of indestructible States. The discussion of centralization and States rights regarding the question of the adoption of the report was amusing and interesting, as it was almost entirely between the Southern governors.

Took luncheon with the President and Mrs. Roosevelt at half past one and after luncheon the President took me out on the rear veranda of the White House (cousin Roosevelt, Millet, and Richardson [8] accompanying) and said anent my VI and VII volumes that I had stepped down from my impartial judgment seat of the earlier volumes and become somewhat of an advocate. During the Civil War I had held the scales even but while I have perhaps properly criticised

---

[8] Wm. Emlen Roosevelt, Francis Davis Millet, Clifford Richardson. (Note by J. F. R.)

the North for their Reconstruction policy I have not blamed the South for the course which she took that made radical measures possible. Her course made any proper policy impossible. Is inclined to think that XIV amendment plan offered the best possible policy. Blames Godkin and Carl Schurz because, after having supported the negro suffrage policy, they condemned the results of it. All right if they had avowed their mistake; but that they did not do. Still held to the negro suffrage policy as being the best. Even now the *Evening Post* condemns the President's action in the Brownsville, Texas, matter, from purely senti- mental reasons. The negro has been hurt, therefore the President is wrong. Carl Schurz and the *Nation* never stimulated the best young men to go into politics and they never had any influence with the crowd. Per- haps all right to say that C. Schurz was almost an ideal senator, but on that level I failed to do justice to Oliver P. Morton. He told with great spirit and enthusiasm Morton's course during the Civil War, speaking of the Copperheads as bitterly as if he had been their personal antagonist. I said Morton was a fighter and perhaps a fighter would appreciate him better than anyone else. The men at the East, the President said, have books written about them in good literary style; they receive the adulation of writers and so get a larger share of commendation than they are entitled to. I supported this by instancing Pierce's Sumner and Pearson's Andrew alongside Foulke's Morton. The President agreed. I was sur- prised at his knowledge of the recent Life of Fessen- den. He told with accuracy and effect the account which Fessenden gave of the Cabinet crises in 1862.

When talking of Morton he said to his cousin (William Emlen Roosevelt): Because Winslow, Lanier & Co. advanced money to Morton in his trouble he is disposed to forgive Charles Lanier for saying that he, the President, is crazy, and furthermore that he is indulging immoderately in drink and that he is an opium fiend.[9] I wish to record here that there is absolutely no foundation for any of these statements. The President took a taste of sherry at luncheon, then tea, and at dinner drank water only. The two previous visits I have made to the White House (Apr. 1902 and Nov. 1905) he drank more because as I remember it he drank champagne at dinner but nevertheless he drank very moderately and there was little champagne or other wine served. This time we had a choice of sherry or whiskey for luncheon and same choice for dinner. Very little of either was drunk. The White House table was simple, the meals four courses but an ample supply of nutritious food.

Morning of May 16. The President says his administration has not gained him the support of the cultivated class, and there are points where it should have done so. But he has received the support of the plain people, of the "one suspender men." And yet he has done things that might have aroused a demagogic feeling. Has shut the people out from the White House grounds in the rear; stopped the public receptions (the three times weekly affairs) and has done a great deal in the limitation of others. Lord Cromer

---

[9] In regard to the President being crazy, it is a charge so utterly without foundation that it hardly ought to be referred to. He is absolutely as sane as any man. He displayed more excitement at the time of my visit in April, 1902, than in November, 1905, and at this time. (Note by J. F. R.)

wrote to him that our work in Cuba was the best colonial work he had known of doing. The President thinks Taft's work in the Philippines equal to Lord Cromer's work in Egypt, only we have gone further in the direction of self-government for the Philippines. Bishop Brent's criticism is that we have not been tyrannical enough. Thinks American public indifferent about the Philippines, or that there is a general desire to get rid of them lest they might hamper us in a war with Japan or indeed be an incitement on the part of Japan to war with us.

Night of May 15. We cannot let in the Japanese. He once thought that we could, but has given up that idea. His efforts have been to get the Japanese to stop emigration. It is working fairly well but not perfectly. An exclusion act may have to come, and that might cause trouble. His reason for the increase of the Navy: they know in Washington what the Japanese are saying in their cups, and there is a desire on the part of a certain class in Japan to go to war with us. But the elder statesmen are opposed to it. The critical financial condition of Japan may be an inducement for the Japanese to go to war before their armament is reduced. The sending of the fleet to the Pacific stopped the Japanese talk of war.

The invitation to the governors grew out of the trip down the Mississippi River last autumn. At a dinner of the governors, a number agreed to come. I understood the President to say that Pritchett and Representative Burton had something to do with the inception of it.

J. P. Morgan not a good financial adviser. James Hill very good, has to keep a look-out, however, that the latter has not an especial eye to his own interest.

At dinner on the 15th, President and Mrs. Roosevelt; Secretary and Mrs. Root, Mrs. Taft, Mr. Meyer, Postmaster-General, Senator Knox, Mr. and Mrs. W. E. Roosevelt, Mr. and Mrs. Richardson.

Fruitful talk after dinner between the gentlemen. I asked if the newspaper and magazine reports of Morgan's taking command were true. The President, Secretary Root, and W. E. Roosevelt said without doubt.

President's account of when he was in New York legislature: Wanted to get the extension of the Grand Central Station. An improvement wanted by the Railroad, needed by the public, and to which there was no objection. He told Senator Depew he would take charge of it. Could not get it reported or brought up, but when he gave it up and Depew worked it through one of the political leaders it went through without trouble. Less corruption in the legislature when he was Governor than when he was member of the legislature. I asked if as much corruption in the American Congress as in the English House of Commons. The President believes the amount of corruption in the American Congress much overstated. Mr. Root said it was difficult to draw the line—there was an imperceptible shading. Seemed to be a general conviction that the amount of corruption was exaggerated.

The President has not a high opinion of the newspapers; in this W. E. Roosevelt agreed. W. E. R. said they were losing their influence. The President reads little but the *Outlook* and *Spectator;* an editorial clipping is sometimes sent to him; has a high opinion of the Kansas City *Star,* but deems William Allen White erratic.

May 15 P.M. Secretary Cortelyou said there were

many things connected with the New York panic which had not got into the newspapers or the magazines, and which were necessary for its complete history: these would sometime be given to the public. The President spoke highly of Cortelyou's work during the panic and said that his impassible face had something to do with his equipoise. Secretary Root desired to know whether Cortelyou had ever played poker.

It was easy to see that the opposition of Speaker Cannon and Representative Burton had not been pleasing to the President.

May 16. Dined with Mr. and Mrs. Bryce at the British Embassy. The only other guest was Mr. Lawrence Godkin. Mr. Bryce and Mr. Godkin as severe on the American newspapers as the President, and I am not sure that their condemnation did not extend to the English newspapers—at all events we spoke of the downfall of the *Times*. Mr. Bryce disposed to question that Arnold the greatest English critic of the XIX century. Spoke highly of Meyer [Myers?] and Symonds.

President's explanation of "I and my people" thank you for your congratulations. This was written by Adee and the President's name signed to it by the Secretary of State without reading it.

During the panic of the fall of 1907, after the acute week Frick (and Perkins or Baker, I don't remember which) came over to see the President regarding the purchase of the Eastern Tennessee and Georgia (I think that the name) Coal and Iron Company stock. The question of competitive concerns and the precise point involved about the proportion of stock. I did not fully understand, but the President had to agree not to prosecute or the deal would not have gone through. This he agreed to, although against the advice of his Attorney-General, Bonaparte. I gathered rather (although the President did not say it or even directly intimate it) that he did not consider Bonaparte a broad-minded man. Of this Frick, etc., transaction the newspapers at the time gave a correct account. Perhaps it was Gary who accompanied Frick, and what they were after was to get immunity from prosecution under Sherman Anti-Trust law.

A letter that followed immediately upon the writing of this memorandum introduces something, as it were, of dialogue to the talk which Rhodes had so greatly enjoyed.

To Theodore Roosevelt

Boston, May 18, 1908.

MY DEAR MR. PRESIDENT:—The wise custom of a bread-and-butter letter enables me to thank you and Mrs. Roosevelt again for your kind and gracious hospitality.

I did not want to interrupt the flow of your conversation or I should on Saturday morning have suggested a qualification of your remark that your administration had not gained the support of the cultivated class; in Boston and Cambridge quite a number of educated men endorse your policy touching the large combinations of capitalists, and in the free discussions, that took place during the past winter around the table of the Wednesday Evening Club, we were numerous enough to constitute mutual support and we thought that we held our own in the argument. I myself—and many agree with me—would have been satisfied with a continuance of the Cleveland-McKinley régime, but I now recognize that was impossible with due regard to the safety of the State and the question for us Conservatives is, was it not better to have the reform made by a man who is sound on the fundamentals than by a ruthless or shifty hand? I deem it probable that the great captains of industry will play fair for twenty or thirty years and unlikely that there will ever be a return to the ante-Roosevelt conditions.

If the present strength in Wall Street is a precursor of improved business in general, Republican success in the autumn is assured. These two considerations will add to your support by the "one suspender men" hosts of people engaged in business who will rejoice that the depression after the panic has been so brief.

With renewed thanks and the expression of my profound respect, I am

Very truly yours,
JAMES FORD RHODES.

To John T. Morse, Jr.

Seal Harbor, Maine, June 21, 1908.
My re-reading of your "Jefferson" was profitable as it recalled some points that I had forgotten and emphasized others. It is a great merit of a biographer to lay stress on salient features, if he is not carried away by a theory and it seems to me that you place the emphasis in an entirely sane and objective manner. It is well worth self-gratulation to have written the Lives of Hamilton, Jefferson, and J. Adams in such a way as to induce the reader to sympathize with each one of them; and that is due to your full appreciation of their good qualities and estimating them by no

[174]

model of perfection, as mugwumps estimate the public men of our day. I wish Jefferson had not had that great faith in "The People," but he could not foresee our vast foreign immigration and the stimulus to large cities from our commercial and manufacturing expansion. Your judgment of Jefferson's power and influence over Congress and the people (p. 264) is well worth pondering. I am disposed to accept it, for you must have well considered the peculiar influence of Jackson and Lincoln. And you wrote before McKinley and Roosevelt. One of the writers in the *Nation* said that McKinley had more power of getting measures through Congress than any President since Lincoln, and that opinion is undoubtedly sound. And I think that we may say that no President since Lincoln has had such a hold on the people as Roosevelt. But he has not like Jefferson commended himself to the mass by "ostentatious shabbiness" in dress (p. 266) nor allowed a mob to invade the White House without decorum as did Jackson.

In your "Jefferson" and "J. Adams" you have unconsciously made an argument for a strong navy in pointing out Jefferson's folly (p. 280) and the sturdy Adams's belief that the United States ought to be "a great naval power" (p. 279).

I am glad that you are led to the opinion that Adams's usefulness to the country was second only to that of Washington. You bring out well his lack of appreciation of Washington.

Your own tribute to Washington (p. 133) is fine and makes one comprehend your sacrifice in giving up the "Washington" to Senator Lodge. "Absolutely unique character in history" is excellent and I imagine that you stick to this still, although, since you wrote those words, you must have made your study of Lincoln.

If you will write no more interesting biographies we must re-read these which we have already from your pen.

If you saw much of the earnest students of American history, especially those connected in one way or another with our Universities, you would know how well they appreciate what you have done as biographer and editor. But they don't know your full service as editor for they are ignorant of your experiences. . . . You must, however, leave a full account of these in your autobiography to be printed towards the end of the century.

To Theodore Roosevelt

June 22, 1908.

Remembering your statement that you rarely saw the newspapers I send you the enclosed clipping, containing a citation from the London *Times*.[10] Let me change the first sentence to, "It is the crowning victory," and I can well believe that the mature historical judgment will in some such manner be expressed; and

---

10 The clipping enclosed was headed "Roosevelt's Greatest Victory," and read as follows: "London, June 19.—The news of Secretary Taft's nomination for the presidency was too late for editorial comment in the morning papers with the exception of the *Times*, which says: 'It is the greatest and most striking of all Roosevelt's many victories. By the unflinching exertion of his personal will, President Roosevelt defeated the undoubted will of the Republican party, and what is hardly less certain the will of the American people. He has chosen to sacrifice his personal ambition to his sense of duty as a citizen. It is a noble act of self-abnegation worthy of the first Magistrate of a people, bred in respect for the law and in veneration for its spirit.' "

there may be added: Washington refused a third term and Jefferson declined to be a candidate for it, but they were old and weary of office, while Roosevelt was young, in robust health and in no way tired of his job.

What may we think of the sagacity of the Wall Street and State Street men who persisted in the statement that you were aiming at a third term?

I congratulate you on the dignity of the proceedings (at any rate up to the meeting of the convention) by which the nomination of Secretary Taft was effected. . . .

To Lord Morley

Seal Harbor, Maine, August 22, 1908.
I am glad that I am not able to get through the summer without some spiritual communion with you, and your new volume of "Critical Miscellanies" has afforded me much pleasure and profit. I like the essays on "Machiavelli" and "Democracy and Reaction" the best, as being a blending of scholarship and thought that adds to one's knowledge and recalls one's own reading and reflections. You have a keen appreciation of our own country, but I am a little surprised and much gratified that you speak of the American Revolution as a mightier event in many of its aspects than the French Revolution (p. 302). Certainly American history and politics for that and the subsequent period are much less studied in England and Germany than the French, and their influence is apparently less; but I am disposed to accept the statement from confidence in your own learning and judgment. And the statement affords me gratification that I have given up my silly dream of writing a history of the French Revolu-

tion and decided to stick to the history of my own country.

I like your appreciation of President Roosevelt. He has done a great work for our country and has been happy in doing it at the right time. Never have our future prospects been so bright as now for the maintenance of social order and a continuance of the betterment in administration. Bryan's election would prove a temporary set-back. It is unlikely, however; and the probability is that we shall have eight years of Taft to consolidate and perfect the work which only a positive man, who loved a fight, like Roosevelt, could have begun.

You have made a splendid and deserved tribute to J. S. Mill. I have marked sentences in your essay which I shall re-read as expressive of my own thought in better language than I could have used. In the autumn of 1906, I visited his "mournful grave at Avignon." I was later well pleased to see that William James dedicated to Mill's memory his recent book on "Pragmatism."

I am sure that I speak for hosts of your friends in saying that we rejoice that you were able to get out of the hurly-burly of the House of Commons and still retain your touch with active political life.

The election of President Taft called forth the following words:

To Theodore Roosevelt

Boston, November 4, 1908.
I congratulate you on the result of the election and express my deep thankfulness to you for your share

[178]

in it. Unquestionably the weak places were Ohio, Indiana, and Illinois, and the difficult condition was the large number of unemployed. We all owe you very much that these obstacles were overcome.

It is another triumph for you. I believe that history will do you as full justice as did the American people yesterday.

Where would the Republican party be today had you continued the Cleveland-McKinley régime?

To Barrett Wendell

Boston, December 16, 1908.
I have read the "Privileged Classes," [11] etc., with much interest, but I do not like it as well as "Liberty, Union, and Democracy." Apart from the questions of education which I do not understand (although I infer vaguely that our higher education is not as good as that in England, Germany and France), I feel in this book a lack of sympathy with democracy while the other was a pæan of it. I know that you say reaction is impossible and that we must submit to the rule of the many. This is nothing but a logical development. The few have had their chance and exploited the many; now the many are exploiting the few; and I think the latter condition means happiness for the greatest number. Either condition may oppress the moderately well-to-do, who want to hand on the torch of enlightenment and at the same time enjoy the good things of life. High thinking demands high living, I think Thackeray used to say. As between the whim of an absolute monarch or his mistress and the dictum of fifteen million voters, I prefer the latter.

---

[11] *The Privileged Classes*, by Barrett Wendell, appeared in 1908.

I must say though that your "Privileged Classes" is a powerful essay and sets one to thinking. The vein of humor running through all of the essays is very attractive.

In the last week of 1908 Rhodes attended the annual meeting of the American Historical Association in Washington. He had asked President Roosevelt in advance if he might call upon him at the White House, and received a cordial invitation to a luncheon recorded as follows in the second of his "Dinner Books."

December 29, 1908, the President gave me a luncheon at the White House at which were present Mrs. Roosevelt, Secretary Root, Justice Holmes, Senator Lodge, James Bryce, Robert Bacon, Captain Henry, A. L. Lowell, and self.

Stone, chief usher, showed Lowell and me the arrangement at table. Lodge was placed next the President and I next Lodge, but when the President went out—he took me out—he looked at the cards and placed mine next to his place, so I sat on his right and Secretary Root on his left. Next me sat Lodge, then Lowell, then Holmes, Mrs. Roosevelt, James Bryce, Bacon, Captain Henry. It was a merry luncheon, and the merriment started early by Mrs. Roosevelt reading a letter from some friend full of advice to the President on his approaching tour, advising him to learn from civilized countries rather than to go into the heart of Africa.

I asked him, Did he find Ferrero reticent? Before the President could reply, Root said: "Reticent! The President found him a remarkably good listener."

Root had failed to get to the dinner, but had a full account of it from Mrs. Lodge, who said the President talked the whole time to Ferrero. "Did you agree with Ferrero's ideas on Roman history anent Cæsar and Augustus?" I asked. "The President did," said Root. "He gave Ferrero his own ideas, and Ferrero assented."

I had rather a pleasant conversation with the President and Lodge regarding Ferrero's treatment of Cæsar and Augustus as to which our opinions were at one. Both seemed to be thoroughly informed about the book.[12] . . .

Hay's volumes of private correspondence were referred to. Mrs. Hay had no idea of editing—abbreviated such names as D. W. and J. Q. A. There is a good deal of cynicism in Hay's remarks on politics. Hay had not accomplished near as much towards the reform of the consular service as had Root. He could not get the Senate to do things for him as has Root. Quite a little friendly discussion between the President and Mr. Bryce as to the extent and effect of this reform. The President's praise of Root was unstinted. There is a remarkable sympathy between the two.

Referred to the late exchange of notes between Japan and the United States. The pour-parlers began about two months ago. The former Japanese Ambassador approved it and was recalled. Then the voyage of the

---

[12] In the preceding November, Rhodes had seen much of Ferrero during his visit to Boston, and had entertained him at dinner in his own house. On the eve of his departure for Europe Ferrero wrote to him, in terms suggestive of Rhodes's kindness to many visitors from abroad: "Je suis un peu fatigué, mais très content de mon voyage. J'ai vu tant de choses et de personnes interessantes. J'espère de vous voir bientôt en Europe et de vous raconter ce que j'ai vu; car vous êtes une des plus charmantes personnes que j'ai vu ici. Il m'a semblé que vous aviez, pour moi historien, une espèce d'affection paternelle."

fleet. Then Japan proposed it. The reception of the fleet in Japan all that could be desired. Newspaper reports true. Nothing whatever occurred to mar the harmony of the occasion.

John Morley wrote to him (T. R.) asking if he could say a good word for the English Government in India. He will do it soon in an address in which the reference will be pat.[13]

Beazley [14] wanted to know if the President would accept his book on the Mongols (History of the Mongols). I told the President about Beazley, and asked him if he would accept the book. From Root— "Don't, Mr. Rhodes. We are now in cabinet meetings actually oppressed by the Mongols."

Lodge said Hay was the most delightful man he had ever met at the dinner table and he also possessed the now lost art of writing letters. I said that Hay was a noble soul.

I omitted to state that the talk about the fleet and J. Morley was after we had risen from the table and the guests had departed. He took me to one side of the room and we sat down and had a thorough confidential talk. I told him when he got back from Africa I wanted him to make a two or three days' visit either in Boston or Seal Harbor and he promised he would.

---

[13] At the end of the note-book containing this passage Rhodes pinned a clipping of a speech delivered by Roosevelt in Washington January 18, 1909, in which he declared, with an accompanying allowance for mistakes in the British governance of India, "the fact remains that the successful administration of the Indian empire by the English has been one of the most notable and most admirable achievements of the white race during the past two centuries."

[14] Charles Raymond Beazley, English historical scholar, and Lowell Institute lecturer in 1908, on "The Teachers and Precursors of Christopher Columbus," had dined at Rhodes's house in Boston a few weeks before this Washington visit.

Again the memorandum was followed by a letter on Rhodes's return to Boston.

To Theodore Roosevelt

Boston, January 4, 1909.

To elaborate what I said to you on last Tuesday; I have just begun writing the history of the United States from Hayes to McKinley (1877 to 1897) and, when that is finished, I purpose to write the history from 1897 to March 4, 1909. The significance of the Spanish-American War I do not yet comprehend, but I do the significance of your administrations. I hope that you will write your own story; it will be of great assistance to historians. You will publish your narrative long before I can finish mine, for I must work up to your administrations chronologically. And indeed I would prefer not to publish an account of your administrations for twelve years or more. When you return from Africa, I shall want to see you as often as I can, and I rejoice at your promise to pay me a visit either here or at Seal Harbor.

I cannot forbear repeating my hearty appreciation of your hospitality to me at the White House, which ended fitly last Tuesday with the merriest luncheon I have ever shared. The insight you have given me into the conduct of the great affairs of state and your enabling me to meet in their hours of relaxation Secretaries Root, Taft, Hay, Attorney-General Knox, and Senator Lodge have been of immense value to me. I thank you for these opportunities and still more for your signal confidence. Yet in reflecting on my five visits since the spring of 1902, what I prize most is your warm friendship, which is to me a great possession. . . .

To Henry Cabot Lodge

Boston, January 15, 1909.

Mrs. Hay kindly sent me the "Letters and Diaries." I have read carefully the first volume and am half way through the second. I regret the abbreviations,[15] but there is so much merit in the work that I am glad to have it in any form. It is a wonderful picture of Lincoln which Hay gives, first during his service as private secretary, second during the writing of his history in Cleveland when our friendship began.

At that merriest of luncheons in the White House when I met you last, I think that I understood you to say that Hay was the best dinner table talker whom you had ever met, and that he possessed the almost lost art of letter-writing. I do not want to bother a busy man like yourself with an answer to this and I will remember to verify the conversation at our next encounter. . . .

While living in Cleveland, Colonel Hay and I dined monthly together in a "Vampire Club." Hay usually did most of the talking in the party of twelve or fourteen. There were two wits who set him off and the talk was very good and very witty. . . .

I hope that you will let an admiring constituent see something more of you before he dies. Lowell, the other member of our trio, is President-elect. It is a wonderfully good choice and I have been very happy over it since it became certain. He has great qualities

---

[15] These were carried even to the point of calling Brown University "B—— University" and Lincoln "L——."

of head and heart and I predict for him a successful administration. . . .

Before the end of May, 1909, Rhodes was again in England, and jotting memoranda of many enjoyable experiences in one of his "Dinner Books." There was a talk with Mrs. J. R. Green, in which the imminence of a war with Germany was discussed; there was a dinner given by the American Ambassador, Whitelaw Reid, at Dorchester House; there was a visit to Sir George Otto Trevelyan at his country house, Welcombe, near Stratford; and there were memorable days at Oxford. On one of these, June 5, Rhodes was one of the three speakers at the dedication of a memorial tablet to J. R. Green at Jesus College; on another, June 8, the Vice-Chancellor of the University conferred upon him *honoris causa*, the degree of Doctor of Letters, for which he was presented by Professor Gilbert Murray. Here, as in all considered appraisals of his writings, his fairness of mind was singled out for praise:— *semper neutrius partis fautor, utriusque candidus iudex et in Nova Anglia et in Virginia, et Bostoniae et Londinii esse censeretur.* A round of dinners and luncheons afforded occasion for the forming and extension of personal relations with the leading historical scholars of England. Rhodes's partial record of it is preserved in one of his letters.

To Mrs. C. H. Toy

Oxford, June 12, 1909.
. . . We have been here for a week and in some way it seems longer because we have done so much.

Last Saturday was the placing of the tablet in the quadrangle of Jesus College in memory of J. R. Green. I received a formal invitation to be present at the ceremony and at the luncheon (Morse Stephens says nothing can be done in England without a luncheon or dinner) and, when I went to call upon Mrs. Green in London, she was desirous that I should read a few words which I did in the quadrangle, following the Vice-Chancellor and Mr. Firth (whose words were effective and wise). That was all in the quadrangle and, hungry in the cold, wet atmosphere, as we all were, we went to the hall for luncheon which was excellent, as are all the repasts in the colleges. After we had eaten and drunk, came a number of speeches. Bury spoke well as did Tout, Smith, Fisher and others. The Principal of Jesus, who presided, was witty, and Mrs. Green made an effective, even a touching speech. The commemoration will always be a pleasant memory.

My degree, with the usual ceremony, was conferred upon me on the following Tuesday. Professor Gilbert Murray made the presentation address and at my wife's request I send you herewith a copy of it.

On that Tuesday evening, Professor and Mrs. Firth gave Mrs. Rhodes and me a grand dinner of 25 or 30 in the Hall of All Souls College, and we count it one of the significant dinners at which we have been present. There was good company, viands and wine and, crowning it all, was the noble room in which we were assembled. Mrs. Rhodes sat by Mrs. Firth and next her was Professor Goudy (Mr. Bryce's successor) who was entertaining and handsome (though 61). The curious thing is that Professor Goudy, though good-looking, resembles Lincoln, who was not. I had the pleasure of sitting next Mrs. Gardner and next me was Dr. Shadwell (there were more men than women at the dinner) with whom Mrs. Rhodes and I are dining tomorrow night at Oriel. . . .

From the Continent he wrote more than a month later:

To the same

Trier a. d. Mosel, 31 July, 1909.

. . . We were about a month in France and, as motoring lends itself to observation and reflection, we are ready with profound thoughts on the state of the country, which will be about as valuable as similar ideas which foreigners express about our own country from superficial observations. From my first coming to France forty-two years ago, I have always loved France and the French, and I would like to see the country prosperous and happy; and it ought to be, for the people are clever, industrious, and frugal, and are capable of great sacrifices. It is easy enough to see that they did not know how to accept the *fait accompli* and to give up all idea of wresting Alsace and Lorraine from Germany. If they had had a French George Washington or Abraham Lincoln, who could have gained their confidence and led them in that direction, they would have been better off today. For they would not have had this enormous increase of debt; they would have an army half of the present size and a snug navy on which they could depend, instead of the utterly demoralized one that they now possess. Nationally it is much easier to see the "mote" in your friendly nation than it is the "beam" in your own; but it is sad to see this highly civilized nation without a rallying point. No King, Church, Constitu-

[187]

tion, Parliament, or Congress which can inspire the people in a stress. When in London it seemed a bit silly that the *Spectator* should say that the cheer which went up when the King's horse won the Derby was something to be remembered, but the *Spectator* was wiser than I, for in that shout lay a loyal expression to him who represented the government.

No one can motor through France for a month without a high regard for the people who have the care of your entertainment and comfort. "Shall I not take mine ease in my inn"—and that ease we took many times in France, where in some uninviting surroundings the food and cooking were delicious and the politeness of the master and mistress of the house added to one's contentment. In only one case were we imposed upon, and that was a charge for rooms at Caen, but after a protest, I think the proprietor made up for the grasping eagerness of his wife by serving our repasts in our salon at the same price as in the restaurant, giving us food and wine at a reasonable price.

If, as I believe it to be true, parliamentary government in France has developed a great deal of corruption and is a failure, many of the good administrative traditions of Napoleon I remain and they are shown in the excellent roads one everywhere finds which makes France the paradise of motorists. The roads are very much better than in England and Switzerland and are well kept up. . . .

Back in Boston in the autumn of 1909 Rhodes found himself plunged again into academic ceremonies, for on October 6 his friend, A. Lawrence Lowell, was inaugurated President of Harvard University. President Hadley of Yale, and Mrs. Hadley, were the guests of Mr. and Mrs. Rhodes for this occasion, involving a number of interesting assemblages. In Rhodes's book of social memoranda it appears that he sat next to Woodrow Wilson at the high table of the alumni meeting following the inauguration, and that "Mr. Hadley made, next to President Eliot, the best speech of the afternoon." If Rhodes's records of the impressions his many guests made upon him are scanty, it is fortunate that one of those guests has written, for the good of this volume, a few words about Rhodes, which may be given appropriately at this point. With many opportunities to observe him, it is thus that President Hadley has seen him in retrospect:

Mr. Rhodes was one of the most delightful men to talk with that I ever met in all my life. He had a singular talent for constructive conversation—for talk that left you with your ideas cleared up and enlarged. This, I think, was due to a combination of two qualities; vast knowledge of the important facts of political history, and a cheerful optimism which underlay all his views and conclusions. It sometimes happens that wide knowledge makes people cynical or even pessimistic. Of such cynicism there was not a trace in James Ford Rhodes. He had observed large fields of human activity and had found them good. Whenever anybody presented a new idea for him to consider, or a new acquaintance for him to appreciate, his eye was always open for the good. In every page of his history this constructive and appreciative instinct is apparent. He told the truth about people and at times told it unsparingly, but his thought was always more of what the man was or did than of what he failed to do.

I remember this specially in our frequent talks about civil war generals in the later eighties and early nineties when controversy raged and reputations were being unsparingly pulled to pieces. He was always ready to find excuses for the man even when the particular mistake could not be excused. I think he always inclined to the theory that a bad general was misplaced rather than inherently incompetent, and it is singular how often he could give good reasons for his charitable view.

But he never asked charity for his own mistakes, nor did he have occasion to ask it. He was one of the most accurate historical investigators that I have ever known. In his thorough collection of all possible sources of information I have seen one or two Germans that equalled him; no men of any nation who surpassed him. A singular instance of this thoroughness came up in my own personal acquaintance. An incident had occurred just before the Republican Convention in 1864 which, if it had become generally known, would have been very damaging to certain prominent political leaders. I had known something of this through personal conversation with eye witnesses and had followed the matter up very carefully as a matter of special interest. From an allusion in Mr. Rhodes's history I inferred that he knew something about it and was anxious to see how much, and in particular whether his newspaper sources of information were the same as my own. I found him not only ready but eager to talk. He said frankly that the incident as it had been represented to him had probably occurred—almost certainly—but that it appeared unwise to him to damage good men's reputations unnecessarily on anything short of a certainty. "As for sources of in-

formation," he said, "I will send for my index newspaper files." "How many newspaper authorities have
you?" I said four. He said, as he looked at his list,
"I have five." I said, "You beat me as usual." He
named his five newspapers. I said, "I have three of
those five and one that you haven't." After looking
them over he said, "Yes, that is all right, but I ought
not to have missed that sixth newspaper clipping." It
shows his high standard of work that that was the thing
that dwelt in his mind at the moment; and the next
time he saw me he ended some conversation about
historical research, "And I can't understand how I
missed that sixth clipping."

He never applied to others quite the same standard
that he exacted of himself. He had worked long
enough to know that it was human to make mistakes.
But when he did see a man whose standards of thoroughness were the same as his own his delight was
unbounded. I remember the enthusiasm with which
he spoke to me not once but repeatedly of John
Schwab's book on the Finances of the Confederate
States. "That," he said, "is first class work. It is a
pleasure to me to read a book whose summaries of fact
I can quote with the same conviction of accuracy that
I should have if I had made the investigations myself."
That was the man all through. Setting high standards
for himself, ready to recognize the good side of others
under all conditions and overwhelmingly rejoiced wherever he found a man who measured up to the standard.

Before the end of 1909 Rhodes, accompanied by
his wife and daughter-in-law, made a visit to Washington, to attend a meeting of the American Academy of Arts and Letters, in which—for all the chaf-

fing it received in its earlier years as a self-constituted group of "Immortals"—he cherished a deep and constant interest. A memorandum for December 13, however, records what he manifestly wished most to recollect in this Washington visit:

Tuesday we three took luncheon with Ambassador and Mrs. Bryce at the Embassy. Mr. Bryce very free in his political talk. Thought no man had done the British Empire so much harm as Chamberlain. We discussed Lecky. He thought Lecky should have opposed South African War. I said Lecky said he had a hard time at home because his wife sympathized with the Boers, while he voted with his party. "He ought to have voted against the war," said Bryce. I: "Lecky said to me that Lord Salisbury told him a week before the declaration or decision, there would be no war." "There would not have been," said Mr. Bryce, "had the negotiations been left with Salisbury, but they were turned over to Chamberlain and war was the result."

The correspondence of 1910 happens to yield but little for preservation. Early in the year Rhodes underwent an operation, from which the recovery was long and tedious. Two letters to Woodrow Wilson reveal the fact that the Princeton honorary degree of LL.D., publicly awarded in 1912, might have been received in 1910 or 1911 had he been able to attend the Princeton Commencement ceremonies in either of these years. The second of the letters to Wilson was written soon after a meeting of the American Academy and National Institute of Arts and Letters in

New York, at which Rhodes received the Institute's gold medal in recognition of his historical writings. This is recorded but briefly in Rhodes's memoranda of the occasion—with allusion to his "lame speech" at the informal dinner on the evening of the award, December 8. A small informal dinner at which he was host on the evening before evidently gave him more pleasure. "Much talk," he jotted down, "about Woodrow Wilson and his campaign.[16] Hadley regards him as a very fine orator." A few days later Rhodes was writing to the subject of this talk.

To Woodrow Wilson

Boston, December 11, 1910.
. . . We missed you but, as we could not talk with you, we talked about you and gave you our high admiration and hearty good wishes in the brave fight that you are making. I marvel at your courage and persistence, instead of taking the primrose path which would have been so easy. When I have known personally a man like yourself it is no wonder that I like to write American history; but it is lucky that I live in cold critical Boston or I should indulge in a spread-eagle strain. . . .

The names of Wilson and Roosevelt are hard to keep apart from 1910 to the end of their lives, and here the one follows promptly upon the other—this time through an entry in one of Rhodes's "Index Rerum" volumes. Roosevelt had recently returned from Africa and Europe.

Roosevelt, Theodore.—Took breakfast, December

16 For Governor of New Jersey.

14, 1910, at Judge Lowell's [17] with him, Mr. Roosevelt, Mrs. Lowell and Judge Grant. Roosevelt full of his European kings. The only man of real ability he saw among the crowned heads was the German Emperor, and he is superficial in his intelligence but has real executive ability. He is such a man as Gov. Draper, only under the same conditions Draper would have been his superior, but Draper has had to earn his living. The Emperor was eager to get Roosevelt's opinion of himself and at last Roosevelt said: "If you were an American and lived in America you would carry your own ward, which is more than I can say for any other of the crowned heads." The German Emperor treated all the other kings with disdain except the king of England. Even turned his back on the Czar with something of contempt.

Amusing tricks in order to gain precedence. A king or prince of one of the Eastern countries got his car put on ahead of the Czar's, next to locomotive, but when it came dinner time the dining-car was on the rear of the train. He asked permission of the Czar to go through his car, which was refused, so he had to get out at a station to reach his car.

Sat next Duke of Cumberland at the "Wake," which he called the grand banquet preceding the funeral of King Edward. "English name but you seem to be German." "Yes, and if it was not for that man there (German Emperor) I would be King of Hanover." The petty jealousies among the kings amusing. The King of Italy a fine fellow. "I wish we had seventy senators just like you." King—"I am educating my son to fit him for the first President of the Italian Republic." All the Monarchs except Germany's and

---

[17] Francis Cabot Lowell.

England's see the shadow of a Republic and fear for their places.

At the Wake Pichon, the French Representative, asked what was the colored livery of your coachman. "Black, I think." "So was mine, and it is an outrage." All these kings and princes had coachmen in liveries of yellow, green, or red. At the funeral, Pichon: "We haven't a glass coach." "I think it a very nice coach; it's yellow; there are three or four steps leading up to it. We have four horses." "It is an outrage, but do get in before *ce petit chinois*. Then think—everyone is put ahead of us, even the Prince of Portugal. I shall make a protest and want you to join me," which Roosevelt steadily refused. "Don't raise a row at a funeral."

But at the breakfast after the funeral Roosevelt sat at the King's table and Pichon at the Queen's. Disappointed in English women. Impressed with Hungarian women. German admiral at head of Navy impressed with voyage of fleet around the world, but— "were you not taking a desperate chance that the Japanese would begin war?" "I thought it was possible, but we were ready and to be ready was one of the instructions I gave Bob. Evans."

Europeans impressed with our naval trip around the world and with our construction of Panama Canal.

Knox bluffed and was not in position to carry out his bluff. We are entitled to open door in Manchuria, but to them (?) Manchuria is Japan's life. Better to concede that than to claim what we cannot enforce. The Japanese government earnestly in favor of peace. Knox a splendid Attorney-General, but runs the State Department as an attorney runs a lawsuit.

Norway with a king as funny as Vermont would be

with a king. No nobility in Norway and little culture in our sense or in the sense of Oxford and Cambridge. King George and his drinking. Roosevelt referred to the reports about himself and to the San Francisco goblet.

Cleveland served him two mean tricks while governor which I did not fully understand. Cleveland grew in office—was bigger as President than as governor. Sustained him as Civil Service Commissioner better than Harrison. Harrison would never go ahead of public sentiment of his party. Cleveland was sturdy and independent. When the silver Democrats went in for Cleveland in 1892 they by no means abandoned silver. "Let us beat the Republicans first and then we can tackle silver."

Roosevelt influential in getting Proctor [18] appointed in Johnston's [19] place. Proctor an excellent C.S. [Civil Service] man.

Addenda and Suggestions which occur to Robert Grant.—He spoke of the German Emperor's tendency to act impulsively, which got him into difficulties at times; and stated that the Emperor had consulted him about the Algeciras dispute with France, and that he (T. R.) had drafted the terms which were agreed on. At the dinner following King Edward's funeral he met the King of Spain, who said, "I congratulate you on your military achievements, but regret that it was at the expense of my countrymen." "I never met braver soldiers, your majesty, than your countrymen; but I

[18] John R. Proctor, of Kentucky, appointed Civil Service Commissioner 1893.

[19] George D. Johnston, of Louisiana, Civil Service Commissioner, removed 1893.

cannot say as much for their leaders." The King threw up his hands and said, "Yes—Yes." (As I remember it) Pichon said, *"Voyez les Chinois"*—objecting to the fact that the Chinese officials were in a coach ahead. The third who occupied the coach with him and Col. Roosevelt was *le prince de Perse,* a shrinking little oriental. Pichon showed Roosevelt deference, but on entering the coach put out his hand to prevent the *prince de Perse* from taking the seat beside him, and glared across at him during the drive. At the dinner following, the "Wake," the Kings sitting near Roosevelt showed great curiosity regarding him. They had never seen a sovereign before who was also a military leader, a shooter of big game, and a man of the people. They would say to him, "What was that story you told in Vienna? My sister-in-law wrote me about it." And the German Emperor came over and said, "Roosevelt, tell us that story you told me," etc. He thought that another cause besides the goblet for the stories of his drinking was his would-be humorous remark to some visitors, "I should be a prig, but for my vices of drinking to excess and gambling." I think (but am not sure) it was one [of] the minor European Sovereigns who had his special car put on ahead of the Emperor. In connection with Japan (besides what you have written) he regretted recent Pasadena episode where the American women declined to go to the dance for the Japanese fleet. Stated that during his administration an arrangement had been made with Japanese officials to limit the emigration in Japan, i.e., before the emigrants started, rather than before they arrived. The Japanese leaders wish peace, but may be stampeded by mass. Said the advice given him by some English authority (was it Ian Hamilton?) not to stir up the Japanese until they had exchanged their present martial fitness for industrialism, had prompted him to send the fleet and find out her intentions. "We shall have six months' start anyway," he said.

Roosevelt after the election of 1910 [had a] feeling of bewilderment. It was the small shop-keepers who beat him, and he thought they were his supporters.— Norman Hapgood to Mrs. Toy, April, 1911.

The following letter illustrates Rhodes's familiarity with matters bearing on the subjects of his writing even when he made but a partial use of the facts he had mastered. It was addressed to the President of the Carnegie Foundation for the Advancement of Teaching, who had been President of the Massachusetts Institute of Technology from 1900 to 1906. Beginning as it does, "Dear Henry," it justifies a quotation from a letter written nearly three years later to Dr. Harvey Cushing, originally of Cleveland, who had then recently come from Johns Hopkins to the Harvard Medical School. "Dear Harvey"—it began—"For so I must address you, and you must call me James or Jim. I will tell you why. When Mr. Pritchett first came here he felt that he was a little 'out of it,' as the men called one another by their Christian names, Fred, Henry, John, Jim, etc., and he said that to 'keep our end up,' as we were from the West, we must do likewise: hence Henry and James. It is a good example to follow." Though Rhodes never became the "Jim" of his early Cleveland days to his intimates in Boston, there were those to whom the "James," duly reciprocated, became entirely natural. He was not at all unaware of his own "Western accent." In writing to Judge Grant about "The Chippendales" in 1909, he spoke of the years he had passed in Boston "as an observer from the 'wild and woolly West,'" and on re-reading the book in 1924 declared, "The efforts of those outside to get within the charmed circle are well depicted, and I am glad indeed that the rich man of the book is from Maine and not from Ohio." Only a "Brahmin," he said, would have written it, and went on: "As you plainly show, the great defect of such a caste is to become narrow; but really I should have liked to belong to it, indulging in the prophecy that, as I mark the contrast of the present with the past, we are all going to the 'demnition bow-wows.'" In this final remark a spirit that characterized only his closing years revealed itself. Back, then, let us turn to 1911 and "Dear Henry."

To Henry S. Pritchett

Boston, February 17, 1911.

Differing with you, the espousal of the Agricultural College bill by Justin S. Morrill seems so in keeping with his life, aims, and character that it does not need any special explanation. Perhaps something is due to childish recollections, as since I was twelve or fourteen years old I have watched Morrill's career with interest. He with a brother Vermonter was at my Father's to a Sunday dinner in the early sixties, and the three went into the library to take before meat a nip of some rye whiskey on which my Father prided

[199]

himself. I was permitted to hear the conversation.
Morrill took a generous drink and after filling his glass
with water thus apostrophized it: "If a man drink
brandy he will live about one year, if he drink gin he
may last three years, but let him drink good old rye
and he will live forever." Had Morrill been familiar
with Bobbie Burns he would have added his tribute to
the spirit of malt:

> "It's mair than schools or college,
> It chucks us full of knowledge."

Senator George F. Hoar knew Morrill well and was
very fond of him. In Hoar's Autobiography (Vol. II,
p. 85) you will find a beautiful eulogy of Morrill.
Hoar in his later years was given to flattery. Nevertheless were I to write a characterization I have little
doubt that I would arrive at the same result as our
highly educated, bookish senator. I regretted that I
could not say more about Morrill in my History, but
as he was not a political leader or a debater I could
not enlarge much on his work; and it did not fall
within my plan to give an account of his Agricultural
College Act. In Andrew D. White's Autobiography
(Vol. I, p. 200) you will find a tribute to Morrill in
this connection. Mr. White knows more about this
matter, I think, than any man living except yourself.
When my first volumes were published he was eager
that I should devote considerable attention to this subject, as was also my friend Edward G. Bourne. . . .
I forget what I wrote to Mr. White, but I told Bourne
that the history of education was not in my line and
that someone would arise who would specialize in it
and do it very much better than I could. My prophecy

is realized in yourself. I suppose you know Mr. White. If not I shall be glad to give you a letter of introduction. His conversation in the line of reminiscence is very interesting, and if sometime when he is in New York you should happen to spend an evening with him at the Century you would get a valuable dissertation from him on the Agricultural College Act and on Morrill. A talk with him would be more satisfactory than writing to him to Ithaca.

In the *Forum* for November, 1897, are some private letters to Morrill printed. I do not remember that they touch upon the Act in question but they will be worth your looking up.

I do not know of any biography of Morrill. . . .[20]

You will observe that Senator Hoar speaks highly of Morrill's services in connection with the National library. He was chairman of the Senate Committee on the library at the time of McKinley's inauguration, and Mark Hanna wanted to get the library for the inauguration ball, to which Morrill interposed a decisive objection. Hanna was irate. I do not remember what he said, but it must have been something like this: "The damned old senator. He thinks his library should be used for nothing but books."

The answer to your question concerning the tariff bill is easy. Morrill was chosen because he knew more about the details of the tariff than any man in the House. He was the McKinley or Dingley of his time. John Sherman was chairman of the Committee of Ways and Means, and, as that Committee had more put upon it than it has now, he did not want an additional burden: nor were the infinitesimal details of the

---

[20] A Life of Morrill, by William Belmont Parker, was published in 1924.

tariff much to Sherman's taste. He devolved that
work therefore on Morrill, who introduced the bill
into the House on March 12, 1860. The House passed
it at that session, but it did not go through the Senate
until February, 1861, after the secession of a number
of the Southern senators. You will find a brief account
of this in Sherman's Recollections, Vol. I, pp. 182, 183
—also see p. 180. See also Vols. II and III of my
History.

I shall read your history of this phase of education
with great interest, and I thank you for your offer of a
sight of your original material on the subject. I have,
however, put everything before 1877 behind me. I am
now living in the period of 1877–1897 and have more
original material at hand than I have eyes to read or
brains to assimilate. . . .

In connection with the following entry in one of
Rhodes's "Index Rerum" volumes it should be said
that his treatment of the Morgan-Belmont syndicate
contract for replenishing the gold reserve in 1895, in
the volume, "From Hayes to McKinley," [21] was based
on a study of the subject from many angles, including
that of a conversation with J. P. Morgan more than a
year later than his talk with Bishop Lawrence. This
entry is typical of a habit of acquiring and recording
possibly useful information from all accessible sources.

Morgan, J. Pierpont, and the gold deal of 1895.
Talk with Bishop Lawrence on March 29, 1911: About
two months previous he, Morgan, and Olney at dinner
at Sherry's. In 1895 financial men of New York

[21] See pp. 431-438.

wanted him to go to see Cleveland. Morgan went to Washington, and had a long talk with Olney. Olney told him about the law of 1862. Morgan went to the White House. Cleveland reserved and offish, said he lacked power to make a deal with the syndicate. Then came the question, "Why do you not bring gold under the Act of 1862?" Morgan said he himself was so worked up during the interview that on going into the President's office with an unlighted cigar he did not light it, but after a while he looked and it was all in fragments at his feet. Bishop Lawrence thinks Morgan believes this one of the great accomplishments of his life. Olney asked Morgan why he did not set all of this down: that it was history. Morgan said he did not care to make a record of such things. Bishop Lawrence said that when Morgan was in the right mood he was a delightful and consecutive talker, "would talk all night." The great point with Morgan was to prevent gold going out of the country, and he assured Cleveland earnestly that he would do his utmost to prevent this. In this conversation Bishop Lawrence told me Mark Hanna had given him the account of the nomination of Roosevelt (V.P.) and how near Root (*sic.*—Bliss?) came to it. Bishop Lawrence wishes that Harvard had conferred the LL.D. on Morgan before Yale. When the question of confirmation was up before the Overseers, it was objected to that the degree was offered because Morgan was a rich man. Bishop Lawrence said if that were the qualification he would not favor it. But Morgan had served his country as a patriot in 1895. He was the best of the capitalists in the Anthracite coal strike, and he was very efficient in the panic of 1907.

Lawrence asked who wrote the Venezuela message?

[203]

Morgan pointed to Olney—"that is the man." Olney said he did not write it but made emendations to the original draft. Morgan seemed to intimate that the emendations were the main thing.

Bishop Lawrence was on a visit to Mackaye-Smith at the time of the Venezuela excitement: at that time the Smith and the Cleveland children were intimate. On the Sunday after the message Mackaye-Smith preached against the message. An invitation of the Cleveland children to the Smith children's party was withdrawn. Bishop Lawrence at a reception at the White House. Was told (I think by Olney) that the President would like to invite him upstairs to supper but could not without inviting Smith, and he would not ask Smith.

The summer of 1911 found Rhodes again in Europe. In an August letter to Barrett Wendell there is a trace of the same sentiment that led him, as we have seen, to seat himself with such seriousness in Jefferson Davis's pew at Richmond and to visit and revisit the scenes of Gibbon's beginning and ending his masterpiece of history. This time it was Eckermann's "Conversations with Goethe" which led him to write to Wendell, "For the fourth or fifth time I have read it this summer both in the English and the German. It appeals to me more than Boswell, inasmuch as Goethe was so much greater than Johnson. His broad mind and catholic sympathy are illuminating. On our trip we stopped two days at Weimar, my third visit, and there is no place where I love the literary associations more except Stratford."

Three other letters of this summer may be given more nearly in their entirety.

To Barrett Wendell

Innsbruck, June 5, 1911.

Your letter of April 15 I received at Venice, and today on arrival I find yours of 19 May, which I have read with great interest. Your remarks on Chinese civilization find in me a response which your comparisons do not. How you would have enjoyed a certain luncheon that the good Mr. Charles Norton gave in honor of John Morley! One of the other guests was President Eliot and the conversation was very good. Mr. Norton was in a pessimistic mood, and after consigning Senator Hoar to one of the deepest dungeons of hell and deprecating generally everything that was going on broke out with, "Well, Morley, I think our civilization is a failure." As, in a way, I had charge of Mr. Morley we took the electric cars and rode to Harvard bridge which we walked over. I must premise by saying that when he arrived in Boston the only gentleman with whom Mr. Morley had a previous acquaintance was Mr. Norton. As we walked on Mr. Morley said: "I did not like the way my old friend Norton talked today. This continued and continual criticism of everything does not appeal to me. But what a great man is Eliot and how his constructive work, how his effort to make the best of conditions, is a real advance and entitled to imitation and approval."

Predictions are uncertain and I shall never make any, yet it must appear to a visitor from Mars as if Germany, the U. S. and England (I hope and think)

must be excepted from your pessimistic generalization.
I believe the mass of the human race have never had so
good a time as they are now having in the U. S., and
that, take it all in all, materialistic conditions were
never so good.   In your illuminating letter you draw
a grave indictment of the people you so much admire.
Dirt and filth, in the teaching of the microbic theory
of disease, do not accompany the highest civilization.
And you quite left out of account Christianity! . . .

To William H. Taft

Evian-Les-Bains, August 26, 1911.

Reciprocity went through,[22] and you are the hero of
it.   If Canada adopts it, the results, unless I am much
mistaken, will be so beneficial to both countries that
the work of the men who have had a hand in it will
be gratefully appreciated.   If the teaching of history
and economics is worth anything, our country has
reached a point where every wise and careful reduction
of the tariff will redound to the good of the greatest
number.

Your movement for arbitration deserves the admiration and help of every lover of peace.   War is so horrible and now so useless that the ruler who outlines a
policy to make it highly improbable between civilized
nations will reach high fame.

Reciprocity and arbitration are two matters that the
mass of the people can understand.   If I were a politician seeking advancement I should not want to op-
pose either. . . .

---

[22] On July 26, 1911, President Taft signed the Canadian Reciprocity
bill resulting from efforts instituted by him.   The Liberal government
of Canada, appealing soon afterwards to the country on this issue,
was defeated.

To Mrs. C. H. Toy

Ouchy-Lausanne, September 3, 1911.

. . . We sail from Liverpool September 23 and shall be at Queenstown on the morning of the 24th. Our ship is the *Mauretania*. It does not now look probable that there will be a recurrence of the labor troubles which have delayed so many ships especially the sister ship *Lusitania*. We were quite anxious during the strike which I followed with keen interest regretting that I was not in some quiet resort in England so as to be more in touch with it. These outbreaks of savagery where the worst elements of the community come to the front interest me much. I have studied two of them critically which happened in our own country and I read all the English papers I could lay my hands on. I did not see the warrant for the statement in the *Nation* that "men and women throughout the streets of Liverpool crying for blood," but there is no question that the situation there was desperate. So far as I can learn the police and the troops acted with moderation and great credit, and Churchill did his duty as Home Minister. I felt sorry for Mr. Asquith at having this trouble follow his grave political contention, and I think the misunderstanding occurring at the famous interview must have arisen from his nervousness and being worn out. I wish indeed he might have been the hero of the settlement instead of Lloyd George who, I think, is politically very much of a rising man. So far as I know the settlement was a fair one. The railroad employees are wretchedly underpaid, compared with our wages, but not with those of Germany and France. I suspect,

however, that Germany is ahead of us all in certain
social legislation looking to the care of aged and worn-
out laborers. . . .

I cannot claim the credit of having sent you *Le
Temps.* I do not wonder you are interested in it, as
it is a high class journal. My friend Tardieu has attracted the attention of all Europe by his articles on
the Morocco question, which he probably understands
better than any other journalist. I am sorry that the
dispute has caused a renewed outbreak of the bitter
attacks on England in Germany. I cannot get it out of
my head that those two great nations should be friends,
but I am too ignorant and naïve to understand the
whole question. I cannot believe that the German
Emperor wants war as he has always been for peace,
but is it magnanimous to push poor France to the wall?
I have been a constant reader of the *Times,* which
seems to be as well edited as ever, and perhaps my
native conservative views are intensified by the ultra-
conservatism of the Thunderer. . . .

For the months of 1911 following Rhodes's return
to the United States there is no more significant bit of
record than a December entry in an "Index Rerum"
volume relating to the visit from Roosevelt which he
had bespoken long before.[23] On December 13 it appears from his memoranda of social engagements that
he gave both a breakfast and a dinner in his guest's
honor. Of Roosevelt's talk during the visit, three
months before he "threw his hat into the ring," there
is the following memorandum:

---

[23] See *ante,* p. 183.

Theodore Roosevelt arrived in Boston at 3 P.M. on Tuesday, December 12 and remained with me until Thursday, December 14 at 10 A.M. He does not want the nomination for the presidency, and is doing nothing to secure it. He feels that the fight will be a hard one. The matter of waiting until 1916 had of course occurred to him. Thinks if the Democrats win in 1912 it will be easy for a Republican in 1916. But some governor or senator or some one may come up to attract public attention. It is easy to see that he does not feel friendly to President Taft, nor has he a hearty liking for La Follette.

He is opposed to the arbitration treaties. No use. Look at the House of Representatives abrogating the Russian treaty. I thought he heard the news with glee that the peace meeting in New York was broken up.

One of his books "The Conspiracy of Cataline," by Boissier.

He is not friendly to Germany. He seemed to feel less near to them than any of the peoples he met abroad. They are not capable of a broad humanitarian impulse like the English, Americans, or French. The cruelty of the Turks to the Christians did not seem to affect them as cruelty, but how the Turks will affect them internationally. At the breakfast a chorus of assent from Diehl and Schofield. Mr. R. was delighted with the breakfast—with the opportunity to meet these young academic people. They were equally delighted with him.

I think Mr. Roosevelt appreciates the seriousness of war. I do not believe he would want to go to war unless he thought he had a good chance of winning on the first go-off. If we went to war with Japan and lost the Philippines we could not get them back. He would like to get rid of the Philippines honorably, but we must not let them be taken from us. The German Emperor is a capable administrator, of superficial knowledge—a great bluffer. Proud of the things in which he has a superficial knowledge—not very proud of the matters in which he excels.

Thinks a lock canal necessary. One ocean is lower than the other. The only question how much of a lock? All the foreign engineers for a sea level canal. All the American engineers for a lock canal.

Early in 1912, before responding yet again to the beckoning of Europe, Rhodes gave token of his satisfaction in his permanent abode.

To Charles Francis Adams

Boston, February 9, 1912.

. . . I read with great interest what you say about Washington. As you have had the best of both Boston and Washington societies, I am entirely willing to accept your judgment. Coming here from Cleveland, however, I have found Boston society very attractive. Having been made a member of four dining or supper clubs (one of which is the Saturday) I find that I meet some choice spirits in an easy, hospitable way. The great University adds much to the interest of my life; and the visitors from England, France, and Germany keep me in touch with the outside world. Being entirely satisfied, there is no use of my making a change, so that I shall pass the rest of my days here, and in this house unless the Progressives and Socialists should take all of my money. . . .

To Mrs. C. H. Toy

Florence, March 31, 1912.

. . . The interesting account you gave of your visit to Washington made me envy you being in the midst of things, for nothing appeals to me so much as American history and politics. It does not show culture to say so, but the Middle Ages and the Renaissance and their glorious products pale with me in comparison. For it seems to me that Mr. Bryce is right when he wrote in his last edition: "That America marks the highest level not only of material well-being but of intelligence and happiness which the race has yet attained will be the judgment of those who look not at the favored few for whose benefit the world seems hitherto to have its institutions, but at the whole body of the people." So the manner in which we are working out our social problems in comparison with England, Germany, France, and Italy seems to me more important than to measure the contribution of the Middle Ages to civilization, or to tell whether they were or not an age of light or darkness, or to discuss whether "The Music Lesson" was painted by Giorgione or Titian. I feel sure that we are coming out all right with neither the sacrifice of liberty nor order and with the results of civilization intact. So I read with keen relish Mr. Cannon's opinion of Mr. Woodrow Wilson, and thought he was very funny about the Saul of Tarsus conversion. I feel sure that General Crozier (whom I knew slightly) would have said to Mr. Cannon if it would not have been too impolite: "It is true that Mr. Wilson has written books and expressed decided opinions different from those of his speeches on

the stump, but, Mr. Cannon, how would you like your
promises to Mr. Morgan and other Wall Street mag-
nates, when they were pressing you for the presidency
in 1908 to beat Taft, to be contrasted with your sympathetic speeches to the farmers and laborers of your
district when you go thither to ask for their votes?"

I may have told you of a little talk at the Wednesday
Evening Club, and if so you must attribute its repeti-
tion to the forgetfulness of age. Sitting opposite Mr.
Brooks Adams when presidential candidates were being discussed, the tone unfavorable to Mr. Wilson, I
said, "Mr. Wilson is a gentleman of honor and intelligence." "Oh ho!" said Mr. Adams with a scornful
laugh, "I never heard anyone say that before." I
replied, "I will amend my statement: up to the time
he ran for governor of New Jersey, Mr. Wilson was a
gentleman of honor and intelligence." "Oh ho!" said
Mr. A., "I fancy you are alone in that opinion." "I
have heard President Eliot say the same thing." Perhaps I misjudge Mr. Adams, but I interpreted his con-
temptuous gesture to mean that such an endorsement
was of no account. I returned, "I am not certain, but
almost so, that President Lowell shares my opinion."
That stopped the colloquy. Next day I met Mr.
Lowell on the street, told him the conversation and
asked if he agreed with me. Of course he gave a decided yes but added, "I cannot see how Mr. Wilson
reconciles to himself his complete change of opinion
from the academy to the stump." But as Lincoln
said, "Nobody knows what this gnawing feeling for
the presidency is until he gets it." . . .

The ensuing letters gain significance when it is remembered that Theodore Roosevelt announced his de-

cision to enter the presidential contest in 1912 while he was visiting Judge Grant in Boston.

To Robert Grant

Cannes, April 11, 1912.

I can never thank you enough for yours of 22 ult., which reached me three days ago. It is an interesting, candid, and graphic account of a historic event which I shall file away with my confidential papers, perhaps to be used at some future time by one of my grandsons. As for me, I shall never do what I had dreamed of doing, writing two or three volumes, entitled *McKinley and Roosevelt*, devoted to their administrations. For if a man makes in 1912 "an unnecessary, a possibly fatal blunder which for the time being at any rate bids fair to destroy his value as a great political asset" (I am using your words which I cordially endorse) that blunder cannot but hark back upon his work as President and make more difficult a justification of his questionable acts. I am grieved. An idol that I cherished fondly is broken. Disclosing his inmost thoughts, as he did to me last December, I had hoped against hope that he would eventually come out mildly for President Taft. For he gave me plainly to understand that he should not announce that he would accept the nomination unless there was clearly a drift of sentiment toward him; that it might appear that President Taft's chances for the nomination were so great that it would be wise for him to keep silence. When I heard of his announcement that came out on the day that he was with you, looking upon him as a shrewd politician as you do, I fancied that he could see the drift toward him. But it seemingly turns out that he was mistaken. Now if he has judged wrongly in this, he may be mistaken about our being on the eve of an economic revolution. At all events, I have not the confidence in his political judgment that I had three months ago.

Noyes (financial editor of the *Evening Post*) had a thoughtful article in the *Atlantic* two or three months ago in which he said that not since 1848 had Europe been in such a feverish state, denoting a social upheaval, and that now the U. S. shared the feeling of unrest. Meeting Bury (a great scholar, Regius professor of History at Cambridge) in Rome, I mentioned this speculation which he thought had much support. A thoughtful Swiss concierge at Menton told me that Europe was on the eve of a general war which the rulers would bring on to prevent a rising of the poor against the rich that would otherwise ensue. We know that there was a marked conservative reaction after 1848, and there is no reason to believe that there will not be another after Mr. Roosevelt's economic revolution.

In announcing his candidacy, personal ambition has swayed Mr. Roosevelt. Although a great admirer and student of Washington and Lincoln, he has failed to manifest any of the unselfishness and magnanimity that so distinguished them. He is no longer the great political asset that he was. And this is a great pity! For he would have been of the highest use in guiding a social revolution or in arousing the patriotism of the country in the event of a foreign war.

But perhaps this economic revolution may not occur. It sometimes happens that events widely prophesied do not take place. If the present improvement in business is real and if we have good crops, Mr. Taft may be elected. Roosevelt and Wilson can thrive only on calamity, which would produce an economic revolution. As a wise German said, The social question is a stomach question.

It seems as if I were losing a great chance in not being in the thick of events at home, as you were, instead of wandering about this old country dipping in a most superficial way into classical times, the Middle Ages, and the Renaissance. I did not want to come abroad this year and I am now seeing what I missed. . . .

To the same

Cannes, April 11, 1912.

By a later post I have your two favors of 26 and 27. I knew of course that you meant that Mr. Roosevelt was in earnest and sincere. I thank you for the privilege of reading your letter to discreet persons. I have made the correction indicated above in your letter.

I am interested in your account of the Howells dinner. I shall gladly hear your account of your conversation with the Cardinal. I thought that he made a good speech at one of the banquets during the President's visit.

I acknowledge the receipt of Mr. Roosevelt's Columbus speech. I had already read it carefully in the *Outlook*. It was less radical than I supposed from the hostile comment, but some of it seemed to me foolish. To advocate a recall of the judges where in Ohio they are elected, I believe, every five years is a different matter from advocating the same principle in New York and Massachusetts. But I suppose that deep thinkers read between the lines and know that

when Mr. Roosevelt has accomplished the recall of
the State Judges he will advocate the recall of the
U. S. judges, those of the Supreme Court included.
His attacks on the decisions of the U. S. Supreme Court
and the N. Y. Court of Appeals are mischievous and
savor of the demagogue rather than of the statesman.
It is an infinite pity! Mr. Roosevelt might have been
very great had he embraced the principles laid down
so ably, lately by his friend Senator Lodge. He had
apologized so much for his Denver speech in 1910 and
had been so adroit in his defence that I was a bit surprised that he should iterate the same doctrine. . . .

To Barrett Wendell

Cannes, April 12, 1912.
Your very interesting letter of 28 ult. came yesterday. It keeps me in touch with Boston, where I have
wished many times to be so as to be close to the exciting political events which are taking place. I quite
agree with all that you say concerning Mr. Roosevelt.
I regret his course. . . . For the first man in the land,
as he was when he returned from Europe in 1910, to
fight for the nomination in a vulgar way as Senator
La Follette and Mr. Wilson are doing means a tremendous fall, and I never thought he would do it. I
was green enough to think he would stand aside unless
there was an unmistakable and decided call for him.
For myself I see an idol shattered and I have had no
such political grief since Senator Hanna died, when
of course there was in addition the sorrow for the
loss of a personal friend and a long-time associate.
Mr. Roosevelt is fascinating at his best, cultivated,
courteous, considerate, thoroughly at home with those

[216]

of his birth, breeding, and education, and it is a pity
to see him appealing to a mob. When he visited me
last December one of the books he read on the train
was Boissier's "Conspiracy of Cataline." Was he
thinking then whether he might and how he could
sway the mass? Why did he not take the advice of his
trusted friends Senator Root and Senator Lodge?
What a wonderful record Senator Lodge is making
and how he ought to win the admiration of all that is
best in our State and City! . . .

To Mrs. C. H. Toy

London, April 28, 1912.
. . . I am interested in all that you say about
American politics, and in Mr. ——'s "vealy" opinion
of Mr. Wilson. . . . Mr. Wilson's appeals to the mob
are censurable, but so are Mr. Roosevelt's, whom I
know and like better; but Mr. Wilson has little or no
idea of the right of private property, and when he believes, as I think he does, that private property is
mainly robbery his course becomes logical. I dep-
recate his change of opinion and his feverish craving
for the presidency, but those things do not make a
man "tricky and dishonest through and through."

I know that I am getting old, as public affairs trouble
me much more than they used to. The quarrel between the President and Mr. Roosevelt is lamentable,
but since the news of the *Titanic* disaster, which we
received at Avignon, I have been able to think of little
else. . . .

In Paris, owing to a pathetic letter I wrote to the
Hotel, we got a bed-room at the Ritz, and Mrs. Rhodes
ran into Ambassador Herrick with the result that he,

Mrs. Herrick, and we had quite a conversation, keeping us from the Louvre whither duty was directing our steps. The Ambassador and his wife were just moving into their fine "hôtel" which they had taken from Mr. Bacon, and they asked us to luncheon last Tuesday and we went, having the honor of being the first entertained at their beautiful house which has a garden that was inviting on this lovely day. Mr. Herrick is very entertaining, and the long conversation I had with him on politics in the U. S. posted me up on matters of which I was ignorant. . . .

Mr. Herrick's coming has excited much comment in the Paris press, much stress being laid on the statement that he was a multi-millionaire. I read one of the articles to Mr. H. and asked if he was a m.m., to which his answer was a decided no. . . . I fear I am becoming a worshipper of wealth, for the style in which our ambassadors in Rome and Paris live seems to attract me; but nothing approaches our Mr. Reid in his Dorchester House, on whom I had the honor of calling Friday at his request. The principal thing I did was to write my name in my volumes that he possessed. He had had the volumes bound by the best London binder (I could not help thinking of the young men in the Princess Cassamassima) and I have never before seen myself in so fine a dress. If I were young I would like to live in such a house for a year and dream of it ever afterwards.

The main thing we have done here has been dining with Sir George and Lady Trevelyan (whose names I pronounced right this time) at their London house in pursuance of an engagement made some weeks ago by letter. On Thursday we went there to call and spent an hour in pleasant conversation. Sir George took down Macaulay's Livy, which was full of lead-pencil comments; these and the date showing how he was drawing inspiration for his Lays of Ancient Rome. On Friday we went to dinner. The other guests were George Macaulay Trevelyan and his wife, Mr. and Mrs. Andrew Lang, Lord and Lady Courtney (whom you met at Mrs. Oliver's when he was a Commoner), Sir Courtenay Ilbert and a young man, whose name I do not remember, a writer for the *Times* and connected with a publishing house. Sir George took Mrs. R. out to dinner and she sat between him and George M., both of whom she found highly agreeable. Having read two volumes of George M. she could discourse on Italy and on W. R. Thayer's Cavour. I sat between Lady Trevelyan and Andrew Lang and had much talk with Mr. Lang about his translations of Homer, having to confess that I had not had time to read his original pieces. This in no way affected the *entente cordiale,* as afterwards he told me politely and frankly that while he knew I was a writer on history he really didn't know what I had written. On the other side of Lady Trevelyan sat Lord Courtney, whom I found less radical than in 1902 and whose talk was entertaining. Lady Trevelyan has lovely unaffected manners; she has a high sense of duty and it is a pleasure to hear her talk. She told me something about Sir George's life when Chief Secretary for Ireland. Altogether it was an agreeable evening and when Mrs. R. broke up the party at eleven we felt that we had had a pleasant and profitable time. . . .

The occasion of the visit to Oxford to which the following letter relates itself was the delivery of the course of university lectures published in 1913 in the smallest of Rhodes's volumes, "Lectures on the American Civil War Delivered at Oxford." Except in minor particulars the book contains little that would not naturally be found in a drastic abridgment of the third, fourth, and fifth volumes of his "History of the United States." But the lectures themselves, delivered on May 4, 11, and 18, 1912, as the first under a new foundation, a "Lectureship in American History and Institutions," fulfilled their purpose admirably, and the prediction of the *Oxford Magazine*—that the lecturer, as the holder of an honorary Oxford degree, "as the unanimous first choice of the committee in America, which included Mr. James Bryce and President Lowell, and as an authority on his subject, the American Civil War," would be met with a hearty welcome and a good audience—proved valid. Rhodes himself, as the ensuing letter shows, was neither elated nor unduly depressed by the number of his hearers. Before coming to Oxford he had written to Professor C. H. Firth [24] (February 15, 1912), "Please do not give a thought to the size of the audience. I have nearly always lectured to small audiences, and anything beyond them would be a surprise." This was based in part upon experiences with Lowell Institute lectures in Boston,[25] and confirmed the conservative

---

[24] Professor (now Sir) Charles Harding Firth, of Oxford, made the arrangement for Rhodes's lectures there in 1912, and contributed in many ways to the pleasures of the visit. Rhodes dedicated to him the volume of his Oxford Lectures.

[25] Rhodes delivered two Lowell Institute lectures on "Commercial Intercourse between the North and South during the Civil War" in the season of 1902-03, and four each on "Reconstruction and Negro Suffrage" in the seasons of 1904-05 and 1905-06.

estimate of his platform abilities expressed in a letter written about ten years before to Dr. Charles F. Thwing, President of Western Reserve University, declining an invitation to deliver some lectures in Cleveland: "My life has been spent in a business office and in a library. I cannot talk on my legs, and my manner of writing has taken a form illy adapted to be read as a lecture, and I read with neither expression nor effect." At Oxford, however, the personal attentions showered upon him and his wife in the form of dinners, luncheons, and all conceivable opportunities for meeting the scholars and dignitaries of the University, might well have overcome him. Yet the memoranda in his "Dinner Book" betray nothing but enjoyment—an enjoyment which one can share in following him to London on the eve of sailing and finding such a quoted jotting, in a note upon a luncheon at which Mrs. J. R. Green was a guest as, " 'Turn your wine-cellar into your book-seller.' J. R. G."

To John T. Morse, Jr.

Oxford, May 22, 1912.

I was pleased to receive your interesting letter of April 14, which reached me in London when on the point of starting for Oxford. I wanted to write to you a long response, but until now I have had no leisure and as it is near my home-coming this can be no more than a congratulatory word on your vigorous convalescence and my appreciation of your thought of me.

I read the last of my three lectures on the 18th, and since then have been more serene in spirit, although quiet can hardly be expected. It is a sociable place, and as Taine wrote in 1871, *"Les diners pleuvent."* My wife and I have been out together a good deal and I have been to the college halls and common rooms without her, so that I wonder as Hawthorne did what the English will do in the dinnerless hereafter.

While the hall of my lectures was not filled (in fact never but three times in my life have I found a hall small enough for my efforts), I had a distinguished audience and am well satisfied with the result. I am therefore glad that I came here this year, although I left Boston last February with bitter regret. Of the last fourteen months I have passed nine in Europe, which is too large a proportion for a sturdy American. Yet in contemplating the woes of Italy and the woes of England, I have been oblivious of our own tribulations.

Among the new acquaintances, I have been delighted with Sir William Osler, as he is called here, but I think Dr. Osler is better. He came to hear my lectures and I went to his. We dined at Lady Osler's and his house, and I have met him frequently and found him in every way attractive. He took me the other day through the Bodleian Library (of which he is a Trustee) to the library of Christ Church (of which he is a fellow) and through the Clarendon Press (of which he is a delegate). This last visit was the most interesting of the three. The Superintendent is a vigorous talker, a North country man, with an accent, much like my own Western speech, and as Dr. Osler's word here is open sesame he took delight in showing us about. I liked to see the printing of the Bible, the Prayer-Book and the great Dictionary. The Oxford paper is of course renowned, and I wish that I might

[222]

have had your opinion of it as compared with that on which you printed the Life of Col. Lee. The India paper is used for their best work, and when I said, "Oh, that is the paper of the Encyclopedia Britannica" you should have witnessed the scorn on the Superintendent's face. "That is very different from our paper. Nothing has done the cause of good paper so much injury as the ads of the Encyclopedia fathered by Cambridge University." You may see the rivalry between the two institutions! I wanted to know, but I thought a minute and so put the question indirectly: "Is the India paper all rag?" "No," was the reply, "and I am not going to tell you what it is made of. When Gladstone was Prime Minister he made us a visit, and in showing him about he asked, 'What is the India paper made of?' 'Mr. Gladstone,' was my reply, 'you are Prime Minister and the most powerful man in the United Kingdom, but you cannot know this secret.' Now when Gladstone asked the question it was somewhat perfunctory, and he really did not care much about it, but when he ascertained it was a secret he worked hard afterwards to discover it but he never found out."

We are sailing for home on the *Mauretania* June 1st. I shall be in Boston at two different times before settling in Seal Harbor. Perhaps I may see you. . . .

On quitting the *Mauretania* in New York Rhodes must have gone direct to Princeton, for there he was on June 8, the guest of his friend Professor W. M. Sloane, to whom he was closely bound by their common interest both in history and in the American Academy of Arts and Letters. The occasion of this visit was

[223]

the deferred bestowal, on June 11, of the Princeton honorary degree of LL.D., about which we have seen him in correspondence with Woodrow Wilson, now about to be nominated for the presidency of the United States. The terms in which Dean West presented him for the degree constitute an estimate of his work which should hold a place in any detailed account of his life:

James Ford Rhodes, first American political historian. Environed from childhood in the rush of our developing American life, he has stood aside a little from the scene to view the enfolding of that life and to explain what and how it has come to be. Discarding all prejudgments of tradition and bending his powers of analysis to the one task of discovering and following out the central determinative lines, he has written down things as they are without passion and yet in words of vivid, poignant reality—the late-born American successor in the great school of political history founded by Thucydides.

If dinners "rained" at Oxford, Rhodes must have thought that academic functions were beginning to do the same in America, for eight days later, on June 19, he visited Providence and was one of the speakers at the Commencement luncheon of the alumni of Brown University, which in 1914 conferred upon him the honorary degree of Doctor of Letters. In 1916, smarting under his financial loss through investing in the stock of the New York, New Haven and Hartford Railroad, he recalled the first of his two visits to

Brown, apropos of a fellow speaker at the Commencement luncheon, against whose appointment to the Supreme Court of the United States he was soon to protest in a letter to Woodrow Wilson: "Brandeis and I," he wrote to Mr. John T. Morse, Jr., August 21, 1916, "were invited four years ago to the Commencement of Brown University, he to make a speech and I to read a harangue. We marched together in the procession and were together in friendly converse for more than an hour. What a pity that instead of airing to him my knowledge about England and Oxford, I had not asked him about New Haven and sold my N. H. in Boston the next day! But I had no confidence in Brandeis, immense in J. P. Morgan."

Instead of selling his New Haven stock on June 20 Rhodes attended the Harvard Commencement, with much satisfaction in the degrees awarded to friends and in the speeches, and proceeded promptly to his beloved Seal Harbor.

To William Roscoe Thayer

Seal Harbor, July 14, 1912.

. . . My wife and I had a delightful four weeks in Oxford where there is so much to talk about that present politics are hardly mentioned. If I may judge from my own friends and acquaintances, newspapers are only cursorily read and the attitude toward the press is the same as that we are accustomed to in the cultivated circles of Cambridge and Boston. I love Oxford. Outside of Boston and Rome I think it the most satisfactory place on earth. I might have lived there happily had I gone there at thirty. But now no place outside of the United States could be endurable for a period of years. I hated to go to Europe this year, but now that my lectures have been read with a fair degree of success I am glad that I went to Oxford. My secondary purpose was to make a book of them, and I am now enjoying the work of their annotation.

The two conventions gave us two interesting weeks. The result of the Democratic is the better. There is a cloud on the title of the renomination of President Taft. I regret this much as I would like to see him President for another term if a padlock could be placed on his lips. I could see little chance of his election before the convention; there must be less now.

Mr. Roosevelt's chance in running independent seems problematical. Many think the real contest will be between him and Governor Wilson. My own opinion about the future is worth little, but I believe that if the election were held today Wilson would be triumphantly elected. But he is one of the "d—d littery fellers," has written many books, and what may result from their careful study by his opponents remains to be seen. If it had not been for Mr. Roosevelt's and Mr. Taft's abominable pre-convention canvass one might rejoice that the country had to choose among three such able and sterling men. Both platforms are admirable, and one wonders how they could have been made so good during the hurly-burly. If I have read them aright (both are too long and touch on too many topics) there is nothing about the initiative and referendum. Neither favors judicial recall and both lean against it. Personally I like the Republican platform on this point better, being a disciple of Senator Lodge so far. On the other hand I like the Democratic

[226]

tariff plank better, in which I shall not agree with our cultivated senior senator. . . .

To the same

Seal Harbor, September 1, 1912.

Your very interesting letter of August 12 was duly received. You deserve a long essay on political conditions in the U. S., but as you are coming home so soon I will send to you only a brief word. Your position as a mugwump is admirable. I do not see how a good mugwump can do otherwise than vote for Mr. Wilson. I am not sure whether you are a tariff reformer but if you are, the Democratic platform and Mr. Wilson's speech of acceptance will be an additional incentive. Believing in a systematic downward revision, I am tempted to vote for the Democrats. They have shown courage in putting the tariff question to the fore, for I am not sure that tariff reduction is wholly popular, and if the Democrats get control of the Senate and the House I think we shall get the proper legislation. Mr. Underwood is undoubtedly the ablest man in the House of Representatives and is showing excellent constructive ability. I do hope he will not be compelled to go into Mr. Wilson's cabinet but will remain in the House. Those of us who vote for Mr. Wilson must be prepared for Bryan in the State Department, for, by all political rules, that position must be offered to him by Mr. Wilson. For the routine and most of the other work he will probably be a sad failure in comparison with Mr. Hay and Mr. Root, but he is a strong advocate for peace, which will counterbalance his deficiences. In my renewed study of our Civil War I am led to the belief that nothing

worse can happen to us than a foreign war. And it is
the easiest thing in the world to keep out of one. If
you carried out your plan of going into Italy you must
have seen the disastrous consequences of her war of
conquest.

I have written as if Wilson's election was certain.
It is not, but it is probable. Mr. Roosevelt's election
is possible. It does not seem to me that President Taft
has any chance. I think the question that will be
presented to voters in Massachusetts or election day
is who do you prefer to have carry Massachusetts,
Wilson or Roosevelt? Wilson's conduct since the nomination has been exemplary, and, if Roosevelt goads
him to some extreme utterance, we must take into account the provocation and forgive him. . . .

To Mrs. C. H. Toy

Seal Harbor, September 24, 1912.
. . . We enjoyed Mr. and Mrs. Lowell's visit very
much. Only once before since he has been President
have I had the full and frank talk that I had a fortnight ago. It is gratifying to see how easily and how
well he is filling his great position. It really is remarkable when one considers the greatness and wisdom of his predecessor. Mr. Lowell was enthusiastic
about the new library and the three Freshmen dormitories. I hope that his health and strength will always
be as sound as now, for his debonair energy is fascinating. We talked well into the night and all of the next
day. . . .

We discussed thoroughly the political situation
and I was gratified to know that we agreed on the
tariff, as I suspected he looked favorably on protection.

But he favors a downward revision. We paid much
attention to Mr. Roosevelt, and of course our attitude
could be one only of sorrow not of anger. We were
of one mind on every point and of course the issue will
be, unless something extraordinary occurs, that we
shall contribute two votes in the effort to carry Massachusetts for Wilson.

President Eliot has written a powerful political mani-
festo which will probably be published in the New
York *Times* if it has not already appeared. He read
it to me the other day and it is a cogent argument ending with the advice to vote for Wilson. I still think
Roosevelt's election possible, more from the precari-
ousness of prophecy where he is concerned than from
any reckoning of electoral votes. Wilson's election
seems highly probable. I do not feel quite so certain
of it since he snubbed Murphy, as I had counted New
York as surely for him, but I do not see how he can
carry it without receiving a goodly portion of the New
York City Democratic vote.

Do you suppose Wilson said what the *Transcript*
reported? "Rats! Go tell that to the Marines." I
hope not, although the provocation was undoubtedly
great. However, we can forgive that if Mr. Roosevelt's
taunting does not incite him to some radical and in-
discreet utterance. So far as I have seen his speeches,
I think they are well calculated to hold the radical
portion of his own party and to attract Republicans
who are not wholly satisfied with President Taft, and
who are alarmed lest the election may go into the
House.

The book of his Essays came duly and I have read
four of them with interest. I liked the Calendar of
Great Americans best and think his tribute to Lincoln

very noble. A man who will try to emulate Lincoln and draws his political philosophy from Burke and Bagehot cannot fail to make a good President. I omitted to say above that Mr. Eliot regards Mr. Wilson as conservative on many questions in spite of an advanced position on some others. Mr. Wilson is a graceful writer and I have been one of his "gentle readers" since his "Congressional Government" appeared in 1885. Mr. Lowell and I recalled the fact the other day that when this book appeared, we each wrote a review of it and submitted it to the *Atlantic*. Mr. Lowell's article was accepted and mine rejected.[26] Some years ago when we learned of this simultaneous action, we compared the articles and found that we had entirely agreed where we had criticized Mr. Wilson's positions. I believe that Mr. Wilson has recanted some of his opinions then expressed.

I have marked and annotated the Essays somewhat as you requested [27] but I cannot do that very well out-

---

[26] See *ante*, p. 56.

[27] This was a copy of Wilson's *Mere Literature*, the gift of the author to Mrs. Toy, which she asked Rhodes to read and annotate as if it were his own. Since he disposed of his library before his death, this volume, besides the copy of Morley's *Gladstone* already mentioned (see *ante*, p. 163), serves a useful purpose in illustrating his habit of making profuse marginal comments in pencil on the books he read. In this instance many of them are brief jottings of assent, approval, or confirmatory quotation from another source. But there are longer comments, such as the following, upon a passage (pp. 178-179) praising J. R. Green: "It is agreeable to meet an opinion different from one's own. I place Gibbon, Macaulay, and Carlyle above Green. I have always understood that Green was full of inaccuracies, although he had two great guides, Stubbs and Gardiner, and their full notes guided him to his original materials. I suppose Green has had more readers than any nineteenth century historian except Macaulay. He is not a student's historian, J. Winsor used to say to me. As to Green's lack of accuracy see my *Historical*

side of my library in Boston. It is lamentable to be so tied down to your authorities, and I am not sure that shows the best kind of intellectual development. Someone has said that a student could write his best book if he would go at it immediately after his library had been burned. . . .

In Rhodes's other correspondence of this summer there was an interchange of interesting letters between him and Mr. George A. Myers of Cleveland,[28] especially with reference to Ohio politics and the political activities of M. A. Hanna, whose biography by Mr. Herbert Croly had recently appeared. Mr. Myers was in a position to enlighten Rhodes on matters which had not found their way into the book, and Rhodes, at work on his "Hayes and McKinley Administrations," placed a true value upon a correspondent who could provide him with so much intelligent informa-

---

Essays, p. 172. Some one wrote to John Morley when he was editor of the *Fortnightly* giving a list of Green's inaccuracies and asking that it be published. Mr. Morley replied that the list ought to be sent to Mr. Green, the implication being of course that Green had done so much service to English history that he should be given the chance himself to correct these errors of detail."

Still another instance of Rhodes's way of annotating the books he read is found this time in a vein of self-criticism, in a copy of O. G. Villard's *John Brown* now on the shelves of the Massachusetts Historical Society library. "Nov. 12, 1910. I have cursorily examined this book and gone over my own account. I see nothing to change in my own account. I think Mr. More's [?] praise too high, but I do not know what I should think could I get into the spirit in which I wrote my account, which must have been in 1890. It was while I was living in Cleveland. As I have read it now the narrative seems dull, the author apparently being overweighted by his material. For such a book as this the examination and discussion of authorities was necessary, but I have found it dull."

[28] See *ante,* p. 62.

tion. In many of Rhodes's letters to Mr. Myers his views on current political matters are set forth, both in 1912 and later, with a special frankness and directness. Of those views in general it is time to say a word.

In a letter to Mr. Worthington C. Ford (January 31, 1922) Rhodes recognized in himself both "an old-fashioned Democrat (which I once was)" and "a Roosevelt Republican (which I am)." We have seen how completely he was an admirer of Roosevelt during his presidency and how deeply he deplored his course in 1912. With the underlying admiration and personal liking that remained, it was not unnatural for his political allegiance to swing substantially back. The "old-fashioned Democrat" in Rhodes must have grown in some measure out of the strong Douglas atmosphere of his youth. Even so late as 1900, when his third volume appeared, he wrote himself down in his discussion of the tariff and protection [29] not at all as a Cleveland coal and iron man, partner and kinsman of Mark Hanna, might have been expected to do, but entirely in the vein of the tariff reformers of the Cleveland period. In the régime of McKinley and Hanna personal affiliations and a rooted dread of the Bryan alternative accounted adequately for his Republican "regularity." But it was quite in accordance with views he had long held that when Woodrow Wilson, at a time of unworthy dissensions in the Republican party, presented himself as a candidate, long known and admired on other than political grounds, and now

[29] See pp. 30-38.

recommended especially by a policy of tariff reduction, he should win Rhodes's support and vote. In 1916 it appears that Wilson's course with respect to the "Adamson Law," involving what Rhodes regarded as a dangerous surrender to Labor, caused him to vote for Hughes. But he was of those, as we shall see, who thought well of Wilson's conduct of national affairs before and during the American participation in the World War. He hoped, as we shall also see, for the entrance of the United States into the League of Nations. Realist as he was in practical matters, and affected undoubtedly by his close personal relations with Senator Lodge—of whom he could nevertheless exclaim in a letter of May 11, 1919, to Mr. George A. Myers, "I fear Senator Lodge is making a bad leader of the Republicans"—he accepted the outcome of the League contest with something more of complacency than he could command when the Eighteenth Amendment to the Constitution was adopted. In this and in other expressions of the drift of modern civilization as his days drew to an end, and his own strength, and with it his natural optimism, began to fail, he found elements of unhappiness quite alien to his life in its entirety, and therefore requiring no extended representation in the pages that are to follow.

If the foregoing summary of Rhodes's variations of political allegiance suggests a lack of constancy to either of the dominant parties in the United States, it suggests at the same time, and perhaps even more strongly, the same quality of mind which caused him, as a writer of history, to weigh the merits of opposing causes and leaders as they presented themselves in turn, and, with due allowance for the personal considerations which meant much to one of his sympathetic nature, to arrive at the conclusions rather of an "independent" than of a partisan.

Rhodes was never more characteristically modest than in the expression of his views about current politics. I remember asking his opinion one day about the probable outcome of an impending election, and receiving the reply: "Now ask me anything you please about what happened in the years beginning with 1850, but don't ask what is going to happen, for I can't tell." In the same vein he is found writing to Dr. F. C. Shattuck (July 2, 1913), "I have made such a failure of prophecy that I have abandoned the business, and I now confine myself to records of the past." There was no quotation that seasoned his letters more frequently than the cautious saying of Hosea Biglow contained in the very next letter to be used. From the summer of 1912 onward, however, his correspondence, like American thought in general, was bound to concern itself increasingly with matters of passing politics.

The ensuing letter gives the reader to understand that a letter to Wilson immediately upon his election has not been recovered; it reveals also Rhodes's readiness to admit a "misconception."

To Woodrow Wilson

Boston, December 19, 1912.
DEAR GOVERNOR WILSON:—When I wrote to you November 7, I said I would write again with my views

on the reduction of the tariff. This promise was based
on a misconception. When the Dingley tariff was
enacted Senator Hanna said to me that the duties in
the different schedules were so well adjusted, owing to
the care and knowledge of Dingley, Aldrich and President McKinley, that if necessary a horizontal reduction by percentage could be made with equal justice
to all the protected industries. Thought on the subject during the last month has convinced me that we
are too far away from 1897 to work out a reduction
of the tariff by that plan.

I have nothing to say then except to repeat what I
wrote previously, that it is important that the downward revision be made speedily in order to take advantage of the present revival of business.

Since writing to you last, close money has been the
important factor in causing the semi-panicky condition
of the stock market. The prophecies of coming disaster emanating from Wall Street and State Street may
be disregarded, although I think the financiers there
dread a panic more than anyone else. But two wise
men in academic life, who have a large knowledge of
practical affairs, have expressed to me their belief that,
on the twenty-year theory, a financial crisis is due in
1913 and that conditions are pointing that way.
Neither of them considers the disturbance in 1907 a
first class panic.

I differ from them, but my whole prognostication
of the endurance of the present period of prosperity is
based on the belief that 1907 was a real panic like
that of 1893 and 1873 and 1857. But I am going to
adopt the wise advice of Hosea Biglow "Don't never
prophesy—onless ye know." . . .

To Charles Harding Firth [30]

Boston, January 5, 1913.

. . . I thank you for your kind words about my Oxford visit. I have no pleasanter memories than those of my last three sojourns. I would fain go thither again before I die, but I am approaching sixty-five and what more writing I do must be done within the next five years. I have almost finished reading the proof of my Oxford Lectures which will be published simultaneously in London and New York soon after February 1st. My publisher has tempted me to write a one-volume history of our Civil War which I shall soon begin. I should have turned a deaf ear to the temptation had I not been full of the subject from the study necessary for my Oxford Lectures. . . .

Morse Stephens has just been here in attendance on the Meeting of the American Historical Association. I saw a good deal of him and my wife and I thought that he was looking very well. The Meeting in 1915 will be in San Francisco during the fair celebrating the completion of the Panama Canal. Stephens will then be the President of the Association and many of us will try to go there to give him a good greeting. Our meeting just ended was memorable from Mr. Roosevelt being our President. I was thrown much with him and had two long talks in which the subject of present politics was not referred to. His manner was in every way deferential to all the historians whom he met, and he showed how charming he can be. It was lucky that I did not meet him before election or I fear

[30] See *ante*, p. 220 n.

that I should have been won by his fascination. But I cannot help wishing that he had kept out of politics after his return from Africa. . . .

To Henry Cabot Lodge

Boston, February 9, 1913.

. . . Mr. Roosevelt was President of the American Historical Association and delivered here in December an admirable address. I saw much of him during his sojourn. The charm and reticence of his manner and the actual self-suppression have left on me an enduring impression. Perhaps you will enjoy a little colloquy with W. R. Thayer. "Theodore, I like your Progressive principles and I would gladly have voted for you, but I cannot stand your advocacy of a high protective tariff." "William, any man who has written as good a Life of Cavour as you have has a right to vote for whoever he damn pleases."

Mr. Roosevelt came here to luncheon on the Sunday and I put on either side of him Von Eucken (the German visiting professor) and Legouis (the professor from the Sorbonne). Legouis was prepared to be fascinated and he was not disappointed. Von Eucken came with a great prejudice against Mr. Roosevelt and went away completely won by his deference and the charm of his manner. . . .

To George A. Myers

Boston, May 28, 1913.

. . . The drop in Boston and Maine and New Haven Railroad stocks has caused a great deal of prospective suffering. I myself am a large victim in New Haven, and I do not think just now that the lot of an investor is a happy one. Some men from here may tell you that the depression here comes from the promised tariff bill, but that is not true. The trouble with the railroads is bad management, optimistic buying of trolley lines and steamboats for the future, and vicious attacks on the management by the Federal and State authorities. . . .

To Frederic Bancroft

Boston, September 4, 1913.

. . . I don't know who told you, or whether you evolved it from your inner consciousness, but you are egregiously mistaken in supposing that I voted for President Taft last autumn. On the contrary, I not only voted for Mr. Wilson, but after August 15 I told everybody who asked me that I was going to do so. One man's vote is of little importance, and it is not necessary to go into any elaborate reasons why I bolted. It was sufficient that the issue of tariff reduction was plainly made. I have favored that for more than twenty years and, believing in it, I voted for it with enthusiasm. The tariff bill will probably cost me in money considerable (I mean with the income tax added), but without going into details I believe the principle of the bill, as it left the House, is excellent and that if the Republicans can be kept out long enough to give it a fair trial, it will redound to the greatest good of the greatest number.[31]

---

[31] After a Wednesday Evening Club meeting of February 5, 1913, Rhodes wrote in his "Dinner Book": "Topics: the unrest! the income tax, all opposed to the income tax and the high exemption except me."

When I voted for Wilson I knew that it meant Bryan for Secretary of State, but I had no idea that he would be so thoroughly incompetent in the Department and make the office a byword and reproach from captious English journals. What a "mushy, mushy" individual he has proved himself to be! But God maketh the wrath of men to praise him, and how we may all rejoice that Bryan has made himself so ridiculous that he can never be President. The representative of the proletariat, of the horny handed sons of toil, of the poor who desire to despoil the rich should never have confessed that he could not live on $12,000 plus the income on $170,000. Fortunately, when any serious question has come up like the Mexican, the President himself has taken the matter in hand and, guided by the wise counsel of J. B. Moore, has proved himself wonderfully efficient for the emergency. When you have spoken of Bryan as the Apostle of Peace you have said the best you can say for him, but he is unstable as water and did, I believe, secure the necessary Democratic votes to ratify the Treaty of Peace and give us the Philippines.

I am well satisfied with the President's course (barring Bryan, which I recognize was a political necessity). Of course I do not endorse the signing of the Legislative bill and the removal of Cameron Forbes, but one cannot have every detail he wants, and it is quite possible that in both of these cases the President is right and I am wrong. You are right to qualify your praise. I remember how enthusiastic you were for Cleveland in 1892, and yet soon after he was inaugurated in 1893 when he let J. Quincy play ducks and drakes with the civil service how bitter you were in your criticism, writing to Mr. Schurz, "We have been buncoed!" I shall myself, however, be satisfied if Mr. Wilson does as well as Mr. Cleveland (in spite of Venezuela). . . .

I remember very well the talk of yours and George H. Monroe, how you vied with one another in condemning and damning President Roosevelt, and how I lay back in my chair amused to think how the writer of so good a biography and the writer of so good editorials in the *Herald* (for Monroe was chief editorial writer, not literary editor) could be so unfair to so excellent a President. The longer I think of it, the more convinced am I that on the whole Mr. Roosevelt made a very good President. When he returned from Africa, like many great men before, he allowed his ambition to get the better of his judgment and the counsel of his best friends. But he is a fascinating man and his conduct last winter at Boston can be described in no other way than charming. . . .

I am glad that you met Mr. Firth. I have known him for eighteen years and he is in every way a splendid fellow, who gains continually on acquaintance. I do not see the point to your sneer, who can blame the English for not caring for our history? Mr. Bryce said they would find in it rich lessons of moral and political philosophy. I suspect that they could learn considerable from us as to how to run a democracy. At all events, they seem to be making a mess of it. . . .

To Mrs. C. H. Toy

Boston, December 25, 1913.

. . . I have heard much about Secretary Bryan recently, the best thing and one which gives me some hope, is that he is very greedy for money. I said that last night to Ellery Sedgwick, who has just met him at dinner in Washington, and who used to have a brief for him, and he did not deny it. My hope is that he will see that his interest and dividends will fail to come in if the government continues to prosecute in an inquisitorial way corporations and business men who are trying to make an honest penny. It may be that the President's letter to the Attorney General indicates the turn. If it does, your present of the little bank may be a joke; just at present, it tells the living truth. But I never could see why any one should object to having the truth brought home to him. . . .

Mere letters of travel are still to be avoided, but the spirit in which Rhodes, with his wife, was wont to betake himself to Europe is so well illustrated in the following letter that it must not be omitted.

To Harvey Cushing

Grenoble, May 24, 1914.

It was kind in Mrs. Cushing and you to bear us in mind and send me the wireless when we were out to sea. We wish that you had been along with us. You would have been a welcome addition to our party and I think you would have enjoyed it. Mrs. Hanna, Miss Phelps, President Hadley and Mrs. Hadley, Mr. and Mrs. Henry White with ourselves, made up one table, and it was a luncheon and dinner party every day. The food and cooking on the *Rotterdam* were excellent, but Mrs. Hanna in her lavish way had brought on board provisions and wine and, as the second steward was very attentive, the repasts were good and

[241]

the talk, as the French say, was *bruyant*. But it was highly enjoyable and I hated to leave the ship.

I have often heard the tired professional and business man say that the only way that he could get a rest was to cut loose from all of his affairs by going to Europe. I never appreciated that until this time. Before leaving home I was a good deal disturbed by private financial losses and the general financial outlook as well as the Mexican muddle, but I have put all of that behind me. I look at my letter of credit and my book of American Express Company cheques and, as long as they last or appear to be lasting, I am happy. Then I am so much occupied with routes and the automobile, with hotels and the maîtres d'hôtel and portiers that I have no time left to think of American finance or Mexico. I read the scrappy Paris *Herald* each day and am thankful things are no worse. If a man is tired or nervous let him take a motor trip in Europe. The fatigue and strain of it will obliterate all the other, and he will have a good appetite and grow healthy and strong and wonder the reason why.

I did not mention in the proper order that Mr. Hadley was going to Oxford to deliver the final course of Lectures on American History and Institutions. We have heard from both him and Mrs. Hadley. The lectures were well attended and I know were highly appreciated. They were going to stop with your friends Sir William and Lady Osler.

We have motored from Rotterdam here and were going to Avignon, but the weather becoming very hot induced us to give up going farther South and now we are on our way to Switzerland via Aix; and as we never tire of Switzerland we shall be quite contented to pass the month of June there. . . .

To Mrs. C. H. Toy

Les Andelys, July 5, 1914.

I was very glad to get yours of 22 June, and we were both more than pleased with the citations from the letter from the White House. With you, I think it wonderful that the President is bearing up so well under all the strain of events since the Mexican trouble became so serious. We are so sorry about Mrs. Wilson. We take it the trouble all comes from the fall. The advice I gave you to write nothing but pleasant things to the President was easy. From your point of view, there is so very much to commend in his course that it is both truthful and agreeable to emphasize (the fountain pen has given out and I am writing with the hotel ink) the points that you approve as in the case of the Repeal bill. From one of the President's speeches, it is apparent that he feels keenly the criticism he has received, and really it is (so it seems to me) the part of his friends to give him all the appreciation and encouragement possible. . . .

What delightful studies you are having in English biography and history; I dipped once into Lord Russell's Fox and was charmed with it, but as I remember it the charm came from Fox's letters and not from the commonplace connections of Lord J. Russell. For Sir G. Trevelyan's Fox, I remember reading it when immersed in business, and it seemed to me one of the most delightful books I had ever read, and the impression comes back to me now as I touch upon his treatment of affairs in England during our glorious Revolution. But since you heard from ———— and ———— strictures of Sir G. T.'s "American

Revolution" I fear that you have been prejudiced against him. And indeed so have many Americans who think he "cracked up" America too much. Dr. Cunningham did not like Sir G. T.'s partiality (?) nor does Mr. Firth, and perhaps your ——— and ——— are right and I am wrong. It will not bother me at all, as I have been wrong so many times in my life, and once more will not discourage me. . . .

Rhodes was in Europe when the World War began. Unfortunately his experiences and thoughts at this time are unrecorded in the letters and other memoranda from which the substance of this volume is drawn. Writing recently to Mr. Andrew Squire, of Cleveland, the Hon. Myron T. Herrick, American Ambassador to France in 1914, as again at present, has, however, provided a welcome bit of record: "At the beginning of the war, Rhodes was in Germany.[32] He managed to get to Dieppe in his motor car just before the battle of the Marne, and was successful in securing passage across the Channel with my assistance, but was unable to secure permission to take his car with him. He telephoned to me and I arranged to have the car taken over, and he wrote me a charming letter from England in which he quoted from Shakespeare, ' 'Tis a mad world, my masters!' "

In Rhodes's "Dinner Book" the record of a Boston engagement for the evening of April 14, 1914, is followed immediately, with no suggestion of intervening

---

[32] Mr. D. P. Rhodes amends this statement with the information that his parents and he were at Granville in Normandy when the war broke out.

events, by another of October 1. For the remainder
of the year dinners and other engagements continued
to "rain"; yet as 1914 neared its end he wrote (December 20) to Mr. John T. Morse, Jr., "New York
makes merry on the first of the year, while we do not.
Why anyone should make merry for the incoming of
1915 passes my comprehension."

Nevertheless it held much to engage his lively interest. Early in its course (January 11, 1915) he
made the following entry in his "Dinner Book":

Breakfast at Dr. Bigelow's to meet Mr. Roosevelt.
I drew the inference that Mr. R. was for the Allies,
though he did not say so in so many words. He had
luncheon with Münsterberg the day previous. M. told
him that the President sent McCombs to him to ask
if his (the President's) course was satisfactory to the
German Americans. Coolidge [33] was at the luncheon,
and said there was no general talk about the war; did
not know what there was aside.

Roosevelt would like to be President for one year—
would be willing to be impeached afterwards; he did
the Panama business when Hay and Root were away
("Councils of war never fight," he said). "You will
be impeached." "I can stand the impeachment if we
get Panama."

Bitter on the President's protest against England.
Protest against the violation of neutrality because we
lose some trade, and no word about the violation of the
neutrality of Belgium. If he had full power from Con-

---

[33] Professor A. C. Coolidge of Harvard was one of Dr. Bigelow's
guests on this occasion.

gress could raise a division of 12,000 men equal to any division on earth. The Allies will probably win, but the Germans may. Bad for this country if Allies win, on account of Japanese invasion; worse if the Germans win.

When ———— died the news was brought to John Hay; "Of course *de mortuis nil nisi bonum,* but really I am glad he is dead. He was a low-down, dishonest cuss."

Two letters of February, 1915, should be mentioned, though more than that would be superfluous. In the first Rhodes acceded to the request of William Roscoe Thayer, then editor of the *Harvard Graduates' Magazine,* to print in that periodical the Phi Beta Kappa "oration," "Lincoln in Some Phases of the Civil War," which Rhodes had already written for delivery at Harvard in June. "I ought not to have accepted the invitation," he said, "as I read badly and should never attempt what is called an 'oration'; but, for various reasons, I have such an idea of the high honor of being a Phi Beta Kappa orator that I could not resist the temptation." The second of these letters, addressed to Daniel Wait Howe, of Indianapolis, acknowledged his presentation of material bearing on the Dred Scott decision [34] brought to light after Rhodes's treatment of this subject in his second volume. It was especially in this sentence that Rhodes revealed that absence of "pride of opinion" which was one of his marked characteristics as a scholar: "I am a slow

[34] See D. W. Howe's *Political History of Secession to the Beginning of the American Civil War* (1914).

thinker and cannot say whether I shall arrive at the opinion you so elequently express on p. 344, but I shall not allow another edition of my II volume to go to press without, at any rate, presenting your side of the question." A third letter of the same month should be given in its entirety.

To Sir George Otto Trevelyan [35]

Boston, February 28, 1915.

Yours of January 9 from Welcombe was duly received. I wish indeed I might see that enchanting place again. It looked very beautiful last September when my wife and I drove into it, and how much more charming it is when the host and hostess are present!

We all read your son George's article in *McClure's* with much interest.[36] He always gets a hearing here, and his is one of the articles you hear discussed at dinners and at clubs.

I am sorry on its own account that the *Spectator* took a bellicose attitude toward this country, as it is a weekly journal highly esteemed here, and it seemed strange to see it in company with papers, whose names I have forgotten, that taunted America with being all for the dollars and losing sight of the moral issue involved. I suppose these papers (except the *Spectator*) are the yellow press of England and entitled to no more respect than are the Hearst newspapers here. I might call to their mind what your

---

[35] Like others to its recipient, and a few other correspondents, this letter, in a rough draft, is found among Rhodes's papers.

[36] "When the War is Over," by George Macaulay Trevelyan, *McClure's Magazine,* December, 1914.

Prime Minister said at the outset of our Civil War when we were fighting for our life and the destruction of slavery: "We do not like slavery, but we want cotton and we dislike very much your Morrill tariff." Two thoughts for the moneyed interest and one for the moral cause! I think we are doing better. I am inclined to agree with your *Times* which, when speaking of the food and money sent abroad from here, said, "In all history there has been no work like it. Never before have we received from another people proof so moving of interest. . . . The American self-sacrifice and warm kindliness have sunk deep into our hearts."

This city, which is only a sample of the East and (I think) of the whole country, has relief funds constantly being collected for the Belgians, French, Poles and Red Cross, and during the past week a large meeting was held to raise money for English and Canadian families of British soldiers. The *Times* is right when it speaks of self-sacrifice, at all events as far as Boston is concerned, for business is bad and hardly any industry here has profited by the war. Some local troubles have heightened the distress in New England and the majority of people whom I know are straitened in their means; and it seems quite likely our own unemployed have been neglected in giving aid to the suffering abroad. I doubt very much whether the United States is as rich a country as England, in spite of our capacity for growing food and cotton.

If I were with you for half an hour I could show you that there is nothing enigmatic about Bryan, as he wears his heart upon his sleeve. He is unfitted for Secretary of State, although from his high personal morality, his sincere religious views, and his power of oratory he has immense influence, west of the Alleghanies, on the voting millions. He has incurred the enmity of the German-Americans, and at their meetings of sympathy for Germany his name is frequently hissed. President Wilson is his own Secretary of State, and he has two very able counsellors in the State Department. Probably what makes his attitude seem enigmatic to you is that, while personally his sympathy is very strong with England, he feels it his duty to maintain the neutrality of our country. So far as I know, in this policy he has a large part of the country at his back (but not Mr. Roosevelt).

To understand opinion in this country we must get rid of the notion that either party is manœuvring for the German-American vote. In the first place, the elections are too far off. No important election occurs until the autumn of 1916, when a President, a House of Representatives, and one-third of the Senate are chosen. In the second place, were the elections near at hand, it would be dangerous for either party to contend for one foreign vote because it would alienate another. The result would be either a stand-off or a disaster.

The ten million German-Americans here sympathize almost wholly with Germany; those of English ancestry, East, West, and South, with the Allies. The English and Canadians here of course support the mother country, and the Italians are against the Germans and Austrians. The Irish are divided, but the majority are for the Allies. I cannot tell you about the Bohemians and Poles.

Jacob Schiff, a leading German-American banker in New York, said, "I think Germany has reason to feel that the people of this country and the press have not been fair in their attitude toward it." . . .

When Mr. Roosevelt was here in January I took breakfast with him and his host. He looks well, has a clear eye and complexion, and his usual fascinating manner. He has just published a book, "America and the World War." There is a story about that he contracted an incurable disease in Brazil, but I do not credit it. . . .

On April 14, 1915, Mr. George Macaulay Trevelyan, now Regius Professor of History in Cambridge University, was the guest of honor at a dinner of the Tavern Club in Boston. In the dinners of this club, whether to distinguished visitors or for its members only, Rhodes took a keen satisfaction—more often as a listener than as a speaker. Rarely, if ever, trusting himself to offhand speech, he was wont to read what he had to say. Among the memorabilia of the club I find a copy of his remarks at this dinner to Mr. Trevelyan, and take from them the first and the last paragraphs, about a third of the whole:

One evening I heard a cultivated English gentleman say, George O. Trevelyan writes better than his uncle, Macaulay, and George Macaulay Trevelyan—our guest—writes better than his father. What a trio! Two inherited the art of writing. All three were Trinity College, Cambridge, and there received training in the mastery of their tongue. William Everett, who also went to Trinity, and had an intimate acquaintance with George O. Trevelyan, used to say Cambridge teaches men to write excellent poetry and Oxford teaches them to write brilliant prose. Had we dared to risk offending Everett, we should have in-

[250]

quired, "How about Macaulay and the two Trevel-
yans?" The German professors who used to come
here in the days of peace intimated with a supercilious
air that while Harvard might be mentioned in the
circles of the learned, Cambridge and Oxford did not
turn out scholars. I wondered what scholarship was,
and if it implied a lack of erudition to prefer the histories written by Cambridge and Oxford men to those
which saw the light in Berlin. I remember a professor
in the University of Berlin once saying to me, "The
teaching of economics in Oxford is all gosh"—he
meant, bosh. William James told the incident of a
don showing a German professor about Oxford, endeavoring to explain the system and at the end of a
wearisome half-day, when he thought he had given a
clear account, the German professor asked, "But what
do you teach here?" Somewhat nettled the don replied, "Well, we teach an English gentleman to be a
gentleman." . . .

Those who have read Trevelyan's biography of John
Bright must have been amazed at his knowledge of our
Civil War. But he grew up with it. When he spoke
to Clio of the "men who stormed the rifle-pits of
Missionary Ridge" he was telling what to him was
more than a twice-told tale. Nearly thirty years ago
John Hay, visiting Sir George at his Northumberland
home, told after dinner a battle story mentioning
neither the combatants nor the place of combat. The
General-in-chief, so Hay probably said, with the commander of one of his armies that was in action, stood
on a hill watching their charge: they gained the first
line of rifle-pits where the orders were to stop and
reform. But they kept on and rushed up the mountain
side. "By whose orders is this?" asked the com-

mander-in-chief. "By their own, I fancy," replied the commander. So the soldiers went on, reaching the last range of rifle-pits, when the three Trevelyan boys, one of whom is our guest, interrupting Hay, burst out, "Missionary Ridge! Missionary Ridge!"

To Woodrow Wilson

Boston, April 22, 1915.

MY DEAR MR. PRESIDENT:—Admiration of the thoroughly patriotic and American tone of your Tuesday speech [37] leads me to an expression of approval of the neutral position you have taken in this terrible European War. I am trying to consider your speech and course from a historical point of view, and I have not found it difficult as, making just now a fresh study of Lincoln, I am asking what he would do and say in a similar case.

I believe that posterity will heartily approve your Tuesday speech and your foreign policy. Fortunately you have not that long to wait for appreciation as, unless I am greatly mistaken, you have the country at your back in your sane and dignified attitude.

An unvarying supporter of your foreign policy, I have had occasion to commend it in my letters to Sir

---

[37] This was an address, on April 20, 1915, delivered in New York to members of the Associated Press. It was chiefly an exposition of the policy of neutrality for the United States, and contained such words, expressive of Rhodes's feeling at the time, as these: "The basis of neutrality, gentlemen, is not indifference; it is not self-interest. The basis of neutrality is sympathy for mankind. It is fairness, it is good will, at bottom. It is impartiality of spirit and of judgment. I wish that all our fellow-citizens could realize that." See *The New Democracy: Presidential Messages, Addresses, and Other Papers* (1913-1917), by Woodrow Wilson, Vol. I, pp. 303-304.

George O. Trevelyan and, from an intimation made to me last week by his son, I feel sure that my most significant letter found its way to Trevelyan's warm friend, Sir Edward Grey.

I have just read the Secretary of State's reply to Count von Bernstorff. Its friendly tone, decisive character, and gentle sarcasm could not be improved. With the expression of my high respect, I am,

Very truly yours,

JAMES F. RHODES.

To George A. Myers

Seal Harbor, August 12, 1915.

. . . I cannot now tell when my Short History of the Civil War will be published. Since coming here I have worked like a nailer on it and can begin to see its completion. Until yesterday the weather was so vile that it was conducive to literary work. We are beginning now to have sunshine and warmth and I shall be able to take considerable open air exercise, which I need to recuperate after a severe illness of May and June last, when I was attacked with great vigor by the colon bacillus, but the surgeon, the nurse and I, with the assistance of much hexamethylenamin, downed him and here I am. I was much disappointed to be ill at that time, as I was very busy in Massachusetts Historical Society matters, and I had accepted long ago the invitation to deliver the Phi Beta Kappa oration at Harvard during Commencement. But I pulled myself together and was able to read my paper (oration so called) on June 21, although I was not as strong as I could have wished. . . .

President Wilson is making an admirable President

and deserves re-election. He has acted with great wisdom in keeping our country out of the European war. It is none of our making, and while my sympathy is as strong as any feeling can be for the Allies, we are not called upon to send our best young men to battle for what England and France are fighting for. . . .

To the same

Seal Harbor, Maine, September 20, 1915.

Referring to yours of September 1 I am surprised that, no matter on how excellent authority you should think "that it is more a matter of luck than diplomacy that has enabled Mr. Wilson to steer us clear of the shoals of war." The President is wearing out his brain and nervous system to keep out of this horrible war, and he should have the praise of every business man. He is enabling you to take in daily your shekels and, what is better, to keep the fine young men who resort to your shop from going to the front to be food for powder as is the case with the noble young men of England and France. You should thank Heaven morning and night that Mr. Wilson is in the White House instead of others that I might name. The President so far has done nobly. I hope that he may have strength and force to continue. You must not forget that as Brand Whitlock writes, "Generally we are less afraid to fight than we are not to fight." The President has somewhat the same task as had Washington, and while he cannot be compared with the Father of his Country in ability or character, yet let us give him credit for trying to imitate that great man. . . .

To Sir George Otto Trevelyan

Boston, December 4, 1915.

Illness has prevented an earlier answer to your courteous letter of October 19, and I must now ask pardon for writing by an amanuensis.

I was distressed to read of the death of Lord Welby, whom I met at your beautiful Stratford home on my visit to you. You, he, the Duchess of Devonshire, and I had a bout at whist in the evening when I remember I played badly. But the afternoon had been full of interest. You took us a pleasant drive and we walked back over the fields. I remember two of your sage remarks, one that Bancroft wrote history by ejaculations, and the other that Charles Adams started at every hare that crossed his path. Mr. Adams's wide intelligence and varied interest made him a delightful companion, but had he concentrated his attention, he would have finished the large life of his Father on which he had been at work for a long while.

My illness prevented me from seeing Senator Lodge before he went to Washington and from hearing his public eulogy on Mr. Adams. I anticipate reading it with interest in the publications of the Massachusetts Historical Society which also, I believe, will print Mr. Adams's Autobiography; these you will get in due time. . . .

The autumn elections did not settle anything except to give a decided blow to woman suffrage, the referendum votes in Massachusetts, New York, New Jersey and Pennsylvania being largely averse to their voting. The Republicans maintain that the elections indicate the probable choice of a Republican President next autumn, and nearly everyone seems to think that they gave a death blow to the Progressive party, which is Mr. Roosevelt's. The Republicans chose an excellent gentleman for governor of this State [38] and, by their union, have made Massachusetts a Republican State, so that Mr. Lodge's re-election as senator next autumn is pretty well assured. The German-Americans are very severe in their denunciations of President Wilson but, so far as I can see, their talk and action had no influence on the results.

William R. Thayer has published his Life of John Hay which is an artistic biography of a charming man. I remember that soon after your "Early Life of Charles James Fox" was published Hay and I fell to talking about you and he told me why you had decided to continue in public life instead of pursuing your great literary success. He had recently made a visit to you at Wallington and discoursed entertainingly about the Macaulay books which I had afterwards the satisfaction of looking over at your hospitable country-seat. . . .

To George A. Myers

Boston, January 6, 1916.

. . . I saw something of Mr. Robert Rhodes when he was here, but our gatherings were so much of a family nature I had little opportunity to talk with him about national affairs. He implied, however, that in Ohio and generally throughout the Middle West the desire for peace was ardent, whence I think it would follow that Mr. Wilson had the support of the coun-

---

[38] Samuel W. McCall.

try, just as Mr. Roosevelt had it in 1904 when my mugwump and refined friends here were reviling him. The fact of it is Mr. Wilson has had something of the same task at Washington, as he has met with rare statesmanship the greatest crises we have had since the Civil War and the greatest Europe has had "since the break-up of Roman civilization." What Senator Lodge said in his Life of Washington may with a slight change be said of Wilson: "The easy and popular course was for our government to range itself more or less directly with the French and the refusal to do so was bold and in the highest degree creditable to the administration." Little wonder is it that Senator Lodge further writes: "As we look at it now across a century we can observe that the policy went calmly forward consistent and unchecked." Probably that will be the historical verdict on Mr. Wilson.

But the present question is will the plain people demand a second term for Mr. Wilson as they did a third for Washington?

I regret that you still hold to the doctrine of a Protective tariff and the "good old days of Hanna and McKinley" and that you cannot get over your talk of the "empty dinner pail." I see that you have cut loose from the proletariat and entered the ranks of "la haute finance." The *Wall Street Journal,* like you, sighs for Hanna and McKinley and undoubtedly in State and Wall Streets you will find many sympathizers. But since "la haute finance" led me astray in New Haven I have no confidence in their judgment and believe generally that their aspirations are bad. We are safe when we rely, as Lincoln did, on the "plain people."

[257]

James Ford Rhodes

To Sir George Otto Trevelyan

Boston, February 8, 1916.

. . . I read with much interest your letter in the *Nation* with its eloquent plea for classical scholarship, and I wished that I might read Latin with the enjoyment that you do. I took down my Plautus, which is French at the top of the page and Latin at the bottom. I used to read the languages with a certain degree of simultaneousness, but the other day I found myself sticking to the French, so much apparently has been obliterated in my memory. I read the "Comedy of Errors" again, which seems to me superior to "*Les Menechines.*" It may be because years ago I saw the "Comedy of Errors" splendidly acted a number of times. There were two actors, Robson and Crane, who played the Dromios to perfection. Crane undertook the task of imitation, which he did well. I was struck with the amount of care the actors paid to the "business" of the play. Robson told me that the comedy had been given in England a generation before with great success, and they got hold of a Mr. Webb who had played one of the Dromios. He instructed R. and C. thoroughly in the "business" of the piece and, then being an old man, was cast for Ægeon. I remember his somewhat pathetic declamation, what in my boyish days I used to call "mighty fine." At all events the performances have fixed the "Comedy of Errors" in my mind and Plautus seems inferior.

It is fitting that with my enthusiasm for Shakespeare I should address this letter to you to Stratford-on-Avon. You certainly live on hallowed ground. . . .

[258]

During the past eighteen months I have got more good from Shakespeare than from any other author and I rejoice that my native language enables me to read him in the original. . . .

To Robert Grant

[Undated, but 1916]

My philosophy is thus summed up:

"Here is the moral of all human tales,
'Tis but the same rehearsal of the past;
First freedom and then glory; when that fails
Wealth, vice, corruption, barbarism at last
And history with all her volumes vast
Hath but one page."

Barrett Wendell and Brooks Adams saw this years ago. Thank Heaven, my eyes are opened at last—only indeed I wish they were not and that I could think this a holy war.

To Mrs. C. H. Toy

Santa Barbara, California, April 16, 1916.
. . . Is not Mr. Eliot wonderful to maintain in such a high degree so remarkable a physique? It makes the rest of us green with envy. I really wish that he might live forever. It seems as if such a man ought to.
Like you I read Daniel's Great Resolve [39] twice. I found the thought rather close and subtle and not being used to anything solider than history, needed the second perusal to grasp it fully. I agree with you in your

---

[39] A war-time pamphlet by his son.

appreciation and criticism. I wrote to him I wish he
had declaimed against "nationality" instead of "patriotism," as I still believed in the virtue of patriotism,
or at all events I did until two years ago. If a Washington or a Lincoln was at the head of the successful
nation Daniel's idea might be realized, otherwise not.
Will the French abandon the idea of the recovery of
Alsace and Lorraine? I am sorry human nature is
what it is, and many times I am tempted to say with
Mark Twain, "damn the human race."

That is my feeling every morning when I read the
excellent Los Angeles *Times* with its tale of Mexico
and our troubles with Germany. I do not see how
Mr. Wilson stands the strain. I have been looking at
many of the snap-shots in the illustrated papers and
magazines, and I am struck with the aging of his features and a development of grim resolution and suffic-
ing strength. It is a wonder each day to me how he has
the ability to cope with the questions that arise and
dispose of them with, *in the main,* so much wisdom.
Troubles seem to increase instead of to diminish. But
with all the worry and trials of the position, it is an
evidence of the virtue of our system of government
that so many men are desirous of the place of President. There is one thing, as I understand it, that Mr.
Wilson knows and the public does not: the Japanese
are only waiting a favorable opportunity to seize California, Oregon, and Washington. Every move of the
President has to be made with this eventuality in view.
When one visits this country one does not wonder that
the Japanese want such a land flowing with milk and
honey.

When we discussed Daniel's pamphlet we might

have quoted what I have heard you so often cite from Goethe, "entbehren, du sollst entbehren." If ever a man was willing to renounce nothing Goethe was, with his love of the "good things of life." . . .

To John T. Morse, Jr.

Santa Barbara, California, April 16, 1916.

I received yours of the 9th day before yesterday, and I thank you heartily for your graphic account of the April Club [40] dinner. There is something in what Mr. Duncan says of Mr. Adams's Autobiography, but I find myself agreeing with your view, except in one respect. It is a notable story written with sincerity, but it need not have been such a bare disclosure of his soul. Rousseau said of his Confessions that no man was truthful enough to narrate his whole life and he was going to do it. If I remember correctly, they were not published until after his death, but the Parisian critics of our day have found fault with their indecent frankness. So with Mr. Adams. It was not necessary to tell that he had been drunk, and the reiteration of how he had missed many changes becomes tiresome. Still, after making all these allowances, it is a tale of intense interest because Mr. Adams knew how to write. But my Mr. Adams is a more worthy man than the Adams of the biography. As I did not know him until I was past 40, I failed to appreciate some traits that to you were vivid. But I found him an agreeable companion to travel with, a considerate man to work with in the Massachusetts

---

[40] "The Club," a prime favorite among Rhodes's social affiliations in Boston, brought together for monthly dinners through the winter a small, congenial company of his contemporaries and juniors.

Historical Society, and in other historical undertakings and a delightful man at the dinner table whether as host or guest. Mr. Adams had the old-fashioned custom of believing that he must exert himself to make it pleasant for the others, so that he was a wonderful and most acceptable diner-out. I saw much of him in one way or another and he seemed to me a sterling character and a most interesting man. I remember that when we have discussed him we have been of the same mind. Mr. Adams said to me once that he should have begun his serious historical work earlier, and in this I think he was right. It would have been better, if his time on the Union Pacific had been devoted to the study of our Civil War. But he was an all-round man, successful in many things, though not in all. The only point where I might register a difference with you is in your vivid characterization of C.F.A. Sr., because I see in him the successful ambassador and the popular man in English society: although the two are consistent with the impression he made in Boston which you so cleverly describe. Our Charles had a restless mind and from his nature he must dip into many enterprises. I never knew a man who did so many things well.

I have at last found in this place an ideal hotel. Everything in your bed-room should be as neat and clean as at home. The cooking should be of the best, the menu of each day limited but varied enough during the week to give you the full variety afforded by the market. Such is this hotel with a central reading room and dining room, and the sleeping rooms are in bungalows scattered over a large garden of sweet-smelling flowers. . . . The excellent taste displayed in all the furnishing, the good food and cooking make a stay in this glorious climate a delight. I do not think that they can take care of more than 50 or 75, and there seems to be a long waiting list, as when a bungalow is vacated it is immediately filled by another party. . . .

Before returning from California where Rhodes and his wife, both in search of better health, stayed from the end of February to the beginning of June, he received the honorary degree of Doctor of Laws from the University of California. A long summer at Seal Harbor lay ahead.

To George A. Myers

Seal Harbor, Maine, June 11, 1916.

. . . Affairs have turned out as you surmised and Mr. Hughes has been nominated. I am much disappointed in him. I thought that he would stick to his assurance of last summer in which, as I remember the letter, he said that no one on the Supreme Bench should be a candidate for political office. It is a dangerous precedent going to the Supreme Bench for a candidate, but the G.O.P. hungers after the "loaves and fishes" and believes that it can win with Mr. Hughes.

But what is this German American Alliance which supports Hughes, and what meaneth it that three German papers have declared in his favor? I cannot believe that he is pro-German. From his telegram of acceptance, I assume that, had he been President, he would have conducted affairs much as Mr. Wilson has done. It must certainly add strength to his candidacy that under him the country may expect a continuance of peaceful policy. It is not consistent, but it is thorough politics, that the G.O.P. should denounce Mr. Wilson for doing just what they will do themselves should they secure the power. . . .

To the same

Seal Harbor, Maine, August 3, 1916.

. . . Mr. Hughes's remarks on the tariff are reactionary; he can only be pitied that he has felt obliged to declare himself in favor of the woman suffrage amendment to the Constitution.

I agree with you that Colonel Roosevelt's support is evidence sufficient that Mr. Hughes is not pro-German. I can understand his gingerly remarks on the subject by his evident desire not to alienate the German-American vote.

There is much in his character and life that is attractive. I suppose if elected Mr. Hughes will make some such a President as did Mr. Hayes.

Mr. Wilson has the hard lot of being in the limelight, forced to act on difficult subjects while Mr. Hughes can stand back and criticize. If I had a vote in Maine it would be important in the coming State election, September 11, but my vote in Massachusetts is not important as that state is sure to go for Hughes. I should indeed like to get back into the Republican party, but I am not sure whether I shall not be prevented from returning to the fold by its unfairness and partisanship. But it is a long time from now until November. . . .

[264]

To John T. Morse, Jr.

Seal Harbor, Maine, August 12, 1916.

I was very glad to get yours of July 15. It is agreeable to hear of the morning occupation of a gentleman—driving horses and paddling a canoe. Automobiling is a plebeian occupation. I feel that in Boston, still more here. For a long while, we kept motor-cars out of this enchanted isle, but now they are here and every Saturday and Sunday, the butcher, the baker and candlestick-maker of Bar Harbor and Bangor invade our quiet precincts with their horrid machines. Fond of motoring myself, it was nevertheless agreeable to read of horses and a canoe. The taste for the automobile, like that for champagne, is plebeian, and I wish that I might break away from both, but the habits are too strong.

I will say but one word more about the European War. You, Tom Perry, and the majority of the people who side with the Allies are against me, and I must refrain from expressing my opinion. If you read the *Atlantic*, as all good Bostonians are supposed to do, read the two citations in Lowes Dickinson's article in the August number. One from the London *Times* of November 23, 1912, the other from the London *Standard* of August 3, 1914. They express thoroughly my sentiments.

I am sorry to differ with you regarding Thoreau. I think Lowell called him a precious humbug or something of the sort, who with all his preaching of Nature, etc., was never out of the sound of Mrs. Emerson's dinner bell.

[265]

I agree with every word you say regarding Germany's blunder. I feel that all our municipal, state, and national blunders, boiled down to one, are meagre compared with Germany's great mistake. It is greater than that of Napoleon III in 1870, and can be compared with Napoleon I after Jena and Austerlitz, but then the Corsican had done something. How inadequate and foolish William II has shown himself! and yet I have heard him called by good Americans equal in ability to our T.R.

At your suggestion, I have read Mrs. O'Shaughnessy's book [41]—every word of it. It is the most delicious Republican campaign document I have seen and is beyond comparison better than Governor Hughes's dreary platitudes in his address of acceptance. Mrs. O'S. shows by indirection the weakness of the President's Mexican policy. It really makes one laugh when she speaks of the "Kindergarten class at Washington" and "one year of Bryan makes the whole world grin." She showed cleverness, too, when she predicted in 1913 that Villa and Carranza would fight. One of the President's advocates was here a fortnight ago and, without knowing the book, attempted to throw doubt on its authenticity. But the Madam shows her truth by her inconsistencies. After remarking that Huerta's best friends were Martel and Hennessey, and saying that he disappeared twice for a *copita*: that his cabinet meetings consisted of himself and advisers in the shape of *copitas*: and twice when his emotion was too much for him, he must have *copitas* yet his "reputation for drinking is very much exaggerated." What voters women will make! Is

[41] *A Diplomat's Wife in Mexico,* by Edith O'Shaughnessy.

Hughes inspired when he declares for the Susan B. amendment? Really, though, I don't blame the women for thinking they could run things better when they reflect what a mess the trained governors of Europe have made of the civilized world. But Mrs. O'S.'s letters are charming. I have read nothing so delightful since those of Miss Greenough of Cambridge (I forget her married name).[42] She is right (I think) in her inference that the President should not have antagonized Huerta. It was probably Bryan's doing, who showed an incompetence beyond our dreams when he got a chance at governing.

I suppose Huerta believed in the saying, "Claret for boys, port wine for men, and brandy for heroes." . . .

To the same

Seal Harbor, Maine, August 21, 1916.

. . . *Governor Hughes.* I agree with you fully that he ought not to have descended from the Bench and that he has made a "mess of it" in his speeches throughout the West. The *Times* concludes its sarcastic article "If Hughes had stayed at home," with "And President Wilson would not have had occasion to make that blistering comment on the character of Mr. Hughes's campaign—that silent but terrific comment that he delivered, when, having made his preparations for an active fight on the stump, he changed them after watching Mr. Hughes's performance for

---

[42] *In the Courts of Memory, 1858–1875,* by Mme. Lillie (Greenough) de Hegermann-Lindencrone.

two weeks and decided that it was not necessary, and he would stay at home."

Your fear regarding Justice Brandeis is new to me, but is, I think, well founded. When Norman Hapgood was editor of *Collier's* he sounded continually B.'s praises and deemed him eminently fit for the presidency. I think about Brandeis just as you do, but the trouble with our position is that Brandeis is a better man than our great representative of *"la haute finance,"* J. P. Morgan, Sr. I speak feelingly, as I lost a great lot of money in New Haven from overweening confidence in J.P.M. . . . If I had followed Brandeis instead of Morgan I should have been better off financially and not looked irritated every time that one asked me for a benevolent or charitable contribution. . . .

To William Roscoe Thayer

Seal Harbor, Maine, September 7, 1916.
. . . If I were an Englishman or a Frenchman, I would not be a pacifist. As an American I am a disciple of President Eliot as shown in his writings before the European War. I am for peace and lament bitterly the struggle in Europe, but of course my hearty sympathy is with the Allies. I feel sure that Europe is going to the devil. I hope that the United States will be spared such a fate, but I am not certain of it. . . .

To the same

Seal Harbor, Maine, September 19, 1916.
. . . I deplore, as you do, Mr. Eliot's inconsistencies, but perhaps not for entirely the same reason. I still

think he is the greatest man living in America, a
George Washington sort of man as William James used
to say, but G. W. died at 67 while C. E. is 82; and
of course we are not infallible.

I read your stricture on President Wilson *in re* the
Brotherhoods with interest. I think the words you
put in his mouth, so to speak, ought to have been used
by him. I cannot understand why he should have
taken a course at variance with that of any of his
predecessors as you so clearly suggest. . . .

To Lord Bryce

Bretton Woods, New Hampshire,
September 28, 1916.

Your valued letter of the 7th reached me the day
before we left Seal Harbor. I suppose that the opening by the Censor delayed it a little, but it brought
to me highly cheering news. That you could see a
termination to the present terrible conflict and a termination of the right sort was gratifying beyond
measure. "The most tremendous and horrible calamity
that has ever befallen mankind by mankind's own
fault," you wrote early in the struggle, and nothing
has occurred to change your luminous characterization.
And the chief culprit is the German Emperor. It does
not seem right that one man could bring so much
misery on the world and endanger our civilization as
he has done. . . .

Seal Harbor misses Lady Bryce and yourself, and
you were in our thoughts constantly. We like to remember that you passed two summers on our end of
the island, and you had our good wishes in every circumstance. I saw a good deal of President Eliot. Al-

though 82 he is vigorous physically and mentally and, if it were not for the oppression of the European War, he might be said to enjoy life. His interest in passing events is praiseworthy and his remarks are always worth consideration. When I saw him in July, he said that he should vote for President Wilson unless something decided happened to change his mind. Late in August when the Brotherhoods and railway officials were conferring with the President and the President made his speech to Congress, he confessed to being mystified at Mr. Wilson's action. I have not seen him since the so-called eight-hour bill passed, but he had already written for the *Atlantic Monthly* an article which I understand is favorable to Mr. Wilson's election. (The *Atlantic* should be here in a day or two but has not yet arrived.)

President and Mrs. Lowell passed a day and a night with us during their visit to Mount Desert Island. Mr. Lowell is cheerful, energetic, and in every respect a charming companion. He is making a decided success of his presidency. It showed courage on his part to follow President Eliot, who seems to me the greatest man in America, but to use a common and vile phrase, with us, he (Lowell) has made good.

Touching American politics you are quite right in assuming that there is practically no issue between the parties in regard to a policy toward the European conflict, although the President is now finding it difficult to deal justly with England. The bulk of his supporters come from the South and the Irish at the North. The Cotton States feel grievously the cotton situation, and the Irish—well, you know them much better than I do. Just about as you were writing, however, an issue has come up of the utmost importance. From

my point of view the President made a "disgraceful
surrender" to the Brotherhoods and caused a "national
humiliation." (The first citation is from the *Transcript*,
the last from the *Times*, a loyal supporter of Mr. Wilson.) In his canvass in Maine just before the State
election Governor Hughes condemned with emphasis
the action of the President in his negotiations with the
Brotherhoods and the action of Congress in passing a
bill which gave the unions just what they had demanded. Mr. Hughes showed wonderful courage and,
whatever may be the result, political character of a
high order. It had to be tested whether organized labor
was to rule, and perhaps now is as good a time as any
to have it out at the polls.

I quite agree with you that Mr. Hughes made an
error in coming out in favor of the constitutional
amendment for woman suffrage. It is an affair that
had better be left to the States. Many of the Western
States have adopted it, and most of the Eastern States
have voted against it. So far as the experience of the
woman suffrage states goes, woman suffrage does not
seem to make much difference except to render it easier
to pass prohibitory laws. It is doubtful, however,
whether the woman suffrage amendment, if it gets
through Congress, will be ratified by three-quarters of
the states, the number which our wise Constitution
makers required. All the newspapers say that woman
suffrage is sure to come in England after the war. I
hope that they are wrong, as I look with alarm on the
doubling of your constituencies when questions of the
war debt and others of finance and pensions are to be
considered. I do not think on these matters that the
judgment of women is as wise as that of men. We
have been through all that trouble with great success,

[271]

I think, in regard to finance and only moderate, in the view that it might have been worse, touching pensions.

But I should have remembered that you are a busy man and that I ought not to have written so much. . . .

To George A. Myers

Boston, October 18, 1916.

. . . I am for Hughes, but I am sorry that he is putting the protection argument so to the fore. You may rest assured that the Democratic tariff bill is on the whole the best revenue bill that has been passed since the Civil War and the imposition of the income tax (although it hits me harshly) progress in the right direction. Legislation should be for the greatest good of the greatest number. To my mind the President let his foot slip in siding with the Brotherhoods. I do not suspect his motive, and he is probably more long-headed than I am, but I do not like the idea of the President and Congress of the great United States surrendering to a threat. Mr. Hughes showed great courage in attacking the Adamson act and the action of the President right on the eve of the Maine election, and Mr. Roosevelt spoke solid truth at Wilkesbarre. I cannot longer stay out of a party led by such courageous men, although as evidence of not my full conversion, I must write it with small letters, g. o. p. . . . .

To Sir George Otto Trevelyan

Boston, November 19, 1916.

I duly received yours of October 18, and in my *Nation* of this week I heard from you again in your brief and pointed letter touching Macaulay and Defoe.

Since writing to you our presidential election has taken place, and the result was close. We went to bed on Tuesday, election night, thinking surely Hughes had been chosen, and our Wednesday morning newspapers confirmed that impression, but on going down town to the bulletin boards we found that the election was in doubt, and not until Thursday evening was it ascertained to be reasonably certain that Wilson had carried California and therefore was elected. Since the presidential dispute of 1876 the procedure of counting and declaring and recounting (if necessary) the votes has been much systematized, with the result that everything proceeds under State action with regularity and precision. There is hardly a chance for a dispute, but if there is, and the count must go beyond the State to Congress, the Election Count Act of 1887 determines a proper method of decision, so that I do not think we shall ever again be on the verge of civil war, as we were in 1876-77 on a disputed presidency.

The closeness of this election is illustrated by the result in Minnesota, which was only known yesterday to be certainly for Hughes, while our neighboring State New Hampshire has just determined that her plurality is 62 for Wilson. The election showed the great popularity of Mr. Wilson. He is much stronger than his party. . . .

I have just been to New York in attendance on the meeting of the National Institute and American Academy of Arts and Letters and there met Mr. Roosevelt, who read a very good paper before the Academy on Nationalism in Literature and Art. I went with Mr. Roosevelt to luncheon and among the guests was Senator Lodge. While the party was ten, the conversation was general and most of it conducted by Mr. Roosevelt and Mr. Lodge, whose burden was the late election. Both were grievously disappointed at the result, and both were bitterly critical of President Wilson. His election was due to his large silent vote, especially from the farmers, for the reason that he had kept us out of war. He has made us a nation of cowards, desiring peace of all things and the opportunity to enjoy undisturbed the comforts of life. The Eighth Massachusetts boys were mainly Republican; they were sent to the border of Mexico and their ennui during the summer was so great that if there were war, they would have it at no price and they almost solidly voted for Wilson.

Such was the strain of talk which I impart to you confidentially, as you are the friend of both. I did not impart my dissent, as, to tell the truth, I was overawed by the two intellectual giants, as I consider Roosevelt and Lodge.

Roosevelt has a large personal following, not so large as Wilson, and it is the general idea that if he had been nominated at Chicago he would have been beaten worse than Hughes. Still, to a recluse like myself, it looks to me as if Wilson and Roosevelt were for the moment the commanding figures in our political life. Anatole France said that after the present war there would be either Socialism or Chaos. It may be that the President believes this and desires the United States to become gradually under the form of law Socialistic. This I thought when I voted for Hughes. But we shall see. Unless I am greatly mistaken, the President cannot do good work with Gompers as one of his chief advisers.

This is a sombre letter, but I will close with something less so. When I met Mr. Roosevelt on the

Academy platform: "I am glad that you have at last got to one of our meetings. I was more successful in persuading you to the American Historical Association. Do you not recollect that at the last dinner you and Charles Francis Adams 'threw bouquets' at one another?" (They disliked one another exceedingly.) "Yes," said Roosevelt, "but if I knew Adams had written such an autobiography I should have thrown no bouquet." I replied, "You seem to agree exactly with Charles W. Eliot." "Well, then," returned Roosevelt, "I think I shall have to revise my opinion."

To George A. Myers

Boston, November 20, 1916.
[Beginning with an acknowledgment of a letter on politics from Mr. Myers and an allusion to the luncheon described in the preceding letter, Rhodes proceeds:]

From your letter and the talk at the luncheon I have arrived at some conclusions:

I. That the g. o. p. made a great mistake in going to the Supreme Bench for a candidate.

II. That Mr. Hughes made a great mistake in stepping down from his dignified place into the arena of politics.

III. That his first Western tour was a dismal failure and his conduct in California that of an infant!

IV. That the Republican campaign was badly managed with no comprehension of the weak spots.

V. That Mr. Wilson is a very great man, abler than Hughes, stronger than his party, and received his reward for keeping the country out of war. Thus might one go on, but the two great personalities politically are Roosevelt and Wilson, both men of education, culture, and ability. It is a great country to have two such men at the head of the two great parties!

I see nothing for us to do but to be at the back of the President in all foreign matters and to criticize him fully in matters domestic. His surrender to the labor unions was fraught with mischief, but it is idle now to say how the thing will turn out; it seems to me, however, that the President inclines to Socialism, and that his work will tend in that direction. The appointments of Brandeis and Clarke would seem an indication, and it is a cruel thought that our sacred Supreme Bench will be filled with men who will incline to the labor unions and Socialism. . . .

I don't know what is going to happen to the world. The outlook is certainly dreary. Let us hope that we may keep out of the European conflict and have no more than our domestic troubles, which will be quite sufficient. . . .

To the same

Boston, April 17, 1917.

. . . No doubt can exist that we were forced into the war, as, if the German government had not shown an asininity passing comprehension, it might have preserved the peace with us. Different from a good many good people here, I see with regret our country in the war, but really we had no option, as Germany forced the war upon us. I hope that our navy will acquit itself creditably and that we shall be of some assistance in the destruction of the submarines and in the supply of food to Great Britain. . . .

It is difficult to understand the German state of mind. Why the Germans should have shown so great

[276]

a lack of humanity and such brutality is almost incomprehensible. Tacitus wrote centuries ago that the
Germans were barbarians, and apparently their contact with the French, English, and Italians has given
them only a veneer of civilization. Their assumption
of superior knowledge and culture has been a sort of
bluff that imposed upon me and perhaps on many
others. . . .

In 1916 and 1917 there was an interchange of letters
with Mr. George A. Myers concerning an impugnment
of Rhodes's accuracy and fairness in the dealings of
his seventh volume with the subject of reconstruction
in Mississippi. This was made by a prominent member of the negro race, Major John R. Lynch, and was
embodied finally in his small volume, "Some Historical
Errors of James Ford Rhodes." Rhodes avowed himself to Mr. Myers "an earnest seeker after truth, trying to hold a judicial balance and to tell the story
without fear, favor or prejudice." He refused to be
drawn into conflict with his critic: "It is my rule never
to indulge in controversies; such indulgence is a rock
on which some historians have split. But I always
correct errors of fact." In this instance he found that
two errors should be corrected in future printings of
his book, with credit to their discoverer, and wrote
(April 22, 1917) to Mr. Myers: "The difference between Mr. Lynch and me is the point of view. I am
quite familiar with his point of view, and the criticism
of my account is quite familiar to me. It has been
given to me by President Roosevelt, Thomas W. Higginson, Moorfield Storey, and many others. It is the

old story of two warriors fighting about the shield, one saying it was golden, the other silver, because they looked at it from two different sides. The discussion will probably go on to the crack of doom."

To Charles Harding Firth

Seal Harbor, Maine, June 11, 1917.

I have not heard a word from you directly since the beginning of the war, and I wish you could send me a word saying how Mrs. Firth and you are getting on. I think of you often and of Oxford where I have passed so many pleasant days. I go back to my first meeting with you, which I think was in 1896 or 1895, introduced to you by Mr. Morfill at Queens. How much has happened since then, but how all the past is dwarfed by the two years and ten months of war! "Neither party expected for the war the magnitude or the duration which it has already attained," said Lincoln in his second inaugural address, and I can echo those words now. Being in England at its outbreak, I remember the remark of the military expert of the London *Times,* quoting someone of authority, who asserted that the war would last three weeks or three years, and I thought that the duration would be much nearer the shorter period. And it is really terrible what you have gone through. I am very sad when I think of the changed England and the changed Oxford, although I have a feeling of pride that England and France have stood this supreme test so well. I really hope that our country will be of the assistance expected, but I do not know how we shall perform our gigantic undertaking. I call to mind that I wrote somewhere in my History that the genius of the American Commonwealth lies in peace, and what sort of a stand we shall make before the skilled armies of Europe remains to be seen. I think that in the matter of growing and furnishing food we shall equal expectations, provided only that we have a "good growing season." I have been around to some extent New Jersey, New York, Connecticut, Massachusetts, and Maine, and everywhere I see ploughing and planting. Front yards and flower gardens are given up to potatoes and beans. It is a calamity that just at this time there should have been the failure of our winter wheat crop which is our great wheat production, but if we have rain and fair weather at proper intervals, I have hopes that that deficiency will be made up. Spring wheat, Indian corn, potatoes and beans make a good substitute, and the promise of a large hay crop and excellent pasturage is good. Our season is backward, about three weeks behind, and the weather has remained wet and cold. As I write we are in the midst of a three-day northeast storm unusual for this season of year. But I hope that by the time you receive this the prospects will be better. . . .

To Mrs. C. H. Toy

Seal Harbor, Maine, July 9, 1917.
. . . I have seen a good deal of President Eliot, making a long call on Mrs. Eliot and himself, and then seeing him at Mrs. Hanna's at dinner. During our long conversation at his house there was nothing of general interest, although he had many inquiries to make of me of the Massachusetts Historical Society, of the Saturday Club, and of people in whom we were

both interested. If ever a gentleman was entitled to the term, grand old man, he is. His physique, poise, and mental vigor are remarkable, and his power of expression carries one away in spite of one's disagreement. He did attack Dr. Manning on the attitude of the Episcopal Church during our Civil War (from the Northern point of view, of course) and only presented one phase of the truth. But Dr. Manning did not mind, although he was just from New York four hours late. Mr. Eliot is very severe on General Wood, which was not so agreeable to Dr. M. as General Wood is a member of his church, and while on Governor's Island was in his diocese. In spite, however, of the general opinion in New York and Boston, I believe Mr. Eliot is right about General Wood, and he shows great courage in expressing his opinion to Boston-Cambridge Harvard men.[43] . . .

To Henry Cabot Lodge

Seal Harbor, Maine, June 29, 1917.

. . . I am following matters in Washington with great interest and some information. I am glad to see the attitude you have taken on the prohibition question, and that Paul R. Frothingham's open letter in the *Transcript* has not influenced you. I do not know what has got into Mr. Frothingham, who is a level-headed, liberal man. Probably the nervous atmosphere of the times has affected him. When you

---

[43] It was in the month after this letter was written that Rhodes, recording in his "Dinner Book" a "Gentlemen's dinner at Charles W. Eliot's," made the note, "Very pleasant dinner—came home smelling strongly of tobacco smoke"—an amusing variation, in view of President Eliot's well-known antipathy to tobacco, upon Rhodes's more common notations of menus.

say "Germany has not restricted alcoholic beverages in any way, while France gives her soldiers regular wine rations, I think nobody will dispute that the German and French soldiers are of good fighting quality," you state a certain truth. You remind me of what Samuel Butler said in his Note Book, "Man's intellectual development would not have reached its present stage without the stimulus of alcohol—which I believe to be both perfectly true and pretty generally admitted." Ask Dr. George Shattuck if this is not true. . . .

To Charles Harding Firth

Seal Harbor, Maine, July 31, 1917.
It was a joy to see your bold hand-writing on an envelope, even if "Opened by Censor." . . .

Our Government has printed a pamphlet entitled, "How the War came to America," which merits high praise. It puts forward with succinctness the national reasons, and will read well in history. While we go into the war because the Germans would persist in sinking our ships and drowning our men, the large majority of us are glad that we are on the side of England and France. We feel keenly our indebtedness to England and in a less degree to France. Their history and literatures have smoothed over many hours, and the mad attack on them by Germany must be defeated if civilization is to endure. Something must be done to destroy the menace of the submarine, and I hope that the British and American navies may light upon some expedient to do it. I think we are weak in our Secretary of Navy, but the President has great confidence in him and to me Mr. Wilson seems a man of towering ability, determined to do everything to win the war. He has got some of the best business and executive men in the country to assist him on Commissions, but why he does not put some of them in his Cabinet is remarkable; for the Cabinet officer representing the President is an autocrat, and if you have a despot, it is desirable to have a wise one. It is lamentable, because the President has the majority of the nation at his back, who are as earnest as the North was in 1861. Probably we have another Farragut in our Navy, and I am hoping that he will be given a chance. Welles, Lincoln's Secretary, a journalist as is Daniels, maintains that it was he who brought Farragut forward. Possibly Daniels may do likewise. He might give a Farragut a high place, as Farragut was temperate, perhaps a total abstainer. But D. as War Secretary would never have given high command to Grant because he was a drinker, and we should under him have lost the greatest Northern general. I wish our Secretary was a reader of books and could have read in Channing's last volume, "Whether alcohol quickened or dimmed Madison's, Jefferson's, and King's intellects would probably best be left for decision to others." . . . But, as an English friend of mine in Boston who, speaking of England, says, we have to take the best material we can get. This war, however, is a very serious affair for most of us, as we see civilization trembling in the balance, and we cannot afford to make many blunders.

I thank you for your inquiry after my health. I was ill about a year and a half ago, but am now pretty well for a man of my age. As Bishop Greer told his daughter, my only trouble is "Anno Domini." . . .

To Mrs. C. H. Toy

Seal Harbor, Maine, August 10, 1917.
. . . Mr. Santayana's letter was very interesting. You know personally the President so much better than I do that you can better answer his surmise, but I suspect that he is correct in his supposition that Mr. Wilson has shown greater ability and leadership than any English or French public man. While he has, to my mind, a better system of government for conducting a war than either the English or the French, he has shown himself master of the situation and his conduct of the war is to me a marvel. I understand, too, that in spite of his burden, his health is good. Regarding his conduct of affairs since the war began, I look upon him as a man of towering ability. Of course he needs success to go down in history as a great man. While I am not absolutely sure that the Germans will be defeated, I feel pretty sure of it. It is the last hundred million of money and the last hundred thousand of men that will count, said Bonar Law at the commencement of the war. This the United States is furnishing, and the historian may say of Mr. Wilson: he waited until he had a large majority of the country at his back (just as Lincoln with his proclamation of emancipation) and until France was far spent and England needed help, then he went into the war with vigor with the result. . . . .

I say this to friends and they ask, why does he retain McAdoo, Daniels, and Baker? I cannot answer. Other great men have kept around them men of inferior ability because they were susceptible to flattery or because they were jealous of real ability. For my-

self I do think the President should make a change in
the Navy or Treasury departments, but I hear that
McAdoo has the backing of Colonel House, who is a
patriotic and able man. And then I call to mind what
Cromwell said to a pious associate who was remon-
strating with him: "Brother, did it ever occur to thee
that thee might be wrong?"

Of course the collapse of Russia is sad beyond expression. It is not pleasant to think that her keeping in
the right course depends upon Kerensky, who has lost
one kidney and has tuberculosis in the other. . . .

To Sir George Otto Trevelyan

Seal Harbor, Maine, September 18, 1917.
. . . It is on the whole a good thing that the war
has come with a Democratic administration, as it has
had more influence with the Southern States and the
Irish Catholics than a Republican administration could
have had; and the majority of the Republicans, outside
of the German-Americans, are all right anyway. I
look upon Mr. Wilson as a very able man and as the
Allies are certain to succeed, posterity will look upon
him as such and he will receive his just meed. But in
a way he is making it hard for those of us who would
like to support him. I have not had much idea that
an army would do great things but by this time the
Navy should have given an account of itself. I had
been led to believe that the Navy was in excellent shape
and I expected to see some work under the lead and
in co-operation with the British Navy, toward a marked
destruction of the submarines. Twice the Secretary of
the Navy has deceived the country by his sensational
editing of two despatches, reverting to his journalistic

career, and this has destroyed what little confidence the country had in him. . . .

To Henry Cabot Lodge

Seal Harbor, Maine, October 4, 1917.

. . . I am open to conviction, but, from this place of seclusion, I have arrived at the opinion that Congress during the last six months has done its work well—better than either Great Britain or Canada did in the first six months of the European War. The Republicans (all but a very few) deserve credit for supporting the President in all of his demands and the last six months makes a bright page in the history of the party.

I certainly think well of your making a statement regarding the events of the past six months.[44] There are a few mugwumps in the Society and an occasional Democrat. I do not know whether to class Charles W. Eliot as a mugwump or a Democrat, but I think he has in the main sound ideas. . . .

To Sir George Otto Trevelyan

Boston, November 2, 1917.

. . . George Ticknor must have been a fine gentleman, but the iron entered into his soul during our Civil War which he believed to be unnecessary. A true disciple of Daniel Webster, he was ardent for the Union, but as the war wore on he wanted it stopped and became a Copperhead. Charles Eliot Norton, his

---

[44] At the October, 1917, meeting of the Massachusetts Historical Society (October 11) Senator Lodge, then President of the Society, addressed its members, in illuminating detail, on "Recent Congressional Legislation."

nephew, and I am told an inheritor of Ticknor's gracious manner, told me that during the Civil War when he saw his uncle coming, he used to cross the street so as not to meet him and hear his violent abuse of those who were conducting the war. Ticknor was devoted to our Public Library and within these walls he is looked upon as a saint. One reason, I take it, why you are so attracted to him is that he did not have that eager desire for reform which possesses so many Bostonians. Ticknor's Life and Letters is wonderfully interesting and so is his biography of William H. Prescott which is a fine tribute of one gentleman to another. We may delight in the amenities between these brother historians. As John Hay once wrote to me in becoming a historian, one should not cease to be a gentleman.

I like your reference to Senator Lodge. He has been winning golden opinions for his support of the administration and he is silent in public over many things that are done not to his liking. At the October meeting of the Massachusetts Historical Society he gave a talk on the last six months of Congress which was directly to the point and interesting in a high degree. He has a remarkable power of statement and uttered his words trippingly as if he were reading from manuscript. A stenographer took down his remarks so I suppose they will be printed in the Proceedings and you will find them worth reading. . . .

To the same

Boston, January 31, 1918.
Your valued favor of 13 was received yesterday. You have certainly gone to the bottom of the English

censorship, and your explanation of it is entirely reasonable. I shall no longer say a word against it. The only objection was delay, but as all things move slowly now, a delay of one or two days more is really of no account. You and I are perfectly willing to have our letters examined by the English or American government, although we do not want them in the newspapers without our permission. I was interested in your account of the state of our people. I fear we could show you only too many instances of too many persons detailed for a job. If that be the case with Hoover and our Navy Department (as I believe it is), which are the two best managed departments, what must it be with a number of others?

I still stick to my previous impression that our Navy has been splendidly conducted, no thanks to the Secretary, however, and I still believe in Hoover. He has had a difficult job, and has made many mistakes, but his hits have been much greater than his misses, and the general result of his work has been good. He could have put his views before the public more systematically, but that is not so very important and his fixation of the price of wheat was too arbitrary. If the war lasts two years longer it is too late, for he seems to have lost sight of one essential fact, that all this inflation in the circulating medium is bound to lessen the value of money and elevate the price of products and goods. But food is now so important, I grant, that the power of the government might be properly exercised in fixing a price for it, but great care should be taken not in any way to limit the production. We shall see during the coming season what has been the result. But apart from food I believe that supply and demand should regulate the price of

everything. The President (who has many virtues
and I believe is the best fitted of all our public men
for the place except Roosevelt) and his Secretary of
War have a mania for fixing prices, but as they are
not omniscient, much of their work has gone wrong.
The coal situation is an example of a stupendous
blunder. While the severest of winters could not have
been foreseen, a wise legislation would have prepared
for the worst but the Secretary of War (with of course
the President's approval) fixed a price for coal too low
to stimulate the production and until this blunder was
remedied much valuable time was lost.

So all manufacturing industries are dislocated,
schools and churches are closing, and the great question is how may we keep warm in our rigorous winter
climate? . . .

I hope that in my old fashioned view about supply
and demand I have not touched on a controversial
question, and if I have, what might be a just inter-
ference of the State in a "tight little island" like England is a different job in our big country with our
diversified interests.

I am glad you take such an interest in the Massachusetts Historical Society publications. It is the only
learned society to which I give any attention, and
through my friendship with Mr. Adams I have been
actuated to it. You will read with interest J. T.
Morse's review of Lord Charnwood's "Lincoln" at
the November meeting.

I did not want to bore you, but on account of your
apparent interest in American things I am going to
send you a volume on our Civil War which I have
just published. I do this because so many reviewers

of the book have drawn a contrast between the despair during our Civil War and our present discouragement. But you may rest assured that we are good for two years more of it, financially and otherwise. It is regrettable that we could not have furnished our aid sooner, but the delay is due, I think, to the generally peaceful aims of our country rather than from maladministration. Nevertheless, I do not think the administration has been as good as it might have been.

The foregoing letter touches upon two matters that give occasion for a pause in the succession, now long unbroken in these pages, of Rhodes's letters to his friends. At an earlier point he has been seen,[45] on his own showing, at work on a one-volume History of the Civil War undertaken at the request of his publishers, and obviously at some disadvantage to the progress of his larger work on the continuation of his History of the United States beyond 1877. This one-volume work was a much more substantial book than the "Oxford Lectures," and by no means so clearly a condensation of writings previously published. In the very nature of the case, and to a certain extent, it was inevitably that; but it was also something considerably more, for during the years since Rhodes's earlier volumes were written an abundance of fresh material bearing upon the war had become accessible, and this he turned to account for the new book. In its Preface he declared it "not an abridgment of my three volumes on the Civil War but a fresh study of the subject on which I have used my work as one of many authori-

---

[45] See *ante*, p. 253.

ties. Wherever I have transferred sentences, paragraphs and pages I have done so because, after a study of the original authorities, I have found that I could give my conclusions no better than in my first work." In giving a partial list of the new material available for this volume, Rhodes did not hesitate to reveal the handicaps under which he had labored in the volumes published respectively in 1895, 1899, and 1904. "I owe especial indebtedness," he said of his new sources, "to the Official Records of the Union and Confederate Navies; Diary of Gideon Welles; Life of Rawlins, which J. H. Wilson kindly permitted me to use in manuscript before publication; the Letters and Diaries of John Hay; Miss Nicolay's Personal Traits of Lincoln; Life and Letters of General Meade; J. Bigelow, Jr., The Campaign of Chancellorsville; W. R. Thayer, Life of John Hay; The Reminiscences of Carl Schurz."

Thus representing a substantial output of fresh labor, the book was nevertheless a publisher's rather than an author's enterprise, and gained more by proceeding from an established source than it could add to the reputation and authority of that source. By itself it would have brought credit rather than distinction to its author; on the other hand, the distinction the book possessed came to it from Rhodes. Yet that was sufficient to win for it the Pulitzer Prize award for the "best book of the year [1917] upon the history of the United States."

The second occasion for pausing at this point is the allusion to Lord Charnwood and his life of Lincoln.

About a year after Mr. Morse gave his opinion of that biography to the Massachusetts Historical Society Lord Charnwood visited Boston and became personally acquainted with the Rhodes he had already known well through his writings. In March of 1928 I received, in answer to certain inquiries, a letter from him which may be printed here, almost in its entirety, as a token of Rhodes's significance to the generation of English scholars next younger than his own:

I do not know whether it will be of interest to you that I should try to note down my impressions of Mr. Rhodes. And first as to his great book. I wonder whether this has received yet anything like the recognition that it deserves. I was put on to it by Walter Hines Page and his wife, just before I began work on my own book about Lincoln. The enormous help that it gave me personally might prejudice me, but I do not think it does. To begin with the qualities which made it so useful to me are not really the dull and ordinary qualities they might seem,—the sufficiency and minute accuracy of detail, and the painstaking rectitude of judgment. When Rhodes gives you his finding on some disputed question of fact or his judgment on a question of policy or justice, he gives you, without running to immense length, such an adequate and balanced summary of the evidence or the arguments on both sides that in the great majority of cases you know he must be right. What is still more remarkable is that in the minority of cases where you disagree with his conclusion or doubt it, you find your reasons for differing from him have been fully and plainly put at your disposal by Rhodes himself. . . .

Rigid accuracy and the untiring effort to be fair
and upright in large things and in small are not at all
common qualities, and they are not dull qualities either,
for they can only be kept going in a high state of
efficiency by a pretty lofty enthusiasm for one's subject. Thus, though I confess that my use for the
book involved more jumping about and rummaging
here and there than continuous reading, I do not think
that anybody, interested enough in history to read a
longish book at all, would find that the flow of
Rhodes's narrative from 1850 to the end of the Civil
War had been injured at all by this conscientious
workmanship in detail. I think he achieved an impressive record of the march of great events combined
with enough wealth of detail to make the whole business very life-like and real, and I have the hope that
future readers who do not want to be bothered with
a lot of little books on the subject will find Rhodes's
history of the Civil War a great story of that great
period, and an inspiring story,—ranking easily with
the few famous history books in our language (or any
other), as well as far excelling some of them in the
security, which it gives, that there is no gross error,
and no gross injustice, and no gross lack of sympathy
or vision anywhere. . . .

The description "a great book" must of course be
restricted to a certain number of his volumes. I think
it is actually before the term of President Hayes, which
he began by naming as his stopping point, that he
really came to a stop,—producing afterwards a number of "sequels" which are like most sequels.

When I met him he was still doing so, and he was
then distinctly an old man whose big effort was in the

past. I do not know whether there came a time when
his health and strength definitely failed. But there
certainly is a point at which he seems to have been
overcome by the difficulty that necessary materials
were not yet available, that living controversies and
living reputations (to which he was perhaps too near)
were involved, and finally that the whole course of
events was anyway too dull. Perhaps it was my own
remoteness of interest that made me feel some of the
sequel volumes were as literature in a lower class than
what went before,—more likely they really are so.
But the splendid good sense, justice, and sympathy of
the man stood out perhaps all the more in those dull
volumes about dull times. And at the end I think
he brightened up. I think one may look on this later
work of his as showing the possibility and the value,
where possible, of turning the historian's trained
method of enquiry and developed power of justice and
of wide sympathy on to quite recent transactions. And
it strikes me as a very noble effort, on the part of a
man who had certainly begun to feel aged, to carry
on that work of his as near down to the present as
was by any means possible.

I first met him in November of 1918, just after the
Armistice, and it was a memorable occasion to me, a
dinner given to me in Boston because of my Lincoln
book. That book had been received by a great many
Americans with what I felt to be great generosity of
appreciation. One particular review of it had already
appeared which I shall always remember as achieving
a "record" in real personal generosity. John T. Morse,
Jr., had, thirty years before, written the book on
Lincoln which most resembled my own in scope and

general purpose and point of view, so that his was the book which mine, if it was good at all, was likely by the mere fact of being written later, to render obsolete. J. T. M.'s review of me was the one which above all others seemed even to me not merely ample but excessive in its praise of me,—(it was brought to my notice by a paragraph in a New York paper which had the just headline, "Some Sportsman"). Well, to return,—after this dinner and after some words from Henry Lee Higginson, whose memory I greatly revere and who was in the chair, I learnt that James Ford Rhodes (personally unknown to me) was to read a regular criticism of my book. I reflected, "Here am I who have got quite a nice little temporary fame by my book. And here is the very historian the fruit of whose labors I was most assiduously pilfering all the while that I was writing that book. This is just about Judgment Day." He got up and read a quiet, conventional sort of analysis of how I had done,—taking samples from my work and explaining in the simplest but really most searching way why he, as a historian, thought them good work,—all he said was absolutely sensible, and absolutely kind and hearty. In a different way this pleased me almost as much as Morse's praise had done. You will get my point: there are ways of handling a man so that he will feel keenly grateful to you ever after.

After that I had some very pleasant hours with him in Boston and some years later here in London, with him and Mrs. Rhodes,—when he talked to me about Roosevelt amongst other matters. And we once or twice exchanged letters. I saw enough of him to have a very vivid impression of his personality, though it does not follow that I can express it. He was to me a most refreshing man to talk to,—a great scholar of course, and with all that one associates with the terms scholar and gentleman; but a scholar by reason of the great width of sympathy, the geniality, the power of enjoyment and the sound judgment, that he turned loose on to his particular business of scholarship. He was what somebody (Tennyson, I think) called a "big, brotherly man," a very good man to smoke with or drink wine with, his heart open to every sort of simple enjoyment; but all this, as one found, was raised into a real love and enjoyment before all else of "whatsoever things are true, pure, lovely, and of good report, etc." So, at least, in my much too brief intercourse with him I felt. I respected his judgment very highly, but should always, I think, have had complete reliance on his kindness,—but should have been very sorry to be caught out by him in anything mean or small. . . .

At the time of Lord Charnwood's first meeting with Rhodes the two volumes which brought his History to a close had not yet appeared. Having thus anticipated the course of events, let us then return to the letters of 1918.

To Sir George Otto Trevelyan

Boston, March 13, 1918.

I received your interesting letter of February 24 two days ago just as I was on the point of going to call on the Archbishop of York, and telling him that I had just received a letter from you and of Lord and

Lady Bryce's visit to you. We had much talk about
you and them. The Archbishop is a highly agreeable
gentleman, and I wish that his visit could have been
made here in happier times. One would rather discuss with him history and literature, Cambridge and
Oxford, than this cruel war which we can talk about
only with heavy hearts. Nevertheless, we had one
merry moment when he invited me to dine with him
at All Souls when next I went to England, and when
he insisted that at All Souls I should call him Lang
and drop Your Grace or Archbishop. My two calls
upon him were an oasis in our desert of vanquished
hopes. I cannot help repeating Lincoln's words,
"Fondly do we hope—fervently do we pray—that this
mighty scourge of war may speedily pass away." Few
of us have any doubt of the result, any more than
Lincoln and his private secretaries had of the result
of the Civil War. I feel keenly that the right must
win.

The Archbishop proved himself a wonderful orator
and produced a mighty effect on his various audiences.
Believing in the Cambridge-Oxford training, I am glad
to point to him as a striking example. It is a great
thing to be able to reach men's hearts in a time like
this, and our community is better for the few days
that he was able to give to us.

I read all that you wrote concerning Lord Bryce's
visit with much interest. During his embassy here he
fastened the hold he had upon this country, which he
had gained by his successive visits and by his book on
the "American Commonwealth." I remember extolling
it to a young English Tory at the time it appeared,
and he replied, "Of course you like it; he butters you
up so." I must say that I derived from it a great

deal of information, and my acquaintance with Bryce since 1895 has been a source of great pleasure and profit.

Further information confirms me in what I said about our Navy. From all sides I hear that it is in excellent shape in every respect. I hope to see the menace of the submarine checked by the operation of the British and American Navies before the end of the calendar year. When that is accomplished, everything else will seem comparatively easy.

I agree entirely with what you say in regard to fixing prices except as to the necessary food staples. Senator Lodge has shown in an able speech in the Senate how badly the attempts of the government have worked in fixing the price of coal and sugar. I can support everything he says about coal, and, because he is right about coal, I believe him to be about sugar. But grain and meat are in a different category, and I don't think we could have a better food director than Hoover. His ability and single-mindedness are unquestioned, and while I regret that he has fallen victim to the American habit of making a sensational statement on the front page of the newspaper, I cannot expect a man of forty-four to be perfect. . . .

Of the letter that follows it is necessary only to say that it was in answer to the seventieth birthday letter from President Eliot with which this volume began.

James Ford Rhodes

To Charles W. Eliot

Boston, May 5, 1918.

Mr. Thayer kindly handed to me your valued favor of 1st. We all regretted deeply that you could not be with us. For me your absence is mitigated by the permanent record which I now possess of your sentiment.

Environment is a great factor in the life of a bookish man, and no city offers such living advantages as Boston with the vital influence of its great University which, under your administration, became, of one of many colleges, the leading University of the country. "Priests of the mind" George William Curtis called scholars, and an institution of light and learning presided over by a wise and liberal administrator gives to them the idea that their life is worth living. In reflecting on Harvard University and Boston the thought of Pericles on the beautiful works of Athens has often come to me, the daily delight in them banishes gloom. Gloom must more or less be present now, but the scholar has some comfort in his work and in his belief that good results may come from this terrible upheaval.

To A. Lawrence Lowell

Poland Spring House, June 11, 1918.

. . . The President of Harvard University stands in the limelight as does the President of the United States. He is sure to be misunderstood and misreported. I do not wonder that you sometimes feel "uncomfortable," and the great wonder is that you can fill your high office with the serenity and wisdom that

[298]

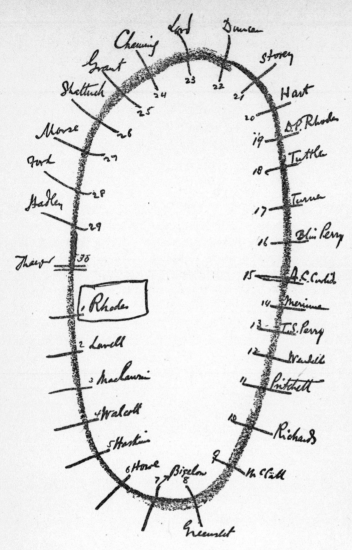

A MEMORANDUM OF RHODES'S SEVENTIETH BIRTHDAY
DINNER
In the handwriting of William Roscoe Thayer

you manifest. Your speech at the "Win the War for Permanent Peace" convention and the platform, which you so kindly sent to me, taken in connection with your confidential talk, show a steadfastness of purpose remarkable in a man, holding at this time a prominent position, who is obliged to express himself so frequently. I thoroughly believe that you have not only the Harvard alumni at your back but also the dominant public sentiment of the country. . . .

To Henry Cabot Lodge

Seal Harbor, Maine, September 7, 1918.
. . . Touching your conditions for peace, I would say Amen to the first three which I understand. As regards the others I would prefer your guidance as you understand the matter much better than I do.

I take exception to your statement that we must go to Berlin and there dictate the peace. It seems to me that as good terms as we ought to ask may be dictated on the Rhine. The Rhine will be a difficult river to cross and the passage will cost an enormous number of men. . . .

To Frederic Bancroft

Seal Harbor, Maine, September 15, 1918.
I am glad that you reminded me in your valued favor of 26 ult., of the approaching anniversary of the birth of Frederic Harrison. I was pretty well acquainted with him, having first got to know him during his visit to this country, which I think was in 1901. He stopped with us a night or two, and my wife and I found him a delightful visitor. We con-

tinued the pleasant acquaintance, and I remember well the last time that I saw him when he took luncheon with us in London and, then 76, said he was nearer 80 than 70. He also remarked that in matters of drink he was a Mohammedan up to 6 P.M., but that did not prevent his helping me out with a bottle of Rhine wine in the days when we thought differently of Germany than we do now. I have read many of his works with delight especially his Cromwell and Ruskin. The latter, he said, cost him a guinea a word. It is a wonderful book. I believe Charles Eliot Norton was asked to write the subjective Life of Ruskin but he declined and let his friend Harrison use his material. I read his last Obiter Scripta in the *Fortnightly*, and found it ejaculatory and in no way equal to his earlier work.

Mr. Harrison was a delightful man; seemed to have known every one worth knowing, and talked about these men in an interesting manner. He was a great friend of John Morley's. I will write to Mr. Harrison as you suggest.[46] . . .

To Sir George Otto Trevelyan

Boston, January 22, 1919.

. . . In Roosevelt we have lost a great man. I cannot tell you how I sorrow at his loss. He was a warm friend, and to him and to Mark Hanna I am more deeply indebted than to any other men. Roosevelt's good points overbalanced decidedly his mistakes. He would have been of infinite use to the party

---

[46] Rhodes acted that very day upon this intention, and wrote to Frederic Harrison a letter of felicitation on his eighty-seventh birthday.

and the country had he not quarreled with Mr. Taft and broken up the Republican party. If he had had some of the magnanimity he so admired in Washington and Lincoln he might have been chosen President in 1916 and on our behalf ended the war. Mr. Roosevelt unbosomed himself freely to you and you know how many times he was wise and far-seeing. If I remember correctly, he wrote to you a letter after the result of the Convention of 1908 which nominated Taft that shows him at his best. Alas! we have no one to take his place! . . .

To Robert Grant

Boston, March 11, 1919.[47]

Your letter in the *Herald* this morning expresses the view of many thinking men. You were good and patriotic to write it. "Factious policy of isolation" is well put. The action of our common friend, Senator Lodge, may well be deplored. He had a great opportunity which he missed, but nothing else could be expected from the leader of an opposing party. Had I his ability, leadership, power of work and expression, I should probably have done what he has done, but it does not seem right to a closet student. . . .

To Sir George Otto Trevelyan

Boston, April 1, 1919.

. . . The question of the League of Nations absorbs all interest here, added to by the debate between Sen-

[47] The date of this letter shows that it was written early in the controversy between President Wilson and the Senate over the League of Nations.

ator Lodge and President Lowell. The hearers were much like those who heard Lincoln and Douglas debate in 1858. The Douglas men thought that their champion got the better of Lincoln and the Republicans thought the reverse. So it was with the friends for the moment of Lodge and Lowell. But the opinion is general that Senator Lodge did not do himself justice in the closing half hour of rebuttal which as challenged party he had; but instead made a stump speech, suitable on the platform during an exciting campaign but not adapted to the audience he had in Symphony Hall. It is dangerous for a man, living in this corner of the country to speak of the sentiment of eighteen million voters plus women but I suspect that the League as defined by Mr. Lowell and still better by ex-Secretary Root will carry the country. The leaders of the Republican party should have supported the League on the lines laid down by them instead of putting up a critical destructive opposition which in a few cases degenerated into harshness. Let us have peace and adopt if possible some plan that shall prevent a recurrence of the events of the past four and a half years. . . .

A brief passage in a letter of April 17, 1919, to Professor Firth in Oxford suggests the diminishing zest with which Rhodes was pursuing his own work: "I published in 1917 a History of the Civil War which you will not care for, but I will send to you next autumn the continuation of my History telling the tale from 1877 to 1899. I shall go on with it if life and health be spared, but I am indifferent whether I publish any more or not."

James Ford Rhodes

To Charles W. Eliot

Seal Harbor, Maine, July 6, 1919.

. . . You are quite right. Having the *cacoethes scribendi* I devote my mornings towards increasing the amount of printed matter already perhaps too large. But what can a man do who has passed the limit of three score years and ten, unless he be in a position to influence actual public sentiment? That makes living worth while, and your expression of cheerful optimism is attractive and I hope may be justified by the years.

As I understand it, I think that the Senate ought to ratify the Treaty and Covenant without Amendment. It is impossible that such a document should satisfy every nation and faction. If you and ex-Secretary Root had been on the Peace Commission, perhaps a better deal for the United States might have been secured, and it may be that the President is jealous of abilities superior to his own; but the best minds attainable have been at work on this scheme, which is one of give and take, and is as good, all things considered, as could have been secured. And the objections, so far as I have been able to understand them, of Senators Lodge, Knox, and Beveridge seem to me slight compared with the dreadful alternative. . . . The idea may be well sustained that Senator Lodge has led his party into a "ditch." Gossip has it that so well is this appreciated by Mr. Root that he has gone to Washington to try to help his personal friend out of the "hole" into which his impetuosity and hatred of the President have placed him.

I sat next to Senator Lodge at dinner last March, and this involved a tête-à-tête of an hour or so. I certainly did not want to discuss the President or the

League of Nations, as I was well aware of his sentiments. It chanced, however, that while waiting at
the Tavern Club I had read an article of his in *Scribner's* on "Familiar Quotations," and we fell to discussing that article and books in general. Senator
Lodge told me that he wrote the paper during March,
1918, at the time that he had heard of the disaster
to the Fifth English Army, and that he put his mind on
the subject as a distraction from his grief. His emotion as he recalled his feeling of those days was cap-
tivating to me, and I was glad indeed that we had not
touched on the topics of the day. The "Familiar
Quotations" was in his best vein, similar to his address
of dedication of the Widener Library. . . .

To Sir George Otto Trevelyan

Seal Harbor, Maine, July 25, 1919.
. . . The prominent topic at Washington is Shall the
Covenant and the League of Nations be ratified? It
seems to me that the Senate Republicans have put
themselves in the wrong by making so violent an opposition. But they dislike President Wilson and with
the presidential election approaching next year, they
do not want to give him any glory toward the settlement of the greatest of wars. While the Senate ought
to rectify the League and Covenant as presented to
them, it is quite likely that it will insist on the reservations suggested by Mr. Root or the interpretations
of Mr. Taft. Mr. Taft insists on the interpretations
only to secure available enough Republican votes for
the necessary two thirds, and his letters seem to me
to present statesmanlike reasons. The cogency of the
Republican objections might be sound were things as

they were thirty years ago but with aeroplanes, dirigibles, poisonous gases and bombs, the Republicans do not take account sufficiently of the dreadful alternative to a non-ratification of the treaty and to the adoption of a League of Nations.

One of my grandsons affected by the bragging of some of his schoolmates was eager to know my politics and I might have said with Odysseus, "I will truly tell you all," and while not saying that I did reply, "Adam, I started life as a strong Democrat, then I became a strong Republican, then a lukewarm Democrat, and now I suppose I am a lukewarm Republican," with which confession of my political faith or lack of it, I will add that my wife joins me in cordial regards to Lady Trevelyan and yourself. . .

To D. M. Matteson

Seal Harbor, Maine, August 3, 1919.
. . . I am in favor of the League of Nations and the Treaty as submitted to the Senate. I would like to see it ratified as submitted but if the necessary two-thirds cannot be obtained then I am in favor, to secure it, of the reservations of Mr. Root or the interpretations of Mr. Taft. Ten years ago I should have opposed mixing in European squabbles, but since then the submarine, the aeroplane, the dirigible, and the poisonous gases have been introduced or perfected so that it is a different world. The alternative to the League is dreadful. There is nothing confidential about my opinion but I should prefer that it does not get into the newspapers as I shrink from that notoriety. But I do not consider the opinion on the present by a student of the past as especially valuable. So

it has proved but one cannot help expressing one's opinions.

To Sir George Otto Trevelyan

Seal Harbor, Maine, August 28, 1919.

. . . To my mind our Senate Republicans are acting badly. To the question Are you not a good Republican, I might reply in the words of Mr. Choate (used on an occasion which I do not recollect): Yes indeed I am a good Republican but because I am a good Republican, it is not necessary that I should be a damnphool all of the time. . . .

To A. Lawrence Lowell [48]

Boston, November 5, 1919

I have your valued favor of 3. I intended to write to you that you need not read the volume nor write a letter about it, but only put it upon your shelves where you might have it for a ready reference. As the Frenchman said, it is the history of day before yesterday of which we are ignorant. It is my intention to continue my history down to March 4, 1909, when Roosevelt gave place to Mr. Taft. This, you see, will stop before 1912 when you and I communed together and at the end of the conference decided to vote for Mr. Wilson.

Senator Lodge's view of President Hayes is the conventional partisan Republican view: that shared by Blaine and Conkling, who hated one another but disliked Hayes. I remember that at the Garfield funeral

---

[48] Clearly in acknowledgment of a letter about *From Hayes to McKinley,* published in 1919.

in Cleveland in 1881 a very nice gentleman, Mr. Henderson, who represented a Republican district in Illinois, told me that he had said to Mrs. Hayes that if she were to run for President she would have his vote. But he added to me, "I hope that we shall never see a man again in the White House so thoroughly incompetent as was President Hayes."

I am inclined to think, however, that I have struck the historical view of Hayes.

I have been told that Senator Lodge voted for Tilden in 1876. . . .

To Sir George Otto Trevelyan

Boston, November 9, 1919.

. . . In the winter of 1902 I was on a visit of two or three days at the White House and the morning after my arrival Mrs. Roosevelt and Miss Roosevelt went away on a visit, so the President and I kept "bachelor's hall" in the White House and I got nearer to Mr. Roosevelt than ever before. Our prolonged talks over the coffee at breakfast still linger in my memory and from that time I began to love the man and the love overpowered any of what I conceived to be his after mistakes. One night at the White House there was at dinner Secretary of State John Hay, Sir Martin Conway, Wellman, the President, and myself, and I can assure you it was a very long dinner for talk. Next day, my visit being concluded, I went to my sister's house in Washington, and as she was married to Mark Hanna, then Senator from Ohio, I have always prided myself on not divulging to either my confidential talk with the President and the Senator, who, while not exactly at odds, did not see weighty matters in the same light. Secretary Hay was at the dinner and after the dinner the following conversation ensued.

Rhodes: That was a nice conversational dinner we had at the White House last night, Mr. Secretary.

Hay: Conversational do you call it? How long were we at table?

Rhodes: About two hours.

Hay: Well, Wellman talked a minute, Sir Martin one and a half minutes, you a minute, and I not more than that, and Theodore talked all the rest of the time. Do you call that conversation?

From 1902 to 1904, the day of the luncheon when we discussed the article of Clio [49] I had not seen the President. So I said: "Mr. President, I have not seen you since I parted from you two years ago. Do you remember the dinner when Secretary Hay was here, when I was stopping with you?"

"Very well indeed," said the President. "Was not John Hay great that night!" . . .

The publication of "From Hayes to McKinley" was the occasion of much correspondence, in one item of which Rhodes's painstaking methods appeared under an amusing side-light. First there was a letter from Dr. Henry S. Pritchett (January 29, 1920), touching "in the interest of historical accuracy" on a questionable point in the new volume. "Referring to the habits of the Chinese," wrote Dr. Pritchett, "you quote from Bret Harte's famous poem on the 'Heathen Chinee' including a quotation to the effect that Ah Sin had

---

[49] An article by G. M. Trevelyan.

concealed in his flowing sleeves 'twenty-four packs,' the same, of course, with intent to deceive. You will agree that twenty-four packs would be going it strong, and would tax even the capacity of the flowing sleeves of the old time Chinaman, for it would involve the concealment of 1248 cards. If you will refer to the original copy of the poem of Truthful James you will find that he states that Ah Sin had concealed in his sleeves not twenty-four packs, but twenty-four jacks." After some further observations Dr. Pritchett proceeded: "Perhaps I should say that this might indicate a lapse of memory, for I am sure that if you will recur to the days before you became a citizen of Boston and a famous historian you will recall that in the noble game of euchre jacks are the desirable cards, because they are the left and right bowers. May I not express the hope—to quote from your friend President Wilson —that this trifling inaccuracy may be corrected in the next edition of your valuable and highly moral history?"

Rhodes retorted that in his edition of Bret Harte (Boston, 1879) the word was "packs" not "jacks," but promised to look into other editions at the Boston Athenæum, and to make the suggested change if it could be justified. "But your arithmetic," he wrote (February 4, 1920), "is slightly in error. In euchre we always took out the cards under the sevens, so that twenty-four packs would involve only 768 cards. Perhaps B. Harte took out all under the tens, which would make the packs even smaller. There is no question, I think, that 'jacks' would be much better, but I do not want to improve on Bret Harte, who probably knew draw poker better than he did euchre."

Dr. Pritchett handsomely accepted Rhodes's defence of himself with "an apology from the Carnegie Foundation." More recently he has written to me, "This seemed to settle the matter, but a few years ago, when the Reminiscences of Bret Harte were published, he referred to the typographic difficulties encountered in the first edition of his poems. One of the humorous mistakes instanced was the fact that in the original edition the Heathen Chinee was said to have twenty-four packs instead of twenty-four jacks! I brought this final proof to Rhodes's attention and he promptly surrendered." Much ado, to be sure, about little, but the *minutiæ* of history have their place beside its larger issues.

To Sir George Otto Trevelyan

Boston, January 17, 1920.

. . . I am feeling deeply the untimely and sudden death of Dr. Maclaurin, the President of the Massachusetts Institute of Technology. A Scotchman by birth, educated in Cambridge, England, spending some time in New Zealand, then at Columbia University, and then here, he has wrought wonders in his administration of the Institute and, as he was not fifty, he had many years of usefulness before him. Well acquainted with him socially, I comprehended his quiet humor and enjoyed immensely his eagerness to get at the bottom of things. As I write, I look across the Charles River at the buildings which will ever be his monument. This is my only excuse for enlarging on so sad a subject but gazing on the frozen river covered with snow the words of Ophelia cannot fail to come to me, "I cannot choose but weep, to think they should lay him i' the cold ground." For his funeral is tomorrow. . . .

To the same

Boston, May 12, 1920.

. . . I was glad to read a good word in your letter for Henry Cabot Lodge as since he opposed the Treaty and the League, as the President wished them, he has been unpopular with a certain set here although I think he has a great hold on the mass. The President, I suspect, is hopelessly ill, while Senator Lodge gained ten pounds during his contest with the President. I called upon the Senator when he was here about two months ago and said to him, "You have been fighting with the beasts of Ephesus." He replied, "I have been fighting with one beast." So does the Senator hate the President. . . .

To George A. Myers

Boston, May 22, 1920.

. . . Senator Lodge is a very able man. The contest has been between him and the President. The President has had a stroke of paralysis: the Senator has gained ten pounds. Naturally any man who comprehends the game should be on the side of the Senator: therefore the ratification of the Treaty and the League of Nations with the Lodge reservations should be the platform of men who hope to save civilization from the wreck which threatens it.

I do not understand what you mean when you write,

"Were Senator Lodge free from the plutocracy influence." He is 70 years old, too old to run for President; he occupies a more enviable position in being leader of the Senate and leader of the Republicans. These positions he has won despite a personal unpopularity in the Senate. He is not liked here by the Independents, who object to him in general and especially for his attitude toward President Wilson, whom he hates as the devil hates holy water. But as you are a good honest Republican it will answer to tie to him. He is a protectionist and a thorough believer in the Republican party. I am on excellent terms with Senator Lodge whose towering ability I cannot help but admire. He was also a great friend of Theodore Roosevelt although he differed from him on essential points, especially on the Initiative, Referendum and Recall.

Theodore Roosevelt was a great president and a great administrator. The more I study him the more I admire him. Thayer has made him out a saint, which he was not, but purely human, which no one would recognize more clearly than he would himself. He was wonderfully attractive, and his sincerity was unquestioned. . . . Thayer is a brilliant writer but not entirely logical in his admiration of Roosevelt. He was an anti-imperialist and therefore down on McKinley and Hanna. He is entirely wrong when he classes Hanna with Tom Platt or Quay. No one understands the difference between them better than you do but you must have a little charity for men who live here in the ideal and do not understand as you do the rough and tumble of life. They are not therefore judges of practical affairs and you will note that defect in their writings. These remarks do not apply to Croly's Life of Hanna which despite some errors is an excellent biography; and in this Mr. Henry White, our ablest diplomat, agrees with me. . . .

Rhodes's remark in the foregoing letter about the physical condition of Wilson and Lodge was not his only comment of its kind. Mr. Charles K. Bolton, Librarian of the Boston Athenæum, of which Rhodes was long a trustee and a member of the library committee, enacted for many years, partly by reason of his Cleveland origin, what he has called the "rôle of an amateur Boswell," and took notes of conversations with Rhodes, which have been kindly placed at my disposal. In one of these bits of record Rhodes, in October of 1919, is found saying, "This is Wilson's third serious attack of nervous prostration—the natural fate of a pugnacious man with a weak stomach." A year later, in October of 1920, Rhodes is reported again, with a certain sad jocosity: "I was for Wilson, but my man got a stroke of paralysis, while Senator Lodge gained ten pounds. I had no choice then, and so I am now for the man who gained ten pounds! Lodge is the most popular man in Massachusetts today with the masses, but not of course with the crowd you and I meet. Our crowd can't forgive Lodge for voting (as I did) for Blaine. Cox will 'shake' the League if elected. He cares no more for it than Harding does."

In Mr. Bolton's memoranda there are also allusions to the crayon portrait of Rhodes, which was drawn in the spring of 1920, and provides the frontispiece of this volume. "Mr. Rhodes came to tell me," wrote Mr. Bolton, April 12, 1920, "that Sargent had drawn his portrait. 'Yes, I've been, and I never was so tired in my life. I sat on that stool for two hours and a half, and now I must go back to be retouched. Sargent at the end appeared to be more tired than I was. I knew him socially before, and now [with a laugh] I know him *intimately*. He talked all the time. He told me what he told you about Rockefeller, and said, "They said I was paid to whitewash him." [50] Sargent did not care for Roosevelt nor for the painting which he did. He is very pro-British and enthusiastic about Henry James. Gosse, you know, is probably truthful in putting James on a lower pedestal than his admirers would approve. Sargent will have none of Gosse.' "

A fortnight later Mr. Bolton recorded some supplemental remarks of Sargent's Boston friend, Mr. Thomas A. Fox: "Tom Fox has much to say of Sargent's sitters. Rhodes the artist liked, and so did him well, 'but forgot to give him a rest, so that the old man nearly fell off the stool.' They differed over T. R., whom Sargent thought ever on parade, and he said, 'I hated Roosevelt, and took it out in doing an extra good picture of Leonard Wood.' "

A single further paragraph of Mr. Bolton's (May 5, 1920) remains to be quoted: "Mr. Rhodes brought in his portrait by Sargent. It is masterfully inquisitorial and strong in detail. It does not quite convey his size and air of bluff geniality, but it's fine. I: 'You look like Andrew Carnegie.' He: 'Sargent flattered me

---

[50] In an earlier note, February 9, 1918, Mr. Bolton had recorded a remark of Rhodes about Sargent and Rockefeller: "Sargent thinks he is a saint and so painted him."

more by saying that I look like Victor Hugo. I never was very fond of Carnegie.' " [51] From this I would dissent only with respect to the word "inquisitorial." The accurately depicted kindness of the face seems accompanied rather with a characteristic penetration.

To John T. Morse, Jr.

Seal Harbor, Maine, July 21, 1920.

Yours of 18 was received on yesterday and my wife and I were touched by your reference to her and her illness. You are absolutely right about Nature. Nature ought to cure her, as she gives it every chance, but it does not work miracles. "God cures and the physician takes the fee," said Ben Franklin. I quoted the first part of the saying to Dr. Lovett on a social occasion and he remarked that the God cures were very slow. So it will be in Mrs. Rhodes's case, but I fully expect that by next autumn and winter she will be herself again. You spoke in one of your letters about my exchanging high ideas with Charles W. Eliot. I have seen him twice since being in Seal Harbor, and our talk has run largely on dentists and teeth.

I wish indeed that some of the "ellicit goods" would stop in Ravenscleft. I could use them to good advantage. I would even drink cocktails. . . .

To Harvey Cushing

Seal Harbor, Maine, August 1, 1920.

Let me congratulate you on the honorary doctorate conferred upon you by Cambridge University. It is

---

[51] A remark confirmed on pp. 146-147 of *The McKinley and Roosevelt Administrations.*

one of those honors well deserved that makes all your friends feel glad. How fine you will look in your red gown as you stalk around at many Commencements which you have before you! I suppose the degree was conferred in Latin. Mr. Howells told me when he was made a Doctor of Letters in Oxford he looked as if he understood every word of it. Dear old Howells was Ohio born like you and me. Of course you have heard the variation of Shakespeare:

> Some are born great,
> Some achieve greatness,
> And some are born in Ohio.

This as I remember it was stated during the Hayes administration. Howells, Sloane and I were one night at dinner at Carl Schurz's and on comparing notes we found that the native place of us all was Ohio. Howells was born at Martins Ferry; Sloane near Steubenville. There were only two other gentlemen in the party. . . .

To Mrs. C. H. Toy

Seal Harbor, Maine, August 17, 1920.

. . . I thank you heartily for the clipping giving the account of the unveiling of the Lincoln statue. It came a propos, as I was writing regarding the relations of Ambassador Bryce and Secretary of State Root. I think they two settled all questions of difference between Great Britain and the U. S. except one. I have just been reading in the *Christian Science Monitor* an account by Cass Gilbert of the way St. Gaudens studied and thought to make a correct statue. The subject possessed him as he travelled from the Pacific Coast to Chicago and if I understood Gilbert correctly,

St. Gaudens went to the Pacific Coast to get an idea of the greatness of the country over which Lincoln presided. "Only one climate from Maine to Florida," wrote Matthew Arnold of his second visit when he failed to gather in shekels and could not understand it. He was like Kipling's Pagett M. P. who visited India in the winter and "spoke of the heat of India as the Asian solar myth." But Kipling makes his entertainer say,

> And I laughed as I drove from the station,
> But the mirth died out on my lips
> As I thought of the fools like Pagett
> Who write of their "Eastern Trips. . . ."

To the same

Seal Harbor, Maine, September 2, 1920.

. . . R. Merriman was full of his trip to England; had seen much of Mr. Bryce and Mr. Lowell. Mr. Bryce seemed very well and put him many questions regarding the contact of Oriental and Spanish civilizations, as to which R. M. is an authority. R. M. could not understand why he wrote such pessimistic letters to President Eliot, which Miss Hopkinson told me was the case. But I suspect he fears for civilization. Certainly England and France are its bulwarks. If they go I suppose we shall go also. A sufficiency of food and coal will not save us.

R. M. thinks Mr. Lowell is making a wonderful impression upon England. He is ready with an answer to every question; is good natured and very clever. It seems he received an honorary degree from Oxford as well as from Cambridge. I knew that one was waiting for him at Oxford whenever he would come

to take it. From R. M. and Jerome Greene I learned
that Mr. Eliot will have an article in the October
Atlantic defending the Wilson administration. Mr.
Greene has heard it and thinks it good. By the way,
do you see the *Atlantic?* If so you must of course read
the William James correspondence and the high com-
pliment he has paid to Mr. Santayana. William
James's letters are charming, and I anticipate reading
the volumes with pleasure. I imagine that I shall like
them much better than the letters of H. James, who
was more egotistical in his correspondence than in his
familiar talk. . . .

I suppose you have seen Norman Hapgood's book,
"The Advancing Hour." Its so-called egotism I find
attractive as it has to do with his experiences as journalist, correspondent, and diplomat and his familiar
intercourse with Mr. Roosevelt and Mr. Wilson. He
has had a wonderful chance in seeing so much and so
many people and deserves credit for giving the public
the advantage of this account. It is really like hearing him talk. That is to say, the familiar part of it.
I am glad to hear from him that the Marx tenets have
proved a failure in Russia. As to what he has to say
about the future and his evident admiration for
Brandeis I am dumb. It is much to his credit, however, that he is hopeful and sees a way out of the
"muss" that we are in, that I cannot help attributing
largely to the German Emperor. . . .

In the ensuing letter to Lord Bryce, as in one that
will follow it before the significant letters of 1921 have
all been set forth, it will be seen that Rhodes was giving careful thought to his final volume, "The McKinley
and Roosevelt Administrations," and to his use of the

material for it with a scrupulous fairness to one of its sources.

To Lord Bryce

Boston, March 11, 1921.

. . . I should value highly the letters of Theodore Roosevelt which you propose sending to me, would have copies made, the originals returned, and only use parts which would be subject to your approval. There need be no hurry about sending them, as I am working along very slowly.

Regarding the other matter, I am partly answered by your luminous article in the *Evening Post* which I have read and reread with care. I can say of you, as you wrote of him, that you go straight to the point as you do in your opinion that a sea-level canal was out of the question. With what weight do your travels as well as your reading enable you to speak!

Assuming of course that administration is better in England than in the United States, did not Roosevelt in his seven and one-half years of office show himself a great administrator, and was not a part of his service to his country, of which you so eloquently speak, in that direction? I can endorse almost everything you say in your article, and eight years ago would have said amen to your remark on the Algeciras Conference averting for a time the "impending conflict." We defend the Compromise Measures of 1850 as putting off the "irrepressible conflict" between freedom and slavery, as in 1861 the North was better prepared than she was in 1850, and the South comparatively less so. Was not Germany better prepared in 1914 than

[320]

she was at the time of Algeciras, and if the war had to come was it not better in 1906 than in 1914? . . .

To John T. Morse, Jr.

Boston, November 25, 1921.

I thank you heartily for your sympathetic words.[52] From 1907 on I have seen much of my sister Mrs. Hanna as we were neighbors at Seal Harbor, where we both passed our summers. Then from 1874 to 1885 I was a partner of her husband's, Mark Hanna, in the coal and iron business, and naturally their house was always open to me, and as our relations were agreeable I saw much of her at that time. Added to these periods the fact that we were brought up to-gether as girls and boys are made us thoroughly ac-quainted and our relations were always pleasant. I shall miss her greatly. . . .

With your great power of generalization you must [count me] . . . as being in no way a good Christian, so far as religion is concerned. I am not a Jap or Chinaman, and therefore belong to a Christian civiliza-tion, which, however, I fear is doomed to destruction, and one reason is that the Church, except the Roman Catholic, has lost its power. The R. C. church will endure, according to Macaulay, when the rest of civi-lization will expire. . . .

Rhodes was habitually reticent with regard to his own attitude towards questions of religion. Brought up devoutly in the Episcopal church, he was always respectful to the faith of others, but made no outward

---

[52] On the recent death of Rhodes's sister, Mrs. M. A. Hanna.

expression of beliefs which ceased to hold a meaning for him.[53] In the intimacy of the Wednesday Evening Club he must have said enough to the Rev. E. W. Donald, rector of Trinity Church, Boston, to warrant his writing to Rhodes as he did on March 30, 1903: "The difficulty is wholly in you. I say it with all the 'sweetness and light' I can muster. A serious trial of the value and stimulus of church-going would, I think, help matters very much." Later in the same year Dr. Donald was writing again: "Who knows but the believing mother may save the unbelieving son!—if Trinity is open. At any rate your history is saved,— that is, has all that is best in it at its best." There was no Sunday-school story sequel to these expressions, but they are worth setting down in evidence that Rhodes's friends were not estopped by any barriers erected by him from touching upon intimately personal matters. Many years later, when, as his letters have shown, he became discouraged about the submergence of the old order beneath the new—even exclaiming in one letter, "The universe has got away from its maker" —it was President Eliot who wrote to him, in words that echo the very tone of the writer's living voice, "May I urge you to dismiss all fears about our civilization going to destruction? That must be a very unhappy state of mind. I could not stand long the

---

[53] It is worth noting that the first recorded communication of Rhodes to the Massachusetts Historical Society (December, 1895) was a tribute to the preaching of the Rev. O. B. Frothingham, whose sermons he "frequently heard, . . . with pleasure and profit," whenever he came to New York in the seventies as a visitor from Cleveland.

harboring of that idea." Rhodes was not one to take
amiss such counsels of a friend, and of his frank relation with this friend there is an illuminating bit of
record in his remarks at the Massachusetts Historical
Society immediately after President Eliot's death: "It
was vouchsafed to me," he said, "to spend a half-hour
with Mr. Eliot shortly before he passed away.[54] His
conversation was of the old days. He asked me if my
boyish days ever recurred to me. He said he had
thought much of these. I told him I was very religious, even pious, when I was young. With a gleam
of his old humor, he said, 'You have got bravely
over it.' "

To Lord Bryce

Boston, December 9, 1921.

I received yours duly of 15th ult., and your idea
of Roosevelt as therein conveyed is different from
mine; perhaps it may be that you consider him up to
his death while I take Roosevelt up to March 4, 1909,
and try to look at him as he was then without a thought
of his quarrels with Taft and Root which I do not like
to think of. I like your characterization of Roosevelt
better in your Literary Review of the New York *Evening Post* of February 19, 1921, than I do in this
letter, but there is probably no inconsistency between
the two. You may rest assured that I shall print
nothing of yours which has been written to me without
letting you see it for your approval.

In my volume which will appear next autumn I have

---

[54] In August, 1926.

cited from your article hitherto referred to your approval of Roosevelt's decision to make the Panama a lock canal. This coming from you I considered of great value.

I have likewise cited from the Life of Roosevelt by Wm. Draper Lewis published in 1919: Mr. Bryce told Roosevelt that he had "never in any country seen a more eager, high-minded, and efficient set of public servants, men more useful and creditable to their country, than the men doing the work of the American Government in Washington and the field" (p. 258). This of course refers to the Roosevelt administration.

We will suppose that was said about the time between Christmas and New Year's, 1908, when we took luncheon with President Roosevelt at the White House and had for associates Secretary Root, Senator Lodge, Lawrence Lowell, Robert Bacon, and of course Mrs. Roosevelt.

I refer in three different places to your unbounded admiration for Secretary Root, the last taken from the London *Daily Telegraph* of July 29, 1920, from your speech at the unveiling of the copy of St. Gaudens's statue of Lincoln.

I have a long citation from your "South America" as to the Panama Canal—one from the same work on the fortification of the canal; also one from your "American Commonwealth" to the effect that in every government we must come to the people at last.

This, I think, is all that I have laid you under contribution for, although I am sure that my volume would have been better had I quoted you more frequently.

I fully agree with you that nations must economize and no way is so easy as to stop building war-ships. War is the greatest of evils, and the Christian nations and Japan must get together to stop it. Perhaps the Washington Conference will in some way effect this. If it does our administration and Secretary Hughes will reap great credit.

It did look last October as if a revival of business had begun, but just now it appears as if affairs had gone back to the same grinding necessity. Generally speaking, the people whom I know are poor and have difficult work to make the two ends meet. Taxes are high and most commodities are low, except what we eat, which seem to be excessive in price. Let us hope that after January 1 matters may look better. . . .

To George A. Myers

Boston, December 27, 1921.
. . . I have finished the last of my History, which extends to March 4, 1909, and shall publish the volume in the autumn. I shall write no more. I began on my literary life in 1885 and when this volume is published shall have had 37 years of it and shall attain the age of 74. Sir George Trevelyan wrote to Theodore Roosevelt that he knew of no good serious book written in English after the writer had passed 70, and I am following pretty nearly his advice. Dr. Weir Mitchell, who desired me to write the Life of Washington, said, however, if I continued on contemporary history I must take the next steamer to Europe. Perhaps I shall be in Europe when this volume appears, as Europe seems to be getting over her stirring-up a bit. . . .

The year 1922, has been chosen as the terminus of the longest section of this book because it was the year in which Rhodes's work as an historian came to an end, with the publication of his last volume, "The McKinley and Roosevelt Administrations." The earlier months of 1922 were passed in Boston, the rest in Europe. Letters written both at home and abroad touch upon current circumstances, and continue to reflect his interest in them and in his friends. But there is little to show for his work as a writer, and comment upon that may best be deferred until a few of the letters of the year have been read. In two of them from Europe he quoted a remark of Lowell's as applicable to himself—thus in writing from France (July 15, 1922) to Mr. John T. Morse, Jr.: "J. R. Lowell counselled to let your mind lie fallow for a while. My wife intimated that never was such judgment so implicitly followed as in my case! that I was doing the fallow 'act' thoroughly." But it was not invariably so.

To Harvey Cushing

Boston, February 22, 1922.

I duly received your address on yesterday and read it with interest and pleasure. What you say about the heroism of Dr. Warren in performing the first operation under ether is exactly what I have had floating around in my mind, but I did not know how to express it; therefore your words came exactly pat. I could not think much of the Morton tribe, but under the influence of Col Warren, whose judgment I respect highly, I did vote for Morton in the controversy that centered around the Hall of Fame. But why not Dr. Warren instead of Morton? This practical sentiment I tried to give form to.

[326]

The history that you give of the Massachusetts General Hospital is to me highly instructive. It is matter of pride that a Clevelander has been able to tell such a story, but I suspect that the highest form of physical science has no city, no state, no nation. . . .

I am glad that your address settles the question that appendicitis was discovered by Dr. Fitz. Nor do I know that the question was ever made except by Brooks Adams. One night at a Tavern Club dinner Brooks Adams asserted positively that appendicitis was discovered by some one else and, knowing the general sentiment and the fact that Dr. Fitz himself was sitting near, I endeavored to change the subject, as I was in a way responsible for Brooks Adams, for the dinner was to Baron Rosen and B. A. was one of the speakers. But Dr. Prince overheard the conversation and determined to have the matter settled once for all; therefore he brought Dr. Fitz into the conversation, who modestly related the incident.

As you give Arthur Cabot an honorable mention, I must tell you that I heard him relate as a witness your operation on General Wood. It was a relation in which wonder predominated. . . .

To Worthington C. Ford

Boston, February 24, 1922.

Mr. Eliot has spoken so well of the "varied character" of Bryce's education, of his power of observation, that no one can add a word to it.[55] He has ex-

---

[55] The tribute of President Eliot to Lord Bryce is printed in the *Proceedings* of the Massachusetts Historical Society for February, 1922, and is followed by tributes from President Lowell and Rhodes.

plained to many of us the power and compass which Bryce showed in his political and sociological treatises. It would be foolish to speak of myself alone, but everyone with whom I have spoken has expressed himself in the same strain. Therefore the illustrations given were excellent, even to those who have not enjoyed the scenery of Mount Desert.

The relation of his conversations with Bryce during his last days was to me pathetic. I noted the "fundamental doubts" which had arisen in Bryce's mind, but the notice was from one who entirely agreed with him, except on one subject that I will not mention. But, Ford, you and I have lived long enough to know that Mr. Eliot may be right and that Mr. Bryce may be wrong.

At all events, it is a perfect address and I shall always be glad that it fell to my lot to preside over the meeting that was so fitly spoken to by Mr. Eliot and Mr. Lowell. . . .

To Mrs. C. H. Toy

Ouchy-Lausanne, September 16, 1922.
. . . Morley's "Recollections" were to most a disappointment. The most that I remember about it was his private correspondence connected with Indian affairs, but it all goes to show that no one should write for publication after reaching the age of 70. I remember in one of Sir G. Trevelyan's letters he writes that he knows of but one book in the English language of any account written after a man was 70. (I believe, however, he did not finish his history until 73.) I told this remark to President Eliot as an excuse for completing my history to 1909, and he was indig-

nant at Sir G. T. making such a remark. Yet I think it will hold good for those not in the class with President Eliot, who is in a class by himself. So perhaps Morley fell down in his "Recollections," and he must be remembered by his earlier work, which is splendid and written in a true literary spirit. . . .

I regret that a closer acquaintance with Henry Adams does not increase your admiration. To me the first chapters of the nine volumes and the last chapters are great. Nearly every college professor of history and advanced students are enthusiastic over H. Adams's history. The great difference (it seems to me) between H. Adams, Brooks Adams, and Charles Eliot Norton is that they saw further into the future than did James Bryce, Charles W. Eliot, and your humble servant when we vainly surmised that everything was going to turn out all right. I am not surprised at all at the pessimism Mr. Bryce displays in his last volume. France and England, I said to him, during his memorable visit of last summer, seem to me the bulwarks of civilization. "I am sorry to hear you say that," he said; and from others who saw more of him than I did I knew of his bitterness toward France. The feeling of enmity still continues, as I learn from Mrs. Grant. The two nations do not seem to get together. Do not ask me which is in the right. But I hate to see *l'entente cordiale* disturbed. . . .

I was struck with the fact of which you speak, that Mr. Bryce thought democracy more of a success in Switzerland than in the United States, and if I remember aright he devoted as much space to Switzerland as he did to the U. S. "Wise paternal government," does characterize Switzerland. One of my favorite remarks is that Switzerland with 16,000 square miles and less than 4 millions population has a volume of Baedeker devoted to it; the same size that he gives to the U. S. with 3,000,000 square miles and 100 millions population. . . .

Mrs. Rhodes, to whom I have reread your letter and my reply, says she agrees with you perfectly regarding H. Adams, that he was a carping, fault-finding individual, conceited to a high degree and thought his own opinion of more value than anyone else's. . . .

To Worthington C. Ford

Ouchy-Lausanne, September 22, 1922.

. . . I duly received your article on the Adamses in the *Quarterly Review* and gave it to Judge Grant, as I knew he would like your views on the subject. I am a bit surprised that you rate "Mont St. Michel and Chartres" so much above the "Education." I read the former twice and the latter three times. I have been to Mont St. Michel and Chartres many times, but it is unnecessary to say I could not see either with the eyes of H. A. or yourself. I am content with regarding Mont St. Michel as very picturesque and Chartres as the finest cathedral in the world. How glad I am that it did not fall in the way of the German invasion as did Rheims!

Your appreciation of the book shows the poetry in your soul. I fear that in the Education the "pose" and the apparent self-conceit led you to overlook the many merits of the book. It really is a great book, and for those who do not like the Adamses possibly faults may be found with it; but it seems to me wonderful.

[330]

I lent my "Mont St. Michel and Chartres" to Barrett Wendell, and he wrote in such high terms of it that I sent the letter to Mr. Adams, to which I had a very appreciative reply that of course I sent to Barrett Wendell, who was a great admirer of Henry A. in literature and of Charles F. in personal acquaintance.

I am glad that you are taking a rest at Plymouth. We spent five weeks at Chamounix and had good weather except for three days. I hope that I shall never see Mt. Blanc nearer to again. It is too overpowering. We saw her on our motor drive this morning, and she is a height to which distance lends enchantment. . . .

To Sir George Otto Trevelyan

Nice-Cimiez, November 12, 1922.

. . . The statue to Queen Victoria is but five minutes' walk from our hotel and where she stopped when she came for the winter at Cimiez is but a short distance beyond. The statue does not flatter her. She was a good woman and a wise monarch. I like to look at the statue, as it recalls for me the salient events of her reign, which was great and glorious. It is not agreeable to allow the mind to dwell on events that have happened since.

We have had our election, and now you are in the midst of one. I remember being in England in 1895 when there was a general election and, as the polling was not on the same day in different constituencies, as I travelled north I assisted (in the French sense of the word) at different polls, and at Glasgow I was offered a ticket and urged to vote (I think) for the Liberal candidate. Arthur Balfour was at the height

[331]

of his fame and had a large meeting which I did not stay for, as with the little influence that I possessed I could get a ticket to the meeting but not a seat. I heard the song, "He is a jolly good fellow" but after uniting a while I returned to the hotel. I spent two months in Glasgow in 1868 and my fondness for the city has always remained. I remember beautiful weather and salmon and strawberries. It was a good year for strawberries, and I recollect that I ate my fill. I ought rather to speak to you of Sir Walter and Bobbie Burns, but the material things of life take the upper place. . . .

To Worthington C. Ford

Nice-Cimiez, December 2, 1922.

. . . I have been reading the Life and Letters of Walter H. Page with intense interest. I knew Page quite well when he was in Cambridge, but I am not certain whether you were there the first time when Page was first Assistant Editor and then Editor of the *Atlantic Monthly*. Page was a remarkable man and added much to his laurels while ambassador to England. He is about the wisest Anglomaniac I have ever known. His letters from London during our neutrality are vivid and convince me that we should have gone to war on the destruction of the *Lusitania*,[56] that is, we should have seized the German passenger ships then in our harbors and so forced Germany to declare war upon us.

Page's acquaintance in England was of the best, and his intercourse with Sir Edward Grey and Balfour

---

[56] The reader will recall that in 1915 Rhodes was in close sympathy with Wilson's policies.

is very pleasant to read about. None of us, I am sure, when we saw him frequently in Cambridge, ever dreamed he would rise to such heights. I saw him and Mrs. Page again in September, 1914, and then I knew that he was a fit and proper representative of us, following so many distinguished men. . . .

The two remaining letters of 1922 bear directly upon "The McKinley and Roosevelt Administrations," published in November of that year.

To Robert Grant

Nice-Cimiez, December 21, 1922.
. . . I am very much obliged for your clipping from the New York *Times,* which is the first that I had seen of it. In fact I had heard little about my book since its publication November 14, when it ought to have appeared. I would not have it come out until after election on account of what I said about Senator Lodge's expression in opposition to President Roosevelt in regard to the government fixing railroad rates. While I think Senator Lodge was right, I feared that the Proletariat that casts the great majority of the votes would not agree with him. I am thoroughly glad that he was elected. What a humbug it is, having senators chosen by the people instead of by the Legislature! . . .

If the *Times* received this last of Rhodes's books with commendation, it is clear from the following letter to the reviewer for the Boston *Evening Transcript* that the volume met with a less cordial reception in that quarter. The letter must be printed for the testimony it bears to the really touching humility with which Rhodes regarded his own work at the end of his long labors. His reversion, for the second time, to the dictum of Sir George Trevelyan upon writing in old age only adds emphasis to his own consciousness of the risks he had run.

To Sherwin Lawrence Cook

Nice-Cimiez, December 22, 1922.

I am much obliged to you and to Mr. Williams for giving me so much space in the *Transcript* of December 6.

About two years ago (when I was 72) I had a talk with ex-president Charles W. Eliot in which I said I should finish my last volume in two years and then I should quit literature and history for I was a thorough believer in what Sir George O. Trevelyan wrote that no man could do well in writing, in at least English, after he was 70. Mr. Eliot dissented entirely from the opinion of Sir G. O. and thought I was very wrong to follow it. Now if your criticisms are just, I was right and Mr. Eliot was wrong.

"Choose wisely out of the mass before you," said Cicero.[57] That the reviewer of the New York *Times* of December 3 believes that I have done. I amassed material for treating every subject you think I have omitted save one, but I was deterred from the treatment of them by the remark of John Morley in a criti-

---

[57] It is worth noting that this saying seems to have been quoted by memory from an entry made many years before by Rhodes in the first of his "Index Rerum" volumes.

cism of Macaulay that he treats well of a lot of subjects that no one cares anything about.

Thanking you for your kind words of my earlier
volumes, I am with kind regards,

Yours very truly,

JAMES F. RHODES

It would be quite misleading, however, to leave the
reader under any total impression that, in the matter
of misgivings with regard to the continuance of his
work at the age he had attained before its completion,
Rhodes "was right, and Mr. Eliot was wrong." Yet
it would be uncandid, and at the same time unfair to
the seven volumes which make up the bulk of his
History, to maintain that the two which followed in
1919 and 1922 will take their permanent place on the
same plane of merit. Indeed it seems as clear that
they will not as it would have been extraordinary, even
miraculous, for them to do so. Rhodes's friend, Mr.
John T. Morse, Jr.—who, by the way, accused him
aptly in one of his lively letters of being "so absurdly
*de*flated with modesty"—made no scruple of writing
of the two later volumes in his Memoir for the Massachusetts Historical Society: "It cannot honestly be said
that they increased his reputation. That this has to
be avowed is no fault of his. The difficulty lay in the
subject matter. Heretofore he had been dealing with
one of the great crises of the century; he came now to
deal with ordinary every-day politics, the intrigues and
wire-pullings, the squabbles, rivalries, and manoeuvres
of mere politicians concerned with questions of common governmental business. Except perhaps for the

[335]

Hayes-Tilden quarrel nothing of more than ordinary interest had to be narrated. It was routine narrative, but in it he showed still his innate fairness of mind, his love of truth and justice, his accuracy and his talent for narration."

This, I venture to believe, is but a partial explanation. Rhodes's earlier vigor had begun to be impaired, with some consequent relaxation of grasp, and the spirit of discouragement about the world in general which came upon him with the World War could hardly have failed to affect his writing. With him, besides, it was not an advantage, but the opposite, that instead of resorting to extensive research for these later volumes, he could trust so largely as he did to his own knowledge and memories, refreshed by consultations with friends; for Rhodes, with an uncommonly quick eye for the striking expressions of others and their adoption for happy quotation, was not himself a master of picturesque phrase. Thus his pages, one by one, lost something of their former enlivening. It cannot be denied, moreover, that his consideration for living, or recently living, persons tended to mitigate his earlier force of exression.

Even taken by themselves the two later volumes possess many merits of authentic record and sound judgment which ought not to be obscured by the frankest recognition of their limitations when they are compared with the volumes that preceded them. But they are not to be taken by themselves. In 1920 the first seven volumes and the eighth, "From Hayes to McKinley," were issued in a new and revised edition under the title, "History of the United States from the Compromise of 1850 to the McKinley-Bryan Campaign of 1896." The volume of 1922, "The McKinley and Roosevelt Administrations," was the only addendum to this definitive edition of Rhodes, and would doubtless have been included in it had its author in 1920 felt confident of his ability two years later to achieve that inclusion.

Regarding the History, then, in its entirety, it is interesting to note that Rhodes's work, with respect to its scope and character, has been compared, and not without justice and authority, to the writings of his admired Thucydides and Tacitus. The discerning in this or that American writer an American Byron, Macaulay, or Dickens, has long, and rightly, been laughed out of fashion, and any attempt to declare Rhodes an American Thucydides or Tacitus would deserve a similar fate. Yet there are parallels between these fathers of history and their remote descendant which need not be ignored. "Like Thucydides," wrote Professor Wilbur C. Abbott of Harvard in the *Atlantic Monthly*,[58] "Mr. Rhodes has written the history of the United States for nearly all of the period covered by life," and this critic went on to quote words of Rhodes's own about the Greek man of business who dealt with historic events that happened while he was between the ages of thirty-six and sixty. "The dean of American historians," to use the further words of Professor Abbott, "has, indeed, performed a task for his country and his generation not incomparable with that of his Greek prede-

[58] *The Atlantic's Bookshelf*, June, 1923.

cessor." For his likeness to Tacitus Professor Abbott has quoted, as applicable to Rhodes, what Rhodes himself once wrote about the Roman historian: "We rise from reading his history with reverence. We know that we have been in the society of a gentleman who had a high standard of morality and honor. We feel that our guide was a serious student, a solid thinker, and a man of the world; that he expressed his opinions and delivered his judgment with a remarkable freedom from prejudice."

These quotations are taken, nearly *verbatim,* from the same Address on History out of which other words spoken by Rhodes, as early as 1899, have already been cited [59] to set forth his conception of the historian's calling. With his "deflated" modesty, Rhodes himself would have been the last to imagine that they would ever be related to the work he was then doing and, for nearly another quarter century, was still to do. But Rhodes, sound, substantial, sagacious, tolerant, and judicial, is eminently one of the writers who must be taken in the large. So taken, his work is found to justify abundantly the high place it made for him among the historians of America.

5.

THE CLOSING YEARS
1923 - 1927

AFTER the publication of Rhodes's last volume a little more than four years of life remained to him. The

[59] See *ante,* p. 96.

ill health that increasingly beset both him and his wife
had been a more constant factor in their lives through
the later years already passed under review than it
has seemed necessary to indicate as the successive occasions for caution and care presented themselves. His
letters have reflected frankly the growing depression
of spirits quite possibly due in some measure—if so
skilled a physician as Dr. Harvey Cushing may be our
guide [1]—to the progress of the arterio-sclerosis which
affects not the body only, and, in Rhodes's case, was
finally to end his life. The sale of his house in Boston, hastened by the threat of building operations in
his own block, and the dispersion of his library, the
removal to a smaller house in Brookline—all accomplished in the winter and spring of 1923-24—were not
encouraging episodes. The world which he had known
and loved so well seemed indeed changing—and, from
his point of view, for the worse—beneath his very
eye and touch. Whether or not in looking back across
the stretch of years, through which he had found and
caused so much of happiness, he could see for himself
the great occasions for satisfaction in the work he had
accomplished and in the friendships that enriched so
many lives besides his own, there the occasions were,
clearly to be seen by others. "Few men in a century,"
wrote Dr. Bancroft to him as his seventieth birthday
was approaching, "are so fortunate, and fewer still have
so thoroughly and wisely enjoyed life themselves and

---

[1] Dr. Cushing is cited to this effect in the Memoir by Mr. John
T. Morse, Jr., previously drawn upon.

also made life much more enjoyable to so many others."

Taking Rhodes's life, then, like his writings, in the large, it was indeed a happy life that was drawing to a close. His faithful and devoted chauffeur through the later years of it accounted by implication for some of this happiness when he told me a saying of Rhodes at the very beginning of their relation as employer and employee: "Now, Merrick, come straight to me when everything is not all right. I like to get the other man's point of view." Thus it is more as a friend than as an employer that he is recalled—a friend with the kindliest of greetings and inquiries at the beginning of every drive, with cordial "good-night," with active, effectual intervention at a moment of dangerous illness in the employee's family. In his own family, though nearly a martinet of punctuality and punctilio, the chivalric and generous qualities of husband, father, and grandfather gave but an intensified expression to the constant consideration for others, the getting of "the other man's point of view," which gave to all his human relationships their distinctive color and glow.

It is not to be thought that he looked back consciously upon such private causes for satisfaction. Nor is he likely to have given much consideration to the larger effects of his work as a writer of history. It is nevertheless the fact that, however resolutely an historian who is read may remain a private citizen, his books effect an influence which makes him more truly a public character than many a figure of the platform and the front page. Rhodes, to be sure, has not been

read in anything like the measure of J. B. Green and
Macaulay in England and Fiske and such an earlier
writer as Bancroft in America. But his readers have
been recruited largely from the class that contributes
most to the direction of public sentiment—teachers,
editors, political leaders—and the opinion of Professor
Dodd already cited,[2] that Rhodes's History has "done
more than any other historical agency—perhaps any
other agency of any sort"—to bring about a better
state of feeling between the adherents of the North
and of the South in our Civil War, is an opinion that
commands a wide assent, and is itself of far-extending
import. On this achievement, whatever pride Rhodes
may or may not have felt in it, others may look back
with admiration.

A few of Rhodes's letters are still to be included in
these pages. Though less firmly and legibly written
than those of the earlier years they continue to show
forth his interest in his friends, and his gratitude for
their interest in him.

To Mrs. C. H. Toy

Nice-Cimiez, January 16, 1923.
. . . Yes, the Emancipation Proclamation was
issued in September, and Lincoln read "High Handed
Outrage at Utica" to his Cabinet before telling them
what he was going to do. I read two papers on the
subject, or rather one paper to two different societies.
I cannot read Artemus Ward well, and so stumbled

---

[2] See *ante*, p. 114.

through it as best I could and the reading (I read the whole Essay of A. Ward) elicited not a smile from the Massachusetts Historical Society. When I sat down next Mr. Charles W. Eliot he said something to this effect: What an extraordinary thing that Lincoln should think it funny. Afterwards I read the same thing at the Thursday Evening Club, and I could hardly get through the "High Handed Outrage at Utica" on account of the peals of laughter that arose. When I sat down Mr. Maclaurin said that I was entitled to credit for giving the T. E. C. some fun, so afflicted were they with serious papers, and, did he not know otherwise, he would know Lincoln had a rare sense of humor from his appreciation of such a sense of it. . . .

But what a man Mr. Eliot is! He is perfectly wonderful in your account of him. . . .

To A. Lawrence Lowell

Nice-Cimiez, March 16, 1923.

In the Paris *Herald* I read of your being in Paris and the great deal that you did there and the honors that were offered you. I should have begged Mrs. Lowell and you to think of the South of France, but just at the time you were in Paris I was laid up with a nasty attack of influenza which made it impossible for me to play host in any degree.

I duly received your book [3] and read it with care and attention. Morse Stephens used to say he could tell that things were done, but he could not tell how opinion led to things which were done. You have cer-

---

[3] *Public Opinion in War and Peace* (1923).

tainly undertaken a brave task in the book. Bearing
in mind that the chapters were originally in the form
of lectures, it is no mean job to make out of them
such a book as this is. It is a live topic. It takes into
account the opinions of the day. I am really amazed
at the account of opinion after the War. The book
could only have been written by one thoroughly informed on affairs in England and France. On England of course I knew that you were informed to the
bottom, but the insight into French affairs astonishes
me. Spending five months in this beautiful country
you have taught me a great deal, and how you got the
knowledge passes comprehension. It is knowledge one
would think could only be had by a daily life among
the people, by reading its newspapers and conversing
with the people on matters therein discussed. France
is, of all countries, the most interesting, and its
provinces various, and each one is marked by some
specific quality.

If Mr. Bryce had been living how he would have
enjoyed the dedication.

It is a fine hit that you make when you say that
the tendency in the U. S. is to make laws and not
enforce them. . . .

To Sir George Otto Trevelyan

Nice-Cimiez, March 24, 1923.
. . . You are quite right. Senator Lodge is a hard-
working man. An eminent physician of Boston said
that he had never known two such brains with capacity
for work as Lodge and Roosevelt, although he gave
the superiority to Roosevelt. Lodge is, however, very
unpopular with the best people in Boston. I can give

you two instances of it. Once years ago he was defeated for Harvard Overseer and Godkin of the *Nation* sent him a despatch saying, Now you see what the best people in Boston think of you! A reviewer of my last volume in the New York *Evening Post,* which was down on Roosevelt and much more so on Lodge, criticised me severely because I wrote that I would not venture to find fault with Roosevelt's railroad policy were I not buttressed by Senator Lodge. Thus, said the reviewer, "He plucks up courage to differ with so great a man as Roosevelt, because he finds himself supported by so small a man as Henry Cabot Lodge." Do you know I think Roosevelt was right in his rating Lodge superior to Sumner but not so great as Daniel Webster.

But such an opinion will make many good people in Boston lose all confidence in Roosevelt's judgments.

Lodge was an intimate friend of Henry Adams and can tell much about him.

If Senator Lodge could have divested himself of that supercilious air he would have found life easier for him. But he came by it naturally. Yet it has stood in the way of his advancement. He would have been chairman of the Committee on Foreign Relations years before had he not been so unpopular with his brother senators. But some of the best men in Boston stick by him: and he had some hold on the masses, though not so much as I thought from the late election returns. You are fortunate in judging Senator Lodge from a distance, and I am lucky in only having been a resident of Boston for thirty-two years and so escaped some of the prejudices. . . .

To John T. Morse, Jr.

Seal Harbor, Maine, August 11, 1923.

. . . Harding's death seems to me a useless sacrifice. If public sentiment is to be represented by President Lowell, Fred. Stimson and myself, we three, sitting on a cool veranda on a glorious summer day, thought that Mr. Harding made a great mistake in taking the Alaskan trip, that he ran too great a risk for what was gained, that it was inexcusable that he should have been served bad food, etc., etc., and now I think we can join you to us three. If he had remained in Washington or gone to a dignified seaside place as did Roosevelt, he would have been living now.

Anent Coolidge—I do not know. I met him twice and at one time we talked together for ten minutes discussing prohibition. Montague [4] tells me that if we had a conversation of ten minutes together we beat all the men he talked with in Washington who affirmed that two minutes exhausted every topic with Coolidge. . . . I can say therefore that he is a very reticent man. . . .

I do not wonder that you are disgusted with the capitalists, but really they are a lot sight better than the proletariat. Their work is not as bad, the benefits they confer on mankind are greater. When the hanging begins it will not stop with the coal barons and the like. It will hit the "damn littery fellers" who do not do an honest day's work but only sit in a study and write. That you are disgusted with mankind in general shows that your heart is in the right place. . . .

[4] Mr. Gilbert Holland Montague, a Mount Desert neighbor.

James Ford Rhodes

To Sir George Otto Trevelyan

Brookline, December 18, 1923.

I wish you a Merry Christmas and a happy New Year. I have not written you before because I was laid up with a bad cold and could not write in a cheerful mood; and I find now that my penmanship bears the mark of age. We are looking forward to George M.'s [5] lectures on England which begin on February 18. It makes a stormy time to cross the stormy Atlantic, but George M. is young and will not mind the rough seas, so comfortable are the ships now-a-days. I have been behind time reading Theodore Lyman's letters,[6] so have just tackled them, and I wonder at the foresight he displayed in 1864 when he wrote, "It is surprising how poorly the Germans show out of their own country, where they are an honest and clever though rather slow people. Here they will plunder and they won't fight. . . . The Paddies on the contrary will go in finely."

I am much interested in going back to our Civil War and therefore getting my mind off from the gloom and sadness of present days.

I brought home from the Library yesterday the new Life of Grover Cleveland of whom I was an admirer, and am prepared for that by reading the Life of Richard Olney which was composed by Henry James, a nephew of the Henry whom you knew and who was much in England. In fact I remember one of my first meetings with him was in London. The attitude of Cleveland in the Venezuela business was to me incom-

---

[5] Sir G. O. Trevelyan's son, George Macaulay Trevelyan, about to deliver a course of Lowell Institute Lectures.

[6] *Meade's Headquarters*, 1922.

prehensible. I take it from talk which I have had with him that Moorfield Storey, who is going to review the book in the January *Atlantic*, will devote a good deal of his limited space to the incident. I say incomprehensible after reading Cleveland's defence and several intimate talks with Mr. Olney whom I knew quite well. . . .

To Gamaliel Bradford

Brookline, April 6, 1924.

I have had much pleasure in reading your article on Pepys in the current *Atlantic*. The sprightly gayety of it is attractive and, after going through it, I recommended it to my wife, who is a much better Pepys scholar than I am. She enjoys the wit in your article and that in the Pepys diary, when Pepys is funny without intending to be, and it needed some such writer as yourself to show this. The conflict between the sensual man and the man of the spirit is abundantly set forth, and at times one wonders which will get the better—his vows or the lusts of the flesh.

Some years ago my wife, Miss Wyman, and myself, had displayed to us the Pepys diary as originally set down which, as you know, is preserved in one of the Cambridge colleges. This was under the guidance of Dr. Cunningham, to whom all in Cambridge was "open sesame" and with whom we took dinner that evening in Trinity. I was glad to have that glimpse of Trinity, as being a student of Macaulay and later a friend of Sir George Trevelyan, I had read and heard much of Trinity.

We miss you very much at the Athenæum. Hurry

to get well and favor us again with your gracious presence. . . .

To the same

Brookline, April 20, 1924.

. . . Messrs. Scribner a number of years ago wanted me to write a Life of Daniel Webster. The subject was highly attractive, but as I was at work then on my History, I had to decline their solicitation. Then after much consideration and reflection, they gave the job to Sam W. McCall, who had not got along with it a great way, as he told me a few weeks before he was stricken with pneumonia from which he died.

Dr. Mitchell, on the part of the Century Company, desired me to write a Life of Washington. I declined this also, giving as reason that I could not go back in time, but must go forward. . . .

To Sir George Otto Trevelyan

Hotel Bellevue, Boston, October 28, 1924.

. . . I liked Macaulay's admiration for the ancient writers, and I imagine it is largely to him that I owe my knowledge of Thucydides and Tacitus. In spite of some errors, Macaulay was a great man, the greatest of English historians, after Gibbon, and that he was an excellent student your biography brings out. What a memory he had! and if memory be the basis of all brain what a brain he must have had. The Boston winter climate does not agree either with Mrs. Rhodes or me, and we have taken passage on the *Duilio* for November 29, expecting to pass the winter on the Riviera. We shall not get to England on this trip, and regret very much not seeing Lady Trevelyan and yourself; but, as you know, old age has its disabilities.

To Robert Grant

Nice-Cimiez, January 29, 1925.

. . . The news of the Saturday Club was grateful indeed. The Saturday is the most famous of Boston clubs, and I cannot understand how C. F. Adams, James Crafts, and Professor Sargent could find the meetings dull. I remember when we tried the experiment of small tables, Charles Sargent, Storey, and I were sitting at one, and the talk ran on Admiral Mahan, when I remarked that he was the most modest of all the celebrated men I knew. Charles Sargent said in a low voice that there was one man present who equalled him, and he pointed to J. S. Sargent who was seated at an adjoining table. There have been other encounters at the Saturday Club I like to recall. . . .

To Gamaliel Bradford

Brookline, January 1, 1926.

Your "Wives" arrived opportunely on Christmas day, and I have enjoyed reading it very much, and so has my "better half," as far as she has got. I have heard her citing in season and out of season your prefix from a French comedy: "We women were the last of God's works: you feel that he was tired," and she has enjoyed more than I the chapter "Confessions of a Biographer." I feel there is too much modesty shown, like that which prevented you from reading before the Massachusetts Historical Society one of your delightful essays, which is exactly the thing to lighten up the proceedings, and no one can read as well as the writer.

The one on Mrs. Lincoln is important from the sidelights it throws on Lincoln himself. What an interesting man he was, and how interesting he is, no matter from what point he is approached! I feel rejoiced that you have quieted much of the "intangible gossip" concerning Mrs. Lincoln, as your judgment is considered sound. . . . The one on Mrs. Blaine shows what a rascal Blaine was and how much he was afraid of death.

Altogether the book is a worthy one, and I congratulate you on your success.

Thus with an expression of pleasure in the achievement of a friend, Rhodes for the last time speaks for himself in this volume. The small sheaf of other letters of the last few years of his life yields but little that is found to claim preservation in print. Nor in these final pages has it seemed profitable to follow, through migrations to France and the Riviera, to Seal Harbor, and back to Boston or Brookline, the steps of one whose health had necessarily become his main concern. His last summer, that of 1926, was passed at Seal Harbor. When he returned in the autumn to the house he had bought in Brookline, the friends who saw him felt that his hold upon life and the interests that meant most to him had perceptibly weakened. The "loud, cheery voice" had suffered a certain subduing, but the smile that embodied the very spirit of friendliness still spoke for something unquenchable within. In Brookline he died on January 22, 1927, in his seventy-ninth year. His ashes were buried, beside his own people, in his native Cleveland.

"When a man has exercised a large influence on the minds of his contemporaries," wrote Froude at the beginning of his biography of Carlyle, "the world requires to know whether his own actions have corresponded with his teaching, and whether his moral and personal character entitles him to confidence. This is not idle curiosity; it is a legitimate demand." These words are as true of a judicial chronicler like Rhodes as of an impassioned chronicler and moralist preacher like Carlyle. As this narrative began with President Eliot's summary of what the subject of it did, it must close, if it has at all achieved its purpose, with a recognition of the fact that what he did and what he was were essentially of the same substance.

BIBLIOGRAPHY

BOOKS

1888   *The Abbess of Jouarre,* by Ernest Renan. Translated from the French by Georges Delon and James F. Rhodes; translation authorized by Monsieur E. Renan (New York: copyright, 1888 by G. W. Dillingham, Publisher, Successor to G. W. Carleton & Co.; London: S. Low, Son & Co.).

1893-1922 *History of the United States from the Compromise of 1850:* Vols. I, II, 1893; Vol. III, 1895; Vol. IV, 1899 (all these volumes were published by Harper & Brothers, New York); Vol. V, 1904; Vols. VI, VII, 1906 (published by The Macmillan Company, who from 1900 became Rhodes's publishers). With Volume VI the title is changed to *History of the United States from the Compromise of 1850 to the Final Restoration of Home Rule at the South in 1877.*

[Vol. VIII] *History of the United States from Hayes to McKinley, 1877-1896* (New York, The Macmillan Company, 1919).
New revised edition in 8 volumes, *History of the United States from the Compromise of 1850 to the McKinley-Bryan Campaign of 1896* (New York, The Macmillan Company, 1920).

[353]

[Vol. IX] *The McKinley and Roosevelt Administrations, 1897-1909* (New York, The Macmillan Company, 1922).

New edition in 9 volumes, *History of the United States from the Compromise of 1850 to the End of the Roosevelt Administration* (New York, The Macmillan Company, 1928).

1909   *Historical Essays* (New York, The Macmillan Company).

1913   *Lectures on the American Civil War Delivered before the University of Oxford in Easter and Trinity Terms, 1912* (New York, The Macmillan Company).

1917   *History of the Civil War, 1861-1865* (New York, The Macmillan Company).

MISCELLANEOUS WRITINGS

1885   "The Coal and Iron Industry of Cleveland," *Magazine of Western History*, August.

"A Review of the Second Volume of McMaster's History of the United States," *Magazine of Western History*, September.

"Wilson's Congressional Government," *Magazine of Western History*, November.

"Some Lessons of History," *Magazine of Western History*, December.

1886   "Samuel S. Cox's Three Decades of Federal Legislation," *Magazine of Western History*, February.

1895   "Remarks on the Death of Octavius B. Frothingham," *Massachusetts Historical Society, Proceedings*, December.

1896 "The First Six Weeks of McClellan's Peninsular Campaign," *Massachusetts Historical Society, Proceedings,* January; also published in the *American Historical Review,* April.

1897 "Remarks by James F. Rhodes, on the Death of Edward L. Pierce," *Massachusetts Historical Society, Proceedings,* October; also published in *Historical Essays,* 1909.

1898 "A New Estimate of Cromwell," *Massachusetts Historical Society Proceedings,* January; also published in the *Atlantic Monthly,* June, 1898, and in *Historical Essays,* 1909.

1899 "The Battle of Gettysburg," *American Historical Review,* July.

1900 "History, Inaugural Address of James Ford Rhodes, President," *Annual Report of the American Historical Association, 1899, Vol. I* (Washington, 1900); also published in the *Atlantic Monthly,* February, 1900, and in *Historical Essays,* 1909.

"Remarks on the Death of Jacob D. Cox," *Massachusetts Historical Society, Proceedings,* October; also published in *Historical Essays,* 1909.

"Some Recent Impressions of England," *Massachusetts Historical Society, Proceedings,* November.

1901 "Concerning the Writing of History," *Annual Report of the American Historical Association, 1900, Vol. I* (Washington, 1901); also published in *Historical Essays,* 1909.

"Tribute to Herbert B. Adams," *Massachusetts Historical Society, Proceedings,* October.

"Sherman's March to the Sea," *American Historical Review*, April.

"Who Burned Columbia?" *Massachusetts Historical Society, Proceedings*, November; also published in the *American Historical Review*, April, 1902, and in *Historical Essays*, 1909.

1902   "Tribute to Samuel Rawson Gardiner," *Massachusetts Historical Society, Proceedings*, March; also published in the *Atlantic Monthly,* May, 1902, and in *Historical Essays*, 1909.

1903   "The Presidential Office," *Scribner's Magazine*, February; also published in *Historical Essays*, 1909.

"Tribute to William E. H. Lecky," *Massachusetts Historical Society, Proceedings*, November; also published in *Historical Essays*, 1909.

1904   "Memoir of Edward L. Pierce," *Massachusetts Historical Society, Proceedings, June;* also published in *Historical Essays*, 1909.

1904-1905 "Negro Suffrage and Reconstruction," *Massachusetts Historical Society, Proceedings*, December, 1904; January, 1905.

1907   "Tribute to Daniel Henry Chamberlain," *Massachusetts Historical Society, Proceedings*, May.

"Tribute to Sir Spencer Walpole," *Massachusetts Historical Society, Proceedings*, November; also published in *Historical Essays*, 1909.

1908   "Tribute to Edward Gaylord Bourne," *Massachusetts Historical Society, Proceedings*, March; also published in *Historical Essays*, 1909.

"Edwin Lawrence Godkin," *Atlantic Monthly*,

September; also published in *Historical Essays,* 1909.

1909   "The Molly Maguires in the Anthracite Region of Pennsylvania," paper read at the first public meeting of the American Academy of Arts and Letters in Washington, December 14-16, 1909: *American Historical Review,* April, 1910.

"Newspapers as Historical Sources," *Atlantic Monthly,* May; also published in *Historical Essays,* 1909.

"Edward Gibbon," *Scribner's Magazine,* June; also published in *Historical Essays,* 1909.

"A Review of President Hayes's Administration," *Century Magazine,* October; also published in *Historical Essays,* 1909.

1911   "The Railroad Riots of 1877," *Scribner's Magazine,* July.

"The National Republican Conventions of 1880 and 1884," *Scribner's Magazine,* September.

"Cleveland's Administrations," *Scribner's Magazine,* October, November.

1912   "Prefatory Note" in *The Abolition Crusade and Its Consequences,* by Hilary A. Herbert, LL.D. (New York, Charles Scribner's Sons).

1913   "Some Humours of American History," *American Antiquarian Society, Proceedings,* April.

1915   "Tribute to Charles Francis Adams," *Massachusetts Historical Society, Proceedings,* April.

"Lincoln in Some Phases of the Civil War," Phi Beta Kappa Address delivered in Sanders Theatre, Monday, June 21, 1915: *Harvard Graduates' Magazine,* September.

"Tribute to Frederic Ward Putnam," *Massachusetts Historical Society, Proceedings,* October.

"Tribute to Samuel Savage Shaw," *Massachusetts Historical Society, Proceedings,* October.

"Tribute to John Davis Long," *Massachusetts Historical Society, Proceedings,* October.

1917   "Introduction" to "A List of Books and Newspapers, Maps, Music, and Miscellaneous Matter Printed in the South during the Confederacy, now in the Boston Athenæum. Prepared by Charles N. Baxter and James M. Dearborn," The Boston Athenæum.

1918   "Tribute to Thomas Leonard Livermore," *Massachusetts Historical Society, Proceedings,* February.

"Tribute to Henry Adams," *Massachusetts Historical Society, Proceedings,* April; also published in *Harvard Graduates' Magazine,* June 1918.

1919   "Tribute to William Roscoe Livermore," *Massachusetts Historical Society, Proceedings,* October.

1921   "Tribute to Barrett Wendell," *Massachusetts Historical Society, Proceedings,* February.

1922   "Tribute to Viscount Bryce," *Massachusetts Historical Society, Proceedings,* February.

"Commemorative Tribute to Barrett Wendell, Prepared for the American Academy of Arts and Letters, 1921." American Academy of Arts and Letters (New York).

1923   "Winslow Warren," *Massachusetts Historical Society, Proceedings,* January.

"On Dr. Eliot's Anniversary," *Massachusetts Historical Society, Proceedings,* October.

"Tribute to Viscount Morley, of Blackburn," *Massachusetts Historical Society, Proceedings,* November.

1924 "Commemorative Tribute to William Roscoe Thayer, Prepared for The American Academy of Arts and Letters, 1924." American Academy of Arts and Letters (New York).

1926 "Tribute to Charles William Eliot": *Massachusetts Historical Society, Proceedings,* October.

1927 "Charles Francis Adams, 1835-1915," in M. A. DeWolfe Howe, *Later Years of the Saturday Club, 1870-1920* (Boston).

INDEX

Index

Glasgow, R. on, 332.

Godkin, Edwin Lawrence, 45, 154, 160, 168-172; R.'s discourse on, 165.

Goethe, Johann Wolfgang von, 94, 97, 142, 204, 261.

Gold reserve, Cleveland's replenishing, 202.

Gompers, Samuel, 274.

Gordon, George A., 134.

Gosse, Edmund William, 315.

Goudy, Henry, 186.

Governors, convention, 167, 170.

Grant, Robert, 57, 194, 213; memoranda on Roosevelt's talk, 196-198; letters to, 213, 215, 259, 302, 333, 349.

Green, John R., 97, 185, 186, 230 n., 340.

Green, Mrs. John R., 185, 221.

Greene, Jerome D., 319.

Greer, David H., 282.

Grey, Sir Edward, 253.

Gross, Charles, 132.

Guizot, François P. G., 21.

HADLEY, ARTHUR T., 159, 189, 193, 241, 242; impressions of R., 189-191.

Hall of Fame, 326.

Hamilton, Ian, 197.

Hamilton, Sir William, 23, 161.

Hanna, Augusta (Rhodes), sister of R., 41, 44, 113, 241, 321.

Hanna, Marcus Alonzo, 41-47, 94, 201, 203, 216, 231, 235, 308, 313.

Hapgood, Charles H., 162.

Hapgood, Norman, 135, 136, 198, 268, 319.

Harding, Warren G., 314, 345.

Harper and Brothers, 28, 66, 67.

Harrison, Benjamin, 77, 196.

Harrison, Frederic, 155, 300, 301; letter to, 108.

Hart, Albert Bushnell, 47, 66, 80.

Harte, Bret, 309-311.

Harvard Graduates' Magazine, 246.

Harvard University, degree for R., 125; freedom of speech, 134; under Eliot, 159, 298; Hadley on, 159; R.'s lectures and connection, 165, 225; Lowell, 184, 188, 228, 270; and degree for Morgan, 203.

Haskins, Charles H., 132.

Hatch, Stella T., 14.

Hatch, U. C., 34.

Hawthorne, Nathaniel, 72, 222.

Hay, John, 26, 45, 81, 84, 181-184, 245, 246, 251, 256, 268, 286, 308-310.

Hay, Mrs. John, 181, 184.

Hayes, Rutherford B., 95, 264, 307, 308.

Hegermann-Lindencrone, Lillie (Greenough) de, 267.

Henderson, Thomas J., 308.

Henry, Guy V., 180.

Herodotus, 88, 89, 97.

Herrick, Myron T., 217, 244.

Hill, Adams Sherman, 65.

Hill, James J., 170.

Higginson, Henry Lee, 294.

Higginson, Thomas Wentworth, 277.

History, in R.'s education, 19, 21; R.'s systematic reading and note taking, 51-54; R. on writing, 56, 72, 84, 90, 94-101, 107; R. on rank, 75, 97; R. on narrative and philosophical, 148-150.

"History," R.'s address, 96, 106.

Hoar, George F., 200, 201, 205.

Holmes, Justice Oliver Wendell, 121, 180.

Homer, 87, 97, 219.

Hoover, Herbert C., 287, 297.

Hopkinson, A. G., 17, 19.

Morfill, William Richard, 134, 278.

Morley, John, Viscount, 116, 117, 128, 164, 182, 205, 328, 334; letters to, 164, 177; on Green, 230 *n*.

Morgan, J. Pierpont, 170, 171, 202-204, 225, 268.

Morgan, Morris H., 143.

Morocco controversy, 208.

Morrill, Justin S., 199-202.

Morse, John T., Jr., 116, 288, 291, 293, 345; on R., 79, 335; letters to, 95, 174, 221, 225, 245, 261, 265, 267, 316, 321, 326; as biographer, 174-176.

Morton, Julius S., 108.

Morton, Oliver P., 168.

Morton, William T. G., 326.

Mt. Blanc, 331.

Mount Desert, R.'s home, 69, 162, 265.

Münsterberg, Hugo, 139, 245.

Murphy, Charles F., 123.

Murray, Gilbert, 185, 186.

Myers, Frederic W. H., 172.

Myers, George A., 62, 63, 231, 277; letters to, 233, 237, 253, 254, 256, 263, 264, 272, 275, 276, 312, 325.

NATION, 23, 154, 168, 272.

National Institute of Arts and Letters, 273; medal for R., 192.

Navy, world tour, 170, 181, 182, 195; in World War, 282, 284, 287, 297.

Negro suffrage, 120, 154, 168; R.'s lectures, 220 *n*.

New York, University of, R. at, 20-22, 34.

New York, New Haven and Hartford Railroad, 224, 237.

New York *Times,* 229, 333.

New York *Weekly Tribune,* 33.

Newspapers, as historical source, 96; political criticism by, 123, 171.

"Newspapers as Historical Sources," R.'s address, 96.

Nicolay, John G., 81.

Norton, Charles Eliot, 152, 205, 285, 300, 329; letter to, 158.

Notebooks, R.'s, 51-54, 118.

Norway, as kingdom, 195.

Noyes, Alexander D., 214.

O'CONNELL, WILLIAM, CARDINAL, 215.

Odell, Benjamin B., 123.

Ohio, as birthplace, 317.

Ohio City, Ohio, 12.

Olney, Richard, 108, 164, 202, 204.

Orphanage, Rhodes house as, 44.

O'Shaughnessy, Edith, 266.

Osler, Sir William, 222, 242.

Outlook, 171.

Oxford Magazine, 220.

Oxford University, 159, 225, 236, 251; Green tablet, 185, 186; degree for R., 185-187; R.'s lectures, 219-222, 226, 236; Hadley's lectures, 242.

PAGE, WALTER HINES, 291, 332.

Palmerston, Henry, Viscount, and Civil War, 248.

Panama Canal, lock type, 210, 320, 324.

Panama Revolution, 245.

Panic of 1907, 171-173, 235.

Paper, of Clarendon Press, 222.

Paris, University of, 159.

Parker, William B., 201 *n*.

Parliamentarism, R. on, 165, 187, 188.

Pasteur, Louis, 150.

Pearson, Henry G., 168.

Index